A Faculty Guide to Addressing Disruptive and Dangerous Behavior

College and university faculty are asked to serve an increasingly diverse and at-risk population of students. They face disruptive and dangerous behaviors that range from speaking out of turn or misusing technology, to potentially aggressive behavior. *A Faculty Guide to Addressing Disruptive and Dangerous Behavior* provides the practical ideas and guidance necessary to manage and mitigate these behaviors. Grounded in research and theory that addresses the interplay of mental health, substance abuse and aggression that may enter the college classroom, this accessible book serves as a necessary guide for busy faculty members facing challenging situations in their classrooms.

Special features include:

- Vignettes from seasoned faculty that provide thoughtful reflections and advice from everyday experience.
- Research-based suggestions and intervention techniques to help faculty better assess, intervene and manage difficult behavior.
- Coverage of special populations, including non-traditional, veteran and Millennial students.
- Discussion of the latest laws and regulations that should affect and inform faculty's decisions.

Brian Van Brunt is Director of Counseling at Western Kentucky University, USA.

W. Scott Lewis is a Partner with The National Center for Higher Education Risk Management, USA.

A Faculty Guide to Addressing Disruptive and Dangerous Behavior

Brian Van Brunt and
W. Scott Lewis

Routledge
Taylor & Francis Group

NEW YORK AND LONDON

First published 2014
by Routledge
711 Third Avenue, New York, NY 10017

Simultaneously published in the UK
by Routledge
2 Park Square, Milton Park, Abingdon, Oxon OX14 4RN

Routledge is an imprint of the Taylor & Francis Group, an informa business

Library of Congress Cataloging in Publication Data
Van Brunt, Brian.
  A faculty guide to addressing distruptive and dangerous behavior/
by Brian Van Brunt and W. Scott Lewis.
  pages cm
  1. Problem children—Education—United States.   2. Learning
disabled children—Education—United States.   3. Behavior disorders
in children—United States.   4. Behavior modification—United
States.   5. School crisis management—United States.   6. School
violence—United States—Prevention.   I. Title.
  LC4802.V36 2013
  371.93—dc23
  2013019231

ISBN: 978-0-415-62827-3 (hbk)
ISBN: 978-0-415-62828-0 (pbk)
ISBN: 978-0-203-10100-1 (ebk)

Typeset in Perpetua and Bell Gothic
by Florence Production Ltd, Stoodleigh, Devon, UK

Printed and bound in the United States of America by Sheridan Books, Inc. (a Sheridan Group Company).

Scott's Dedication

To Kim:
without your support,
none of this is possible.

To my Mom, Paula, and my Grandfather, Justo:
two of the best professors I ever had.

To my kids, Sophia and Justice:
may you find the best teachers and
then become them.

Brian's Dedication

To Bethany,

"you are my constant"
—Sayid, *Lost*

To the world you may be just one person, but to one person you may be the world.

—Unknown

We never know which lives we influence, or when, or why.

—Stephen King, 11/22/63

That's the way with any new idea. It takes the hoopleheads time to adjust. Sometimes I wish we could just hit 'em over the head, rob 'em, and throw their bodies in the creek.

—Al Swearengen, HBO Series *Deadwood*

I look back on the way I was then. A young, stupid kid who committed that terrible crime. I wanna talk to him. I wanna try to talk some sense to him. Tell him the way things are. But I can't. That kid's long gone and this old man's all that's left.

Ellis Boyd "Red" Redding (Morgan Freeman), *The Shawshank Redemption*

Contents

xi

Contributors

Cort Basham teaches Interdisciplinary Studies at Western Kentucky University. He received his Master of Arts in Education in 2001 and Master of Arts in History in 2012, both from WKU. He has been teaching freshman and Inter-disciplinary Studies majors for 11 years. He primarily teaches critical thinking and the purpose of education in first-year experience courses. Content in his interdisciplinary studies courses often focuses on food studies, and he presented "Food as Content for Critical Thinking" at the Association for the Study of Food & Society conference at New York University in Summer 2012. His historical thesis examines the rise of popular prophecy in America and related views on the "end of the world," especially premillennial thought as popularized by Hal Lindsey's *The Late, Great Planet Earth* during the 1970s.

Laura Bennett is a student conduct and behavioral intervention practitioner with over ten years of experience in higher education administration. She has provided education and guidance to faculty and staff in a diversity of campus settings, including the Colorado College, the University of California—Berkeley, and William Rainey Harper College. Laura currently serves as Harper's Student Conduct Officer, where she facilitates the student conduct processes and coord-inates the campus threat assessment/behavioral intervention team. She currently serves on the Board of Directors for the Association for Student Conduct Administration (ASCA) as the first Director of Community Colleges, and has presented numerous webinars and sessions at regional and national events. Known for her willingness to have difficult conversations, Laura has developed a series of workshops for adjunct and full-time faculty members, and serves as a guest instructor on her home campus.

Monica Galloway Burke is an Assistant Professor in the Department of Counseling and Student Affairs and the Assistant to the Chief Diversity Officer at Western Kentucky University. She has approximately 20 years of experience in the field of mental health and higher education administration. Dr. Burke earned a Bachelor of Arts degree in Psychology from Tougaloo College and a Master of Science degree in Counseling Psychology and a Doctor of Philosophy degree in Educational Administration and Supervision with an emphasis in Higher Education from the University of Southern Mississippi. Her primary areas of research include diversity as it relates to student affairs and higher education; the role of networking and mentoring in career development; and workplace dynamics. In addition to Dr. Burke's academic research, she consistently conducts presentations and workshops focused on diversity and the professional development of student affairs and higher education professionals.

Jack Cobb: after spending his first two years of life teething on pilsner-infused pretzels and terrifying the locals of southern Bavaria on moonlit nights, Jack Cobb grew up in Muhlenberg County, Kentucky, a few miles from Paradise, the bulldozed town made famous by folk legend John Prine. He recently completed a book titled, *What You Need to Know before Teaching English in Korea*. His poems, travel essays, and short stories have appeared in *The Christian Century*, *The Cream City Review*, and in *Weave Magazine*. Jack teaches English at ESLI@WKU in Bowling Green, Kentucky. He writes these days mostly in the hopes of someday impressing his wife. He's @martinbluther on Twitter.

David J. Denino has worked in higher education and counseling over the past 36 years and is Director Emeritus of Counseling Services at Southern Connecticut State University. He served as the Associate Director and then Director of Counseling Services for over 30 years. David also supervised the university's health services for a two-year period and led a search for a new medical director during that time. He is currently an adjunct faculty member teaching in the Clinical Mental Health Program at SCSU and has been teaching graduate students for over 25 years. He has taught graduate classes in counseling theory, student affairs, crisis counseling, lifespan/career development, and internship supervision. Currently, David is the Interim Director of the Counseling and Wellness Center at Central Connecticut State University and maintains a private practice in North Haven, CT. He is also a Master Trainer of QPR and has taught the QPR curriculum for several years; he was instrumental in bringing the QPR model to the state university system in Connecticut. David has also been a Red Cross mental health first responder, assisted with relief efforts for hurricanes Katrina and Sandy and has been a volunteer with the rebuilding of the 9th Ward in New Orleans.

Aaron W. Hughey is a Professor and Program Coordinator in the Department of Counseling and Student Affairs at Western Kentucky University, where he oversees the graduate degree program in Student Affairs in Higher Education.

Before joining the faculty in 1991, he spent ten years in progressive administrative positions, including five years as the Associate Director of University Housing at WKU. He was also Head of the Department of Counseling and Student Affairs for five years before returning to the faculty full time in 2008. Dr. Hughey has degrees from the University of Tennessee at Martin, the University of Tennessee at Knoxville, Western Kentucky University and Northern Illinois University. He has authored (or co-authored) over 50 refereed publications on a wide range of issues including leadership and student development, standardized testing, diversity and educational administration. He regularly presents at national and international conferences and consults extensively with companies and schools. He also provides training programs on a variety of topics centered on change management.

Tiffany Laine De Mott discovered her passion for teaching nearly 20 years ago while working as a visual merchandising manager for Pottery Barn. A portion of her job responsibilities was to train store managers to merchandise on their own when she wasn't around. She soon realized the joy that came with helping some-one find confidence in a new skill, so off to graduate school she ran.

In addition to video production and photography, Tiffany teaches several facets of semiotics and storytelling at Cornish College of the Arts in Seattle. When she is not designing or in the classroom, you can find her wandering through second-hand shops with her family in pursuit of vintage still and movie cameras and antique, macabre children's books. She also enjoys dabbling in amateur music composition when she can find the time. Tiffany holds a BFA from Mason Gross School of the Arts at Rutgers University in photography with a focus on narrative, artist books. At the Rhode Island School of Design she earned her MFA in graphic design with an emphasis on digital media while fulfilling a teaching fellowship. She has a Collegiate Teaching Certification from Brown University.

W. Scott Lewis is a partner with The NCHERM Group. He serves as the 2013–2014 president of NaBITA, and is a founder and advisory board member of ATIXA. He is one of the most in-demand higher education risk management consultants in the country. Previously, he served as Special Advisor to Saint Mary's College in South Bend, IN and as AVP at the University of South Carolina, where he was also on faculty. Scott brings over 20 years of experience as a student affairs administrator, faculty member and consultant in higher education. He is noted as well for his work in the area of classroom management and dealing with disruptive students (and parents), and has trained thousands of faculty and staff members.

Mitchell A. Levy possesses 30 years of experience in Higher Education Administration, including 22 years as a graduate and undergraduate professor, having taught 150+ courses. Dr. Levy was awarded Full Professor (Adjunct) status in the Fordham University Graduate School of Education, and at present is an Associate Professor (Adjunct) in the Long Island University Graduate School of Education. Currently, he is the Dean of Students at Atlantic Cape Community College. In addition, he is a member of the National Center for Higher Education Risk Management (NCHERM) Behavioral Mental Health Consultation Team, the National Behavioral Intervention Team Association (NaBITA) Advisory Council and the New York City Higher Education Task Force on Student Wellness and Anti-Bullying. As a consultant, he has presented 200+ workshops, webinars, and presentations regarding emerging issues in Higher Education.

Eric Manley is a Counseling Psychologist at the Western Kentucky University Counseling and Testing Center. He completed his doctoral degree at the University of Memphis. Eric has published in the areas of counseling research, LGBT studies, and working with veterans who have returned to college. Eric is also part-time faculty in the department of psychology and has taught a number of undergraduate psychology classes, ranging from Test and Measures to Abnormal Psychology. Eric's clinical interests include LGBT issues, couples, working with veterans, trauma, career counseling and EMDR. As a member of APA and ACA, Eric maintains his education in psychology and enjoys studying new techniques and theories. In his spare time, Eric enjoys travel, reading, family and friends, and taking care of his three dogs.

Bernard A. Polnariev has continually proven himself over the past 15 years to be a poised academic administrator, researcher, and faculty member with the ability to successfully lead teams, teach, collaborate, and communicate effectively with students, staff, faculty, and all levels of management. He currently serves as the Administrative Executive Officer for Academic Affairs at LaGuardia Community College—charged primarily with supporting learning outcomes assessment and ensuring focused strategic plans for the institution. Dr. Polnariev was previously the director of the Accelerated Study in Associate Programs (ASAP)—achieving community college success with impressive student remediation, retention, and graduation outcomes with the support of a great team as noted in a 2012 MDRC report on developmental student success. He created several assessment feedback loops on essential components of the ASAP model for LaGuardia; ASAP was prominently highlighted in the college's 2012 reaccreditation evaluation report. Prior to functioning in an administrative capacity, Dr. Polnariev spent a decade teaching both undergraduate- and graduate-level psychology courses throughout NYC colleges. He is proud of the many initiatives that he spearheaded, in particular, the Art of Advising faculty professional development seminars for which he and his colleague won the 2011

NASPA's Student Affairs Partnering with Academic Affairs (SAPAA) Promising Practices Award.

M. J. Raleigh has been a college mental health provider, graduate training director and center director for over two decades. Throughout her career she has conducted research, crafted policy relevant to college counseling, and supervised professional and intern staff in the field. Dr. Raleigh has been awarded the ACCA professional development award in 2006 for outstanding service to the field of college mental health and the ACCA president award in 2011. As a member of CAS, ACA and ACCA, Dr. Raleigh continues to reach out to other professionals through webinars, publications and research in the field. In her role as consultant, MJ has presented at conferences and conducted webinars on LGBTQ safe campus, ethical compliance to Title IX and college mental health legal concerns. As an adjunct faculty member with Johns Hopkins University Dr. Raleigh oversees graduate interns as well as teaching courses in clinical practice and theory.

Corrine R. Sackett is Assistant Professor and Director of the Talley Family Counseling Center in the Counseling and Student Affairs Department at Western Kentucky University. Dr. Sackett holds a Ph.D. in Counselor Education from Virginia Tech, and an M.A. in Marriage and Family Therapy from Appalachian State University. She teaches and supervises advanced level graduate students during their practicum and internship placements in Counseling. Dr. Sackett's research focuses on experiences of the counseling process, and the implications for supervision.

Brian Van Brunt joined The NCHERM Group as Senior Vice President for Professional Program Development in January of 2013. He is past-president of the American College Counseling Association (ACCA) and has a Doctoral Degree in Counseling Supervision and Education from the University of Sarasota/Argosy and a Master's Degree in Counseling and Psychological Services from Salem State University. Dr. Van Brunt has taught at a number of universities and colleges over his career. He has offered classes in counseling theory, ethics, program evaluation, statistics and sociology for both graduate and undergraduate students. Brian has served as the Director of Counseling at New England College and Western Kentucky University. He is the author of *Ending Campus Violence: New Approaches in Prevention*.

Carolyn Reinach Wolf is a Senior Partner in the law firm of Abrams, Fensterman, Fensterman, Eisman, Formato, Ferrara & Einiger, LLP and Partner-in-Charge of the Firm's Mental Health Law practice. Ms. Wolf holds a J.D. from Hofstra University School of Law, an M.S. in Health Services Administration from the Harvard School of Public Health and an M.B.A. in Management from the

Hofstra University School of Business. She is admitted to practice in New York State and Federal Courts as well as the U.S. Supreme Court. In addition, Ms. Wolf is currently an adjunct professor at Hofstra Law School, teaching Law and Psychiatry. Prior to practicing law, Ms. Wolf was a hospital administrator and Director of Hospital Risk Management. Ms. Wolf is a frequently invited speaker and consultant to health care and mental health organizations as well as institutions of higher education, specifically university counseling centers and administrators, and professional associations throughout the country regarding mental health law issues. Her topics include: mental health legal issues, health and risk management from a mental health care law perspective, the increasing rate of student suicides, serious mental illness on campus, drug and alcohol abuse, date rape, law enforcement, confidentiality, parental notification, documentation and the increasing liability of campus staff, administrators, mental health professionals and the institutions themselves.

Preface

Welcome to our book. We truly appreciate your willingness to spend time with us on the topic of how to handle disruptive and dangerous behavior in the classroom.

This resource is useful for new and experienced professors and those instructors and educators who work in our colleges and universities. The book contains useful information for both more traditional four-year institutions as well as community and technical colleges. We include a wealth of case studies and personal stories from our years of teaching in a variety of college and university classrooms. Each chapter concludes with thought-provoking discussion questions that help to expand discussion of the chapter's content with your peers and fellow faculty.

The book is divided into four sections: Foundations of Classroom Management, Individual Behavior in Context, Community Referral and Final Thoughts. This organization provides instructors with some clear guidance on how to approach classroom management, highlights the importance of understanding behavior of individuals from their unique perspective and ends with exploring how faculty can best connect student behavior problems to campus resources.

In "Foundations of Classroom Management," the reader will develop a better understanding of the differences between disruptive and dangerous behavior as it occurs in the classroom. Chapters in this section focus on what a professor should be looking for in the classroom and how to develop the appropriate stance and mindset to successfully mitigate the crisis and move the student toward more appropriate behaviors. Chapters are also dedicated to teaching educators the central concepts of threat assessment to help better prepare them to identify the risk factors associated with more extreme campus violence.

Readers will find a wealth of information in the "Individual Behavior in Context" section. This section includes chapters dedicated to the unique populations such as GLBT students, African American students, Millennial, veteran and non-traditional students, as well as those with mental health disorders. The mental health behavior in the classroom chapter includes helpful text inserts that offer advice on what to do and what not to do when working with these students. The chapter on working with African American students also includes advice to better manage microaggressions; those subtle and often unintentional devaluing statements or actions placed on a minority group by those in a position of privilege. There is also a chapter provided on the unique needs of professors and instructors who work with students in online environments.

The final section is entitled "Community Referral". This section highlights the importance of faculty referring chronic and potentially dangerous behavior to the appropriate use of on-campus recourse to ensure proper follow-up and risk mitigation. This section includes chapters on how faculty should refer to their campus Behavioral Intervention Team (BIT) or Student of Concern teams. An experienced conduct officer and friend of the authors', Laura Bennett, shares a chapter in this section to help faculty better understand who they should be referring to the campus conduct and/or BIT.

The book concludes with the "Final Thoughts" section discussing the qualities necessary to effectively manage both disruptive and dangerous behavior in the classroom. Ten core concepts are provided along with illustrative case examples and practical advice on how to best handle classroom behavior problems. These concepts include: displaying confidence, humility, the importance of timing, how and when to use grace and mercy, developing an awareness and curiosity, using active listening, asking clarifying questions, the importance of consultation and how and when to exert control.

Throughout the book, the reader will have the opportunity to read dozens of personal reflections and stories entitled "From the Trenches." These captivating stories arise from experienced faculty from across the United States who share their wisdom and experience in handling behaviors in community college classrooms. These funny, seasoned teaching veterans create narratives that appeal to newly minted and timeworn professors who have been teaching for decades. They offer some creative ideas and approaches to handling a wide range of disruptive and sometimes dangerous behaviors from seasoned professors.

We extend our deepest thanks to our friends and colleagues who offered their stories of success (and failure) when dealing with disruptive and dangerous behavior. Aaron, Bernard, Carolyn, Corrine, Cort, David, Laura, Eric, Jack, MJ, Mitchell, Monica and Tiffany—this book could not have been possible without the gracious sharing of your stories. Your wisdom, insight, thoughtfulness, kindness and humor provide an excellent perspective for new and experienced instructors and professors alike.

We also extend our gratitude to Heather Jarrow, our editor at the Routledge/ Taylor & Francis Group. Her patient and thorough comments have made this a much stronger book.

W. Scott Lewis
Brian Van Brunt

Abbreviations

ACCA	American College Counseling Association
ADA	Americans with Disabilities Act
ASCA	Association for Student Conduct Administration
ASD	Autism Spectrum Disorder
BIT	Behavioral Intervention Team
CAP	Campus Assistance Program
CTD	Concerning, Threatening and Dangerous
DOE	Department of Education
DOJ	Department of Justice
DSSO	Disability Support Services Office
EAP	Employee Assistance Program
FBI	Federal Bureau of Investigation
FERPA	Family Education Rights and Privacy Act
FYE	first year experience
HIPPA	Health Insurance Portability and Accountability Act
IEP	Individualized Education Plan
MET	Motivational Enhancement Therapy
NaBITA	National Behavioral Intervention Team Association
NCHERM	National Center for Higher Education Risk Management
OCR	Office for Civil Rights
PTA	Parent/Teacher Association
PTSD	Post Traumatic Stress Disorder
RAT	Risk Assessment Team
REBT	Rational Emotive Behavioral Therapy
RV	recreational vehicle
SCO	Student Conduct Office
TAT	Threat Assessment Team
VPSA	Vice President of Student Affairs
WDEP	Wants, Direction and Doing, Evaluation, Planning

Part I

Foundations of Classroom Management

Chapter 1

Identifying the Crisis

WHAT IS A CRISIS?

Crisis is contextual.

Let us explain. One of the greatest challenges in responding to a crisis situation is first acknowledging that you are experiencing something outside of your everyday experience. It's difficult to train faculty to respond to disruptive and dangerous behavior without first addressing the idea that each professor, whether male or female, young or old, new or experienced, has a different tolerance for the variety of disruptive and dangerous behavior encountered in the classroom.

Think about what kind of activity you enjoy in your free time. For some, careening backwards in a darkened cavern while being chased by a 50 foot Yeti at Walt Disney World is their idea of a perfect vacation. Others consider this medieval style torture. Our leisure is defined by our individual tastes and experiences. Our response to a crisis is no different. We each have a unique view of what frustrates us in the classroom. Developing an appreciation of "what upsets you might not upset me" and the corollary—what works for you in handling frustrating behavior may not work for me—is a helpful place to start when understanding disruptive and dangerous behavior.

Why is all of this important? It's important because we can't just give you a checklist of disruptive and dangerous behaviors and a corresponding "if a, then b" approach to handling these problems without taking into account the context of your worldview. This applies to both what's considered disruptive and what interventions you bring to bear in a given situation. One professor becomes enraged at a student who doesn't show up for class, while another might pride himself on having a flexible attendance policy and doesn't mandate class attendance. One professor encourages questions during his lecture while another instructor requires students to hold questions until the end of class. One uses humor to calm a disruptive student who acts disrespectfully in class while another may dismiss a student from class for the same behavior.

So where does this leave us? Our goal in writing this book is to create a useful collection of research-based theories and intervention techniques explained through stories and vignettes to identify and manage disruptive and dangerous behavior in the classroom. We will clarify and define those behaviors that fall into the clear categories of disruption (yelling, rude attitude, or racist or misogynist language) as well as those behaviors that cross the line into the realm of dangerousness (direct threats to harm other students, throwing objects, or slamming doors). We will set the stage for an open and candid discussion of those "grey area" behaviors that may frustrate some professors, but not others (attendance in class, asking questions out of turn, use of personal technology in the classroom).

Once we define these behaviors, we will review how to work with these students effectively, how to understand the individual motivations that may cause the behaviors and how to refer these students for help within the larger campus community. These approaches to address disruptive and dangerous classroom behavior are best understood as a loose collection of tools; each applied in a given situation with attention toward the utility and efficacy of the given technique. These are the techniques used by professors to confront classroom behavior and achieve compliance in a manner that keeps the peace and redirects the student's inappropriate behaviors back into the norm of the classroom. In more dangerous or potentially violent interactions, the goal becomes keeping the professor, other students and the student causing the disruption—in that order—safe from harm.

The techniques we discuss will require aptitude and appropriateness in their application. Consider this: You can take a wrench and try to use it to cut a board in half, but that's not the right tool for the job. You would be more successful in reaching your goal by using a saw. Choosing the right approach for the given situation is critical. Yelling back at an escalating, rude or entitled student isn't the right tool (no matter how cathartic it might feel). Embarrassing a student in class who is misusing technology (surfing the web on a laptop or checking text messages in class) isn't the best way to address that behavior. In essence, it's using a screwdriver to hammer a nail into a board. You might be able to get the job done, but there are easier, more effective, ways. We will discuss and explore the variety of techniques and tools available while keeping an eye on how to use them in a practical way.

Another point we'd like to make is the importance of appreciating the unique abilities, knowledge and experience of instructors as they apply a given technique. Some excel at using humor to engage a student without offending them. Others' attempts at humor end up feeling forced and make a crisis situation worse. Some instructors display genuine concern and caring through personal questions. Some treat their students with a degree of humanity and empathy that immediately garners respect. Others attempt this same stance and end up coming off as pushy or prying to the student. The right technique, applied to the right situation with experience and skill is the ideal. A single technique or comment made at the wrong time can lead to an intervention that fails to persuade the student to comply.

There are some essential, foundational qualities to bring about successful management of a crisis situation. These are "tried and true" stalwarts that prove efficacious in almost every situation. An example is approaching a student with respect and patience. Another is a professor who seeks to understand the student's perspective before rushing to offer a response. Setting clear expectations at the start of the class in the syllabus would be a third. These are non-negotiable, effective approaches to classroom management. Like the game of chess, it is easy to learn but takes a lifetime to master.

Some more "advanced" techniques require a bit more training and strategic application for success. In wise and experienced hands, these tools of classroom management are extremely effective in provoking thoughtful consideration and growth within the student. These may include the use of humor or probing and personal questions. They may include one-on-one conversations that closely echo those in a counseling relationship. They may involve giving direct advice, setting inflexible limits and boundaries, or the involvement of the peer group to challenge and motivate the student towards change.

To explain this further, let us offer the following example. Think about martial arts training. Learning one technique well, say a front punch, might be just the thing for some martial artists. They find it serves their needs. In a fight, they respond with this effective and well-practiced attack. The teaching corollary is the professor who listens to students first before attempting to correct their misconceptions (or rude or entitled behavior). This is a tried and true metaphorical "front punch" that will always yield an effective result. Patiently conveying a concern for a student's mental health or showing empathy in response to their environmental stress is always a better way to begin a confrontation. Practice this technique well over time and you could put down this book right now and have about 80% of what it means to handle classroom disruptions and dangerous behavior.

Other martial artists may wish to invest more time and energy to develop, say, "a spinning back fist of certain doom." This certainly sounds very effective (and painful), though learning how to do it well requires much more practice, experience and necessitates a more tactical application. The teaching corollary here may be a professor who uses humor (or even sarcasm) to de-escalate a potentially dangerous student who is escalating in the classroom. It can be very, very effective in the right situation if applied strategically. It also could result in a total disaster if the technique isn't applied correctly.

Carrying the martial arts analogy to its conclusion, any practitioner of martial arts knows the mantra "use common sense before self-defense." That is to say, another common misconception is that we forget the power of prevention, and the ability to avoid a situation by engaging in good preventive practices. While we will spend a fair amount of time on how to manage disruptive situations, we will also spend time on prevention, as it is critical.

We want to clear up a common problem when new professors ask for advice on how to handle classroom disruption. Many have sought council from peers and "wise elders" and they have struggled to successfully use the advice in their own classroom. A memorable professor shared how she was able to get the class back to order when a discussion became too passionate or moved away from the focus of the lecture. She told us, "Well, I just tell them to shut up." And strangely enough, that worked very well for her. Students respected this motherly figure and her use of sarcasm with the class was very effective.

You can imagine if we tried her approach with our classes, many students would take offense and would have called us rude or report us to the Department Head for unprofessional behavior. And this brings us back full circle to the concept of classroom management being contextual and subjective. What works for some, given their background as the setting in which they apply their approach, may not work so well for others.

Another common problem is that, when we utilize "old" methods to work with new problems, we often fail. Many professors have shared with us their frustration about their "tried and true" techniques no longer working over these last few years. It's because the student has changed. We could spend a ton of time explaining why, but you will just have to trust us on this one. The details behind that are for the next book.

Allow us to make one more point before moving forward. We have noticed an interesting psychological phenomenon over the years. It reminds us of the story about the emperor who had no clothes. Remember that one? He ends up parading down the street wearing not a stitch because no one tells him that his magnificent outfit is really just his birthday suit.

Professors are like this sometimes (not you of course—and certainly not us—but some of them out there are like this). Professors get to talk for hours each week, often with very little feedback. They have total control of their course content with very little oversight from their Department Heads. They are praised for controlling their classrooms and being able to do so without assistance. They pontificate, ramble, meander, blather and sometimes just make stuff up. They receive very little direction in how they teach and are allowed to develop their own classroom standards, rules and social mores. It can be a little like *Lord of the Flies* when left unchecked.

This academic freedom can create some truly great professors. It allows them to lead and create based on their ideas and thoughts. It lets them alter direction and change the lecture focus to accommodate a vibrant class discussion. It allows for creative and critical thinking. This freedom has the potential to create unique and wonderful learning environments for students.

However, all this academic freedom can also create some really arrogant, entitled and rude professors that are well defended against criticism, suggestions for improvements or challenges to their fiefdom (again, not you or us, of course). Professors may develop serious blind spots in their teaching techniques and, by extension, their ability to manage classroom disruption and crisis. These blind spots can be institutionalized when professors are encouraged to control their classrooms and handle conflict on their own. There is a subtle message: "good professors control their students." End of story.

Some might say "What about course evaluations? Wouldn't they sort all of this out?" and they would be right. Professors do have an opportunity to get feedback from their performance evaluations. However, students rarely make good use of these evaluations. They are often too tired at the end of class to share any well-thought out reflections. Others don't want to say something negative and hurt the professor's job. A few may "let loose" on their evaluations and say some pretty horrific things about the professor's clothes, teaching style and apparent lack of any social graces. But this is rare and those students' over-the-top comments are readily dismissed as the rantings of the crazed outliers. In the end, carefully considered and constructive feedback is rare to encounter from students stressed out at the end of the semester and forced to fill out a scantron sheet before rushing off to study for their next final.

This is one of the reasons we wrote this book. We want to call some of you out on your behavior because, really, there just aren't that many opportunities for a professor to hear "hey, there is a better way to do that." We know that has been our path over a combined 30 years of teaching. It has only through blind luck, and perhaps some skills learned in our other professions as a college counseling center director and a student conduct administrator that we have been successful as professors. For us, it has been a combination of on the job learning as well as taking advantage of professional development opportunities—everything from counselors to cops to other professors to K–12 teachers—and paying attention to the changing student population.

Perhaps this message will bounce off of your well-defended view of yourself as a teacher. We hope not. We'd ask you to lower your guard just a little bit. Just to see how it feels.

Perhaps we are preaching to the choir and you aren't in need of redirection in your teaching or crisis management methodology. If this is so, then we are glad we see eye to eye. Hopefully you can still find something new and useful in this book.

It may be you are so set in your ways that you aren't looking for a new way of doing things, especially from us or a required reading of a book on classroom management your Department Head put into your lap.

And maybe—just maybe—this book is for you. Maybe you want to be better at handling the conversation with a student who says she is thinking of killing herself. Maybe you wonder if there is another way to deal with a student who sneaks a text underneath his desk than yelling at him or embarrassing him in front of his classmates. Maybe you want to know what kind of behaviors you should handle yourself and what you need to share with your campus Behavioral Intervention Team (this goes by many names) or Student Conduct Office. Maybe you want to be a better teacher. Good, us too.

WHISTLING DIXIE

As a teacher of interdisciplinary courses, including a first year experience course (FYE) entitled University Experience, my chief goal is to teach students to think critically and interdisciplinarily as well as to help them transition into university life and flourish in life after college. The FYE focuses on learning about critical thinking, university culture, academic skills and the practices of a good citizen in a global society.

I have the pleasure of teaching an incredibly diverse range of students in my courses. General sections of the FYE consist mainly of traditional, first-year students from Kentucky and the Southern United States. However, my summer sessions contain tremendous racial and geographical diversity, as they are often heavily populated with student-athletes. These students hail from all over the U.S. and occasionally other continents. This diverse geographical mix coupled with the often strong personalities of Division I athletes make for an exciting and interesting teaching experience, which I enjoy and appreciate immensely.

Challenges do arise, and one challenging disruptive behavior scenario involved a group of football players. It was early into the summer session, and there had been a couple of minor but common occurrences of inappropriate side conversations and the like. But, one particular day I noticed that each time I turned my back to write on the board, a low whistling noise would begin. When I turned around, it would stop. This happened multiple times, as my initial approach to deal with this was to simply not acknowledge "junior high" behavior in a college classroom. But, it soon became clear that this approach was not going to work, and it was beginning to cause others in the class to snicker.

So, I simply said, "Whoever is making the whistling noise, please stop. Thanks." That did not work, either, as it only got louder the next time I turned my back. Not knowing the "right" approach here, I finally said, "Whoever is making the whistling noise, I'd like to you leave." I had never (and have not since) asked a student to leave class, so this is not a common strategy that I employ. Still, no one stood up. I asked again. Nothing. I turned . . . and I heard the whistle start once again. At this point, I said, "Class will not resume until the person who is whistling leaves the room."

Minutes passed. Many students, already uncomfortable with just seconds of silence, were becoming very uncomfortable as time ticked by and I calmly stood in front of the class and sipped coffee. Finally, one of the brawniest of the football players (not the whistler) turned and said, "Whoever did that needs to leave. This isn't grade school." A few seconds passed before the person I suspected was the whistler rose to leave. But, in a somewhat unexpected turn of events, two other fellow footballers rose almost simultaneously and left with him. Two more followed suit. At this stage, I feared a dozen or more people might simply exit the classroom. Ultimately, the standoff resulted in just those five students walking out. I was not sure whether I had helped or hurt the situation at that moment. After the five students left, I apologized to the remaining students, but most seemed to understand and several said, "You had to do something." We resumed class and that day's class went well from that point.

That night, three of the five students who had exited class that day emailed saying that they were not the whistler, but left as a show of unity with their teammate and that they could not let him leave alone (although none named the whistler, either). I met with all five of them after class the following day, and said that I was not angry, but that the whistler should take responsibility for his actions. Of course, being student-athletes, I had the option of simply going to their coach and having him rain hellfire down upon all five of them. But, I also clearly communicated that our class was not football practice, and I did not want to go that route. There seemed to be an understanding, and the whistler eventually owned up to his actions (albeit reluctantly).

I wish I could say that all five went on to do very well in the course, but not all five did. I wish I could say that I know I took the correct course of action, but I cannot say that, either. What I do know is that, when faced with "in the moment" challenges that demand action, there are a raft of options and probably not a perfect one. My personality, the makeup of the class, the timing of the event (it was very early on in an 80-minute class session) and many other factors affected the situation. What I can also say is that I had very few behavioral issues in that class after that day and no lasting damage was done to the class or to my relationship with the five students who left. And, from their point of view, perhaps those guys probably did foster some "team unity" through that event.

Cort Basham
First Year Program/General Education Professor
Western Kentucky University

QUESTIONS FOR FURTHER DISCUSSION

Here are some additional questions to help you better understand crisis and how other professors handle classroom management. These questions are useful for self-reflection or to assist in facilitating a group discussion during a faculty training or orientation session.

1. We suggest that "crisis is contextual." Describe a time where you encountered a crisis event that would have been altered (either worse or better) if the crisis had occurred in a different environment.

2. We offer a controversial viewpoint that some professors may become isolated from helpful feedback and find themselves insulated from other points of view and opinions. Talk about how you agree or disagree with this premise.

3. We argue that each professor or instructor must find their own way of interacting with the class based on their own set of skills and abilities. Talk about the differences you have seen in how other colleagues in your department and at your institution address classroom management. Talk about times these approaches would work for you. Discuss times when they would not.

Chapter 2

What Should I be Looking For?

WHAT IS DISRUPTIVE AND WHAT IS DANGEROUS?

A central question lingers for faculty as they address difficult behavior in the classroom: "Is this kid going to come back into the classroom with a gun and start shooting people?" Given recent news stories involving high school violence and attacks at institutes of higher education, it's no surprise that this question remains crucial to those teaching on the front lines.

The answer? It depends. We must estimate the risk of violence within the contextual baseline of past behavior and understand potential risk factors. There is no be-speckled, goatee-sporting analyst to give us a definitive answer about a student's future violence. There is no psychological test or expert computer system that will predict the next campus shooting. The best alternative, agreed upon by those who study threat assessment and potential dangerousness, relies on understanding the context of the behavior within a focus on the nature, quality and the immediacy of the potential violence. This brings us closer to determining the level of risk and the appropriate response.

Allow us to bring the question forward with some practical examples.

HOWARD: ANGRY AND EXPLOSIVE

Howard is a student in your class who has a low tolerance for frustration. This is the third time he has taken the remedial math class and he becomes easily overwhelmed with the assignments. Howard is known to slam his book shut, curse, gripe and complain about upcoming tests. He has stormed out of the classroom on several occasions. You have tried to understand and be empathetic to his difficulties mastering this required math class, but things aren't getting better. After he receives a failing grade on an exam he stays after class and says, "I don't know what is going to happen if I don't pass your class this time. I won't take it again. If I fail, we are going to have a problem." He doesn't give you a chance to respond and leaves the classroom.

Is Howard the next psychopath, ready to explode and take his classmates with him? Is Howard merely a frustrated student, unsure of how to climb out of a seemingly impossible hole in which he has dug himself? Should his statement be taken as a threat and reported to the campus police or is he talking about reporting you to "your boss" or giving you a bad evaluation? Should his statement be seen as a childlike, rude and entitled expression of a student who has come to the realization he will be taking remedial math for a fourth time?

While Howard's frustration may be understandable, his behavior is not acceptable in the classroom. Howard displays a history of impulsive acting out behaviors such as cursing, slamming books shut and voicing his frustrations despite the presence of social norms and college rules encouraging civil behavior. His ultimate statement to the professor is a slightly veiled threat that requires further evaluation and assessment to determine the potential risk. Howard's behavior is dangerous and requires notification of your campus Behavioral Intervention Team (BIT), campus student conduct officer and/or campus police or security (always being mindful that conduct and police are members of most BITs, so telling one may be telling two or more.). While it may be that Howard is just a disgruntled student frustrated with his math class, he may act this way in all of his classes. Howard may have a long history of making threats like this. The only way to assess whether his threat is "dangerousness" or just impulsive acting out behavior is through a proper threat assessment and connection to your campus BIT.

GRACE: ODD AND THREATENING

Imagine Grace, a student in your Introduction to French History class. Grace is an odd student who is often the butt of teasing from others in the class. She seems to struggle with social interaction, speaks with an odd inflection and often disrupts lectures with off-topic questions and lengthy rants about her understanding of French history. She is smart and often shares insightful comments that would belong in a more advanced and nuanced class. The problem is in her delivery. She comes across as arrogant and disconnected from others in the classroom. You have talked to Grace on several occasions about keeping her questions and comments to a minimum. These conversations don't go well and Grace responds with a sullen and snarky mood for the next several classes. During a discussion of the French revolution and the use of the guillotine, Grace shouts, "I'd like to have you put your head down on a wooden stump and use a guillotine to cut your head off." You ask Grace to leave the classroom. She leaves, slamming the door in the process and mutters "bitch" under her breath.

Grace has made a clear threat against a professor and engaged in some rude and disrespectful behavior in front of a classroom of students. Her outburst will likely have little positive impact on her social status among her peers. How should her threat be handled? Could there be a mental health component to Grace's social behavior? What happens when Grace comes back to the next class section later in the week?

Grace has made a threat against a professor, although "death by guillotine" would likely require massive funding and carpentry knowledge. While the nature of the threat may not indicate a high lethality event (compared to Grace threatening to shoot her professor with her father's .38 revolver he gave her so she would be safe at college), her poor reaction to the professor's redirection of her poor social behavior and off-topic classroom discussions is a concern. Grace may have a history of social difficulties or a diagnosis of a mental health disorder such as an Autism Spectrum Disorder/Aspergers. Reporting her threat to the Student Conduct Office or Behavioral Intervention Team will allow for further investigation and potential referral to support services such as counseling and/or the Disability Support office on campus. The threat, while likely not a high concern for the professor, may be a first step to connect Grace with support services. Though not likely dangerous, Grace's disruption requires some intervention.

DYLAN: UNMOTIVATED AND INTOXICATED

Perhaps you teach a required University 101 class for incoming first year students. When he's in class, Dylan sits as far away from the front of the classroom as he possibly can. He wears a dark grey hoody pulled up over his head and seems to fight the urge (at times, unsuccessfully) to just lay his head down on the desk and take a nap. You've talk to Dylan about his lack of focus and attention in class, showing up without a notebook or pen and his difficulty turning in his homework assignments. During the talk, Dylan smells strongly of alcohol and you notice his eyes are bloodshot. Dylan has little chance of passing your class and you worry about him getting caught up with a bad crowd at college and developing an alcohol or drug problem.

Do you report Dylan? Should you remove him from class? Do you allow his behavior to continue and just have him experience the natural consequences of failing your class? Are there supports to which you can refer Dylan to get some help? How do you handle Dylan's likely negative reaction to being confronted about his smelling of alcohol?

With Dylan's behavior, there is even less danger apparent here when compared to Grace's unlikely threat. Dylan's problem will likely result in his eventual failing of his University 101 class and potentially other classes where his drinking, and lack of motivation would impact his grades. Some type of referral and intervention should be provided to Dylan, whether you go through academic affairs or through the campus BIT. In addition to campus BITs offering some threat assessment capacity, a more frequent utilization of the team is to offer referrals and assistance to students struggling with everything from mental health or substance abuse problems to financial aid, disability, or time management issues. Another possibility is that Dylan simply has connected with the wrong crowd and may be in need of the "Deanly" talk about his commitment to college, balancing academic work and his social life. Adopting the attitude, "You are an alcoholic and a drunk, get out of my class" assumes many things that may not be accurate. A more careful, contextual assessment is needed.

CARLOS: DEPRESSED AND SUICIDAL

Imagine Carlos is a student in your Anatomy and Physiology class. This is a required course for nursing students. It is a difficult course and about a third of the students find the course so hard they have to take it a second time in order to achieve the required C grade to be accepted by the nursing program. Carlos has failed the first test and shared his worry about being kicked out of the nursing program due to a poor grade. You encourage him to study harder and perhaps encourage him to visit the campus tutoring center to assist with his studies. He tells you how important the nursing program is to him and that he has always dreamed of being a nurse. Carlos becomes increasingly anxious in class and begins to struggle in the lab assignments. On a particular dissection project, he runs from the classroom in a state of panic, worried he is going to make a mistake. Carlos fails to show up for the next week and misses a study session before the second exam. He sends you this email:

> *Professor.* Thank you for trying to help me. I have failed and I am a failure. I don't know what I will do, but I wanted to thank you for your kindness if I don't see you again. Please donate my lab dissection tools to a future needy student. I won't need them. Goodbye.

Is Carlos dropping the class or is Carlos thinking of killing himself? Should you report this behavior to someone? Is it appropriate to ask Carlos directly about suicide? Is that your role as a professor?

Carlos presents with a mixture of anxiety and depression. His note suggests two potential suicide concerns (giving objects away and a veiled threat of "I don't know what I will do" and "Goodbye"). While these may be the only hint we get prior to Carlos going home and putting a gun to his head, it may be just as likely that he has decided to drop his A&P class and is thanking his professor and saying goodbye since he no longer will be in the class; his behavior could be a simple expression of shame that he is having to change his major. As with threat assessment, suicide assessment requires further questioning of Carlos such as asking him: "When you say 'I don't know what I will do' and 'goodbye', it makes me think you might be thinking of killing yourself. Is that what you mean?" Given the academic difficulties, apparent anxiety and depression seen in class, a referral to the counseling center or BIT may be in order for Carlos, and a representative from the BIT is likely the best person to ask these questions.

UNDERSTANDING THE DISRUPTIVE

In conversations with our faculty colleagues, we discuss the entitled and immature nature of many of those coming to college, whether to a four-year institution or a two-year community college. Some students seem to lack a general sense of civility and common sense that used to be prerequisites to being successful in higher education. We aren't talking about the extreme John Houseman *Paper Chase* kind of respect. What seems to be lacking is the basic respect of addressing faculty by a proper name and the inability to ask questions without a sense of rudeness or entitlement. In extreme cases, students experience frustrations by yelling, throwing things or storming out of the classroom.

Again, this is *some* of our students. Not all. Like a rotten apple in the center of a bushel of apples, it can be tempting to cast generalities when teaching today's college students. There is a temptation to paint with broad brushstrokes and see a single, poorly behaved student as evidence of a generational lack of respect or focus. We see a student such as Howard and run the risk of seeing other student's frustrations with math through the same lens.

As we continue to discuss disruptive and dangerous behavior, we'd like to offer a caution. Do not extrapolate a single student's behavior to an entire class or generation of students. While each generation may have some unique characteristics based on the time in which they were raised or the prevailing attitude toward parenting, each student brings a unique worldview and subjective context to their behavior. We can only differentiate disruptive from dangerous behavior when we see each student as an individual and avoid overarching statements such as "all these kids lack the kind of respect I had for professors" and "this whole generation is entitled and averse to the kind of hard work needed to be successful at college." These statements create blind spots for us and make our jobs more difficult.

That being said, there are some aspects of generational analysis that do have value and have been able to offer some explanation for these behaviors. Of course, extrapolating the fringe aberrant behaviors coming from these analyses to all members of a generation would be inappropriate, but to ignore them would be to ignore the new and changing norms and mores of a generation with differ-ent impactful experiences—and we would do so to our detriment. For example, the use of cell phones during conversation—unbelievably rude to those from an earlier, pre-cell phone era—is an expectation of those under the age of 25, with no discourteous overtones at all. Another example comes from the study by Sara Konrath that shows that this generation has significantly less empathy when compared to earlier generations (O'Brien 2010). This may explain what we see as a "sense of entitlement."

15

UNDERSTANDING THE DANGEROUS

So, where does this leave us on the central questions concerning what is "disruptive" and what is "dangerous" behavior in the classroom? We've stressed the importance of understanding concerning behavior in the context of past behavior, the situation at hand, and other behaviors (in other venues) you as the professor may or may not be aware of from the student. We'd be more concerned about a student such as Carlos if we learn he has recently looked into a local firing range where he could rent a handgun to kill himself. We would be more concerned if Dylan spent last Friday night in the emergency room after being treated for alcohol poisoning. We would be more concerned about Grace if we learned that she had a recent assault incident.

Threat and risk are best understood in the context of the individual and the environment. Passing information onto the campus BIT is the best way to ensure a centralized group of trained faculty and staff is putting together the pieces of this puzzle. In essence, where you have a view of one snapshot of the student's situation, the BIT has the whole picture (or at least more of it).

On Friday, July 20, 2012, James Holmes shot and killed 12 people and injured 58 others. Holmes was a student at the University of Colorado and recent reports (CBS news, 2012) indicate he had made some kind of threats to his professor prior to the attack. It's this kind of worst-case scenario that leads us to encourage professors to report any potential threats they receive at the time of the behavior.

When addressing a veiled threat or a vaguely suicidal statement, it is important to err on the side of safety. Ask yourself, "What is the worst case scenario here?" and respond accordingly, generally with a referral. While it is unlikely Grace will assemble a guillotine to kill her professor, we can't wait until there is an escalation here in her behavior from simply being angry and upset to acting on her frustrations and communicating a threat to her professor. Plan for the worst and hope for the best. Take any threat or concern seriously and pass it along.

"We want a list of the 'problem' behaviors!" When we train faculty on disruptive and dangerous behavior, this is often what we hear. Despite the fact that all behaviors must be assessed in context to determine risk, people still want a list. So, let us give you a list with this caveat: these are meant to be gen-eralizations and behaviors that fit into either the category of "disruptive" or "dangerous." Both sets of behaviors will require some kind of faculty inter-vention—that is to say, no matter whether you refer or not, some aspect of classroom management must be employed or have been properly employed. Dangerous behaviors will likely require notification of your campus BIT, police, Student Conduct Office, Dean of Student office or campus counseling. Again, since the membership of the BIT likely includes members of one or more of these offices, notifying all may be redundant. But that is okay. Check with the Chair of your BIT or your chief Student Conduct Officer (they may be the same person) to see the best way to refer or report. Remember, the list is NOT meant to be exhaustive, or to replace the previous statements about behavior in context. Our focus in this portion of the chapter is to help faculty know what to look for so they can then intervene, manage and refer.

Examples of Disruptive Behaviors*

- Taking/making calls, texting, using smart phones for social media, etc.
- Students misuse of technology in the classroom. Sneaking text messages from beneath the desk or having a laptop open to Facebook™ or other social media site during a lecture.
- Frequent interruption of professor while talking and asking of non-relevant, off-topic questions.
- Inappropriate or overly revealing clothing in classroom; including extremely sexually provocative clothes, pajamas or sleepwear in the classroom.
- Crosstalk or carrying on side conversations while the professor is speaking.
- Interruptions such as frequent use of the restroom, smoke breaks, etc.
- Poor personal hygiene that leads to a classroom disruption or lack of focus.
- Use of alcohol or other substances in class. Attending class while under the influence of alcohol or other drugs.
- Entitled or disrespectful talk to professor or other students.
- Arguing grades or "grade grubbing" for extra points after the professor requests the student to stop.
- Eating or consuming beverages in class without permission (or against the class norms).
- Showing up to class in strange clothing (dressed in military gear, Halloween costumes when it is not Halloween, etc.).
- Reading magazines, newspapers (yes, they still read them, although usually the campus one), books or studying for other classes/doing other homework.

Examples of Dangerous Behaviors*

- Racist or otherwise *fixated* (not just expressed once to press a button) thoughts such as "Women should be barefoot and pregnant," "Gays are an abomination to God and should be punished," "Muslims are all terrorists and should be wiped off the earth."
- Bullying behavior focused on students in the classroom.
- Direct communicated threat to professor or another student such as: "I am going to kick your ass" or "If you say that again, I will end you."

17

- Prolonged non-verbal passive aggressive behavior such as sitting with arms crossed, glaring or staring at professor, refusal to speak or respond to questions or directives.
- Self-injurious behavior such as cutting or burning self during class, or exposing previously unexposed self-injuries.
- Physical assault such as pushing, shoving or punching.
- Throwing objects or slamming doors.
- Storming out of the classroom when upset.
- Conversations that are designed to upset other students such as descriptions of weapons, killing or death.
- Psychotic, delusional or rambling speech.
- Arrogant or rude talk to professor or other students.
- Objectifying language that depersonalizes the professor or other students.

* A similar list of behaviors that occur in the online community is provided in Chapter 9.

THE MYTH OF THE PROFILE IN REGARD TO DANGEROUSNESS

There isn't a list of characteristics that we can cross off a checklist to determine who the next school shooter will be. Those who have engaged in extreme rampage violence at high schools and colleges over the last decades include good students and failing students, socially well-liked and socially isolated, male and female, bullied and popular, Caucasian, Asian and African American. The Federal Bureau of Investigation (FBI), Department of Education (DOE), Department of Justice (DOJ), Secret Service and a number of threat assessment experts (Albrecht, 2010; Meloy et al., 2011; Meloy & O'Toole, 2011; O'Toole, 2002; Turner & Gelles, 2003; United States Post Office, 2007; Vossekuil et al., 2002) all agree that profiling a certain type of individual won't work when it comes to identifying rampage violence in high school and college settings.

The Secret Service and FBI offer this:

The threat assessment process is based on the premise that each situation should be viewed and assessed individually and guided by the facts. Judgments about an individual's risk of violence should be based upon an analysis of his/her behaviors and the context in which they occur. Blanket characterizations, demographic profiles, or stereotypes do not provide a reliable basis for making judgments of the threat posed by a particular individual.

(Drysdale, Modzeleski & Simons, 2010, p. 37)

18

Another expert in threat assessment, Dr. Mary Ellen O'Toole, recently released the book *Dangerous Instincts* (O'Toole & Bowman, 2011). She introduces the term CTD to represent Concerning, Threatening and Dangerous behavior. She presents several concerning behaviors that are based on her work as an FBI profiler and while not exhaustive, provide an excellent place to start when considering a person's risk. These behaviors are:

> impulsivity, inappropriate or out-of-control anger, narcissism, lack of empathy, injustice collecting, objectification of others, blaming others for failures or problems, paranoia, rule-breaking, use of violence, thoughts and fantasies of violence, drug and alcohol problems, poor coping skills, equal opportunity coping skills and thrill seeking.
>
> (pp. 181–182)

One of her concepts that we have found helpful in understanding those who develop plots of revenge and intricate schemes to inflict harm on others is the "injustice collector." O'Toole describes this individual as "a person who feels 'wronged', 'persecuted' and 'destroyed', blowing injustices way out of proportion, never forgiving the person they felt has wronged them" (p. 186). They kept track of their past wrongs and are often upset in a manner way beyond what would typically be expected. They hold onto past slights, many back as far as childhood and see the world from this "singled-out perspective" and often have poor coping skills to deal with their frustrations.

In 2012, Van Brunt completed a book in which he reviewed over 90 incidents of violence that took place in high schools and at college campuses (Van Brunt et al., 2012). Based on that research, we have developed ten general concepts to attend to when it comes to what kind of behaviors or situations most commonly lead to violence. While not an exhaustive list, this is a helpful starting place for professors to understand the nature of more extreme violence. It also should be shared that these can be classified as warning signs or red flags for further investigation.

TEN BEHAVIORS TO LOOK FOR

Simply raising these red flags does not imply that the student in front of you will be the next Jared Loughner (Von Drehle et al., 2011), Steven Kazmierczak (Vann, 2008) or Seung-Hui Cho (Virginia Tech Review Panel, 2007). However, these are the concepts we suggest to faculty when they want a list of ways to prevent violence in your classroom.

1. *Attend to potential leakage related to a planned campus attack.* This leakage may be overheard conversations, shared comments on social media such as

Facebook™, Twitter™ and YouTube™ postings or a direct communicated threat through a class journal, blog, webpage, e-portfolio. Faculty are in a unique position to "overhear" students who may be planning an attack. The news frequently covers high profile, high body count rampage shootings that occur in educational settings, but often reports little about the thwarted attacks prevented by a student or faculty member who took a threat seriously.

- In January 2011, a Cal State Northridge (Dobuzinskis, 2011) student shared with his counselor a threat against other people. The counselor reported this to the university police, and bomb-making materials and a shotgun where found in the student's room.

2. *Attend to work conflicts and terminations with fellow faculty and academic failures and program dismissals with students.* Emotions run high in these tense conflicts. These events should be seen as potential contextual tipping points for violence. A fellow professor who doesn't receive tenure or who has a poor performance evaluation can allow this frustration to build. A failing grade or separation from an academic program such as nursing or teacher certification could be the catalyst for a desperate student who sees no other way out but to kill or take revenge on those they deem responsible.

- In February of 2010, Amy Bishop (AP, 2010) shot six people, killing three, following a faculty meeting. It was reported she was upset with her treatment in the department and being denied tenure. She had a history of an explosive temper and there remain some questions about the accidental shotgun death of her brother at her hands.

3. *Investigate and closely monitor unrequited romantic relationships that lead to isolated, irrational behavior.* A number of cases involve violence that either began with or were driven by the frustrated passions of unstable individuals. These situations can trigger explosive bursts of anger or methodical and carefully detailed plots of revenge. Faculty are often in a position to witness some details of these intense arguments and fights in the classroom.

- On May 3, 2011 University of Virginia Student George Huguely killed his ex-girlfriend after sending her threatening text messages and emails (Doughty, 2010). It was reported that he kicked open her door and repeatedly banged her head against a wall, that they had a historically tumultuous relationship, and that he had a history of aggressive behavior toward women, including a female police officer.

4. *Look for manifestos or large societal messages that indicate a deeper, entrenched view of the world or call to action.* Many of those who plan violence do so under the rationalization of some greater cause or message they are trying to

communicate. Their attacks and killing are in some way designed to release their larger message or call others to action for their cause.

- Matti Saari opened fire on a group of students taking a business exam before lighting other classrooms on fire in September of 2008 at the Kauhajoki school in Finland (Whitlock, 2008). Saari left notes saying he had a hatred for mankind, for the whole of the human race, and that he had been thinking about what he was going to do for years. He posted a series of YouTube™ clips prior to the attack that were investigated by the Finnish police to no further action.
- Cho (Virginia Tech) sent his to NBC (Virginia Tech Review Panel, 2007), and recently in Aurora, CO, it was reported that the shooter from the theater sent a warning to his counselor/advisor (CBS news, 2012).

5. *Watch for all bullying behavior (perpetrator and victim) and attend specifically to bullying behavior that creates isolation and an environment where a smoldering individual grows more dangerous in his thinking.* All those who are bullied (or who bully) are not destined to become the explosive attacker or the sociopath causing harm for pleasure on a grand scale. However, it is clear that some who are bullied carry these scars and wounds with them and eventually seek revenge. Faculty should attend to and report bullying behavior that occurs in their classroom.

- Damon Thompson (Blankstein & Faturech, 2009), a student from Belize, brought a six-inch kitchen knife into a UCLA lab and stabbed another student three times in an arm and hand and once each in the back and neck in October of 2009. Thompson was taunted in the residence halls, dining areas and the library. Kelbold and Harris (Columbine) were reported to be bullied and to bully others (Langman, 2008).

6. *Identify students who feel hopeless or are irrational in their logic.* Many of those lost down the path toward violence fall out of connection with others who have the potential to refute their pessimistic logic and offer alternative views of the world outside of violence as an escape from pain. Identify students who are isolated and out of connection with others. Find ways to try to engage them and, if such engagements are unsuccessful, consider a referral to the campus BIT.

- In October of 2007, Dillon Cossey (Ruderman, 2007) was arrested at his home after a friend told police about his plan to carry out a Columbine style attack on Plymouth Whitemarsh High School. Bullying led his parents to pull him out of public school at the end of his 7th grade year and home-school him. His mother was arrested for purchasing an assault rifle for him. It is also reported he corresponded on MySpace™ with Pekka-Eric Auvinen (Boyes, 2007) who had followed through on a similar attack in Finland in November of 2007.

7. *Look for gaps in students who need to access mental health services on campus.* While those with mental illness are not more likely to commit violence on campus, a protective factor to prevent this violence can be found by ensuring proper treatment. This involves timely access to the appropriate care in a quantity that can have an ongoing positive impact.

- *Cases with Potential Depression*: David Everson, Jason Hamilton, Anthony Powell, Steven Kazmierczak, Pekka-Eric Auvinen, Asa Coon, Seung-Hui Cho, Victor Cordova, Jacob Davis, Evan Ramsey, Jillian Robbins, James Kearbey and Robert Poulin.
- *Cases with Potential Schizophrenia*: Jared Loughner, Jiverly Wong, Steven Kazmierczak, Latina Williams, Douglas Pennington, Biswanath Halder, Peter Odighizuwa, Michael McDermott, Andrew Wurst, Michael Carneal, Wayne Lo, Arthur McElroy, Patrick Purdy, Edward Allaway and Walter Seifert.

8. *Though rare, be concerned about the sociopath and those that take pleasure in harming others and expressing obsession-filled hate and threats of violence towards individuals or groups.* These behaviors may manifest in teasing behaviors in the residence halls and the classroom, practical jokes that are taken too far and a lack of remorse when caught hurting others.

- Kimveer Gill shot 20 people, killing one before committing suicide outside of Dawson College in Quebec, Canada (Payne, 2006). He romanticized death and his role as the Angel of Death and the Death Knight. He posted dozens of pictures of himself, mugging for the camera as he brandished an assault rifle and other weapons. He wrote, "Head to toe, all black. Boots as black as tar. Cloak lashing to and fro with the wind . . . the disgusting human creatures scream in panic and run in all directions, taking with them the lies and deceptions. The Death Knight gazes at the humans with an empty stare, as they knock each other down in a mad dash to safety. He wishes to slaughter them as they flee."

9. *Pay attention to small hints and dropped information. Those who engage in violence rarely just snap; violence is often the end product of months (if not years) of planning.* It is important to identify those on the path to violence at the early stages of ideation and planning rather than the later stages of acquisition of weapons and implementation (Deisinger, Randazzo, O'Neil & Savage, 2008). Extreme violence is rarely an impulsive decision, rather it is the culmination of much thought and planning.

- Seung-Hui Cho killed two students in West Ambler Johnston Hall before his killing of 30 other students in Norris Hall at Virginia Tech in April of 2007 (Virginia Tech Review Panel, 2007). Cho purchased his Walther P22 online and then picked it up on February 9, 2007. He then waited until March 13 to purchase a second weapon from Roanoke Firearms to comply with the 30-day waiting period between handgun purchases. He carefully purchased clips and ammunition between March 22 and April 1 for both weapons along with chains for the doors. Cho practiced shooting at the PSS Range and Training, an indoor pistol range in Roanoke, VA. He taped his video manifesto at a local hotel on April 8 and practiced chaining the doors on April 14. On the day of the shooting, Cho removed his hard drive and disposed of it, as well as his cell phone. He mailed his video manifesto along with a letter to one of the English department faculty. Cho carefully prepared for his massacre.

10. *Watch for the hopelessness and desperation to escape pain that occurs in suicidal individuals. This also is present in most who engage in extreme violence.* While all suicidal people do not kill others when they attempt to kill themselves, it does appear that most who engage in extreme violence end up taking their own life in the process. The isolation and distorted thinking about escaping pain and, perhaps, a romanticized escape from this world appears to accompany many of the attacks.

   - *Forty Shootings Ending in Suicide*: Wellington Menezes de Oliveira, Clay Duke, Samuel Hengel, Colton Tooley, Nathaniel Brown, George Sodini, George Zinkhan, Anthony Powell, Jiverly Wong, Tim Kretschmer, Michael McLendon, Matti Saari, Steven Kazmierczak, Latina Williams, Pekka-Eric Auvinen, Asa Coon, Seung-Hui Cho, Jonathan Rowan, Charles Roberts, Duane Morrison, Kimveer Singh Gill, Douglas Pennington, Jeffrey Weise, Robert Flores, Robert Steinhäuser, Al DeGuzman, James Kelly, Buford Furrow, Eric Harris/Dylan Klebold, Luke Woodham, Brian Head, Gang Lu, Marc Lépine, Patrick Purdy, Nathan Ferris, David Lawler, Robert Poulin, Walter Seifert and Andrew Kehoe.

QUESTIONS FOR FURTHER DISCUSSION

Here are some additional questions concerning disruptive behavior and the difference between disruptive and dangerous. These questions are useful for self-reflection or to assist in facilitating a group discussion during a faculty training or orientation session.

1. Discuss how you categorize the concerning classroom behavior you have come in contact with during your teaching tenure. We use the two general divisions of disruptive and dangerous. What are the limitations of this approach? What are some of the benefits?

2. Think about some examples of disruptive behavior you have encountered in your classroom. Discuss how many of these examples of disruptive behavior escalated (or could have escalated) into dangerous scenarios.

3. We offer a wide range of at-risk behaviors to consider in order to better assess potential risk. Discuss the top three behaviors you have seen correlated with at-risk students. Are there any other behaviors that you have seen that faculty should be aware of in their classrooms?

Chapter 3

Stance and Technique

EQUANIMITY: FINDING YOUR CENTER

You remember that girl right? The girl with the yellow hair who had a penchant for eating other people's porridge? That little girl offers some useful advice to those looking to find the best kind of stance when it comes to working with disruptive or dangerous student behavior. Finding a middle ground. Not too hot. Not too cold. Aristotle offers a bit of a fancier take on this simple concept. "Virtue is the disposition to choose the mean, in both actions and passions."

That's what we are getting at in this chapter—finding the wise stance as an instructor working with disruptive or dangerous students. We encourage faculty to obtain greater equanimity; a greater balance and grace in the face of chaos.

Our argument is one for the mean. Find a stance based in calmness, confidence and a flexible curiosity when attempting to manage at-risk behavior. Like Goldilocks and the porridge, too hot or too cold misses the mark. A professor who approaches a student with their buttons pushed and ready for a fight is going to be just as ineffective managing the crisis as a professor who approaches the situation with a lack of caring and attention. The "just right" porridge is where the instructor approaches the student with a balanced calm, adjusting as the situation demands.

Imagine a student who is text messaging during the class. An instructor can ignore the behavior, hoping it goes away. He can aggressively address the student in front of the class and seek to discourage the behavior through fear and embarrassment. These are the "too cold" and "too hot" approaches. The middle ground is a caring confrontation with the student explaining the reasoning for the rule, your request for them to comply and a follow up conversation to ensure that they understand why their compliance is important to the overall stability of the classroom community.

I NEED CRAYONS: STAT!

I teach several facets of graphic design including semiotics, visual communication and motion design in an arts college in Seattle, Washington. I've been teaching for about ten years now. As an undergrad, my art school experiences included serial student expulsions from the classroom (never myself) by several snarky professors who didn't think that the work presented for critique was serious or poignant enough. I found this a strange teaching model, but in this context it seemed to be effective.

When I became a teacher, I was one day faced with a student who gave a presentation on something flippant and having nothing to do with the assignment. He wasn't disruptive or violent, just lazy. I kicked him out of my classroom. He dropped out of school at the end of that semester. I realized then that my actions were powerful enough to change the trajectory of students' lives, something that I didn't understand since I was never personally treated in this manner. I was lucky that he didn't have any violent tendencies. My act could have incited more than just withdrawal. I still feel terrible about it.

Years later, I found myself in a situation that was indeed disruptive if not a seed for something potentially dangerous. During a critique, a student who was rather brawny, intense, smart, articulate, abrupt and who was also a combat war veteran, leapt out of his chair and sternly questioned "what the hell are we doing and why?" He was clearly frustrated and furious. The balance of the students, one by one, followed suit. I panicked as the overwhelming fear of a coup developed in my gut.

My initial reaction was to bark back and explain exactly what it was that we were doing and why, but at that point, it would only worsen the situation. I took a deep breath, asked the class to stay where they were and told them that I would be right back. I ran to my office where I kept a bevy of kindergarten-type arts supplies for a different class. I grabbed a giant crate full of crayons, construction paper, markers and play-dough. I went back into the classroom where I found the students brooding and confused. I presented them with the box and commanded them to channel all of the frustration they were feeling into an image making exercise. Much of the work that resulted was wonderfully uncanny.

I later found that the student in question is sweet, intensely self-aware and staunch, the opposite of what I had perceived. He was simply having a bad day. I also realized that the results of the exercise were nothing more than lucky. Throwing toddler toys at angry adults could have been an insulting and disastrous move. Rather than commanding them, I should have invited them.

Since then I've had many a student yawp during a critique. Over time I've learned that the most effective way to redirect the situation is to:

1. Overcome my initial fight/flight response with cleansing breaths while engaging an empathetic ear.

2. Make sure that the cohort listens quietly and respectfully to the student.

3. Validate the student's emotions/concerns.

4. Bring to light the positive possibilities stemming from the student's frustrations.

It's been quite a journey. My own self-awareness recently told me this: arrogance and luck have no place in dealing with emotions. Empathy and validation are always the way to go.

So far.

Tiffany Laine De Mott
Assistant Professor
Visual Communication and Motion Design
Cornish College of the Arts

THREE WAYS TO STAY CENTERED

Take the example Professor De Mott writes in her "From the Trenches" story. As the professor, she could have ignored the entire incident or told the student to leave the classroom. She could have become enraged this student dared to create a dangerous situation in her classroom and yelled at him for his poor behavior. Instead, De Mott rightly demonstrates the importance of finding the middle ground. She controls her own emotions, separates the students from each other and calmly addresses the problem by finding the middle ground. The "just right" approach gives the student an opportunity to calm down and work on refocusing his poor behavior.

This approach is also called "Staying Centered." When managing any situation, it is critical to find your center: geographically, physically, and emotionally. A quick explanation:

1. Geographically—Staying centered geographically means finding the "center" point—or becoming it. If you have ever been to a college keg party (it's okay to admit it—you're reading this alone), you know where the "center" of the party is—the keg. Not the dance floor, not the TV (unless the party was to watch a game), not the kitchen. If it isn't you can make it the center. Simply grab the tap and hold it—don't give out any more beer. It will take five minutes to be the center of attention. In a classroom, the geographic center is naturally designed to be the front of the room where the lecture is going on. Your ability to keep it there is your imperative. When a confrontation occurs, it—or the disrupter—becomes the "center." You must put it back on you. This is not done by shouting or through a show of physical dominance, but instead through remaining calm and in control. The other two aspects of "staying centered" will assist in this.

2. *Physically*—This is easier than you may think. Keeping a neutral body posture is critical. Do not "bow up"—puffing out your chest, pulling your shoulders back, lifting your chin, staring hard, etc. "Bowing up" is simply an attempt—in a very mammalian sort of way—to make yourself appear bigger, an attempt to impose physical domination. Unfortunately, it's also an aggressive gesture, and can move the situation away—often quickly—from the desired "middle ground." But you can't go the other direction either—pulling your shoulders in, averting eye contact, dropping your chin, etc.—this is called "getting smaller" and will only serve to empower the disrupter, and keep them in the "geographic center." So, keep your body even. Shoulders in a neutral posture, chin even, eye contact steady, but not glaring, hands in open positions (not clenched, pointing aggressively or in pockets, etc.). Your voice is equally important here. You want to bring the tone back to the "center." Often dropping your volume to a lower level than normal does this, even when shouted at. This is designed to bring the volume of the conversation back down. No one wants to shout alone. (You may have to repeat this act twice or even three times—but never do it more than three. If that hasn't worked, assume the person is no longer rational).

3. *Emotionally*—this is the hardest one of all. You need to "tend your own garden." This is difficult because it means acknowledging your own personal biases and emotions. For example: Say there is a student who has been struggling in your class. His writing and statements in class are not only inflammatory, but take positions that are irritating to your personal beliefs as well. If he were to act out in class, it wouldn't be unusual for you to be a little less patient. Add to that an argument with your spouse that morning, and you are starting the confrontation even more "off center." In this situation, the breathing exercises become even more critical. Taking a moment in this situation—or even "tending your garden" before you go into each class—is a great practice to "stay centered."

CHANGE THEORY (Prochaska and DiClemente)

One approach to working with the often frustrating and difficult process of encouraging a student in crisis to change their current behavior lies in the work of Prochaska, Norcross and DiClemente (1994). Their book *Changing for Good* is a powerful one that we often use when teaching courses in psychology or adjustment and personal growth. The concepts are universally helpful when looking to answer the question "Why don't I (or this person in front of me) change their behavior?"

Their approach outlines how people move through various stages before becoming ready to make lasting change in their lives. This can help give a sense of perspective and understanding about why a student may be repeating difficult or frustrating behaviors. When we teach these concepts, we ask people to pause before going on and think about a behavior they have tried to change in their life. This can be something they are currently struggling with (perhaps smoking, watching too much TV, not getting enough exercise) or something they have tried to change in the past.

Pre-contemplation: At this stage, the student is unaware that there is a problem and hasn't thought much about change. Faculty can help the student increase their awareness of their need for change through discussion. They also can help the student understand how their behaviors may be impacting their life.

This stage of change is one of the most challenging for faculty to address in their students. The problem, as you may be able to anticipate, is everyone else seems to know that the student has a problem *except* the student themselves. Imagine Kim, a socially odd student who struggles with forming social relationships. Kim often asks off-based questions in the classroom and other students have begun to roll their eyes each time her hands flies into the air to ask a question that often results in a five to ten minute distraction from the lesson at hand. Imagine this occurs prior to an exam and the other students in the class become vocal in their frustrations with her. They tell her to "shut up" and insult her. The professor becomes annoyed at Kim's frequent, non-relevant questions.

If she is in the pre-contemplation stage, Kim is unaware that her behavior is causing other people in the classroom frustrations. She misses the social cues and stays focused on having her questions answered and becomes lost in the content. Kim could also have an awareness of other students' frustrations but falls back on a script her mother taught her in 5th grade that says "don't worry about what other people in the classroom are thinking, just worry about yourself and make sure you ask questions if you have them." In either case, behavioral change will be difficult for Kim until she is able to move from pre-contemplation to contemplation.

An instructor who tells Kim to stop asking questions will likely be met with Kim's confusion and frustration. She sees questions as helpful to the learning process. Kim doesn't realize yet that her behavior in the classroom is both harming her ability to earn a good grade in the class and costing her in terms of her social interactions with her peers.

In helping change this disruptive behavior, the instructor must first talk with Kim and help her understand why her questions are having a negative impact on her grade and frustrating her fellow students. Imagine the following conversation between the professor and Kim:

Instructor: "Kim, thank you for staying after class today to talk with me."
Kim: "Sure, no problem. I actually wanted to ask you something about . . ."

Instructor: "Actually, that is part of the problem. I need to talk to you about the questions you are asking in class. You might not realize this, but many of the questions are not related to the discussion at hand and end up taking time away from the material that I need to cover."

Kim: "I was always taught that if I had a question I should ask a question. No one is going to ask it for me."

Instructor: "Well, that's true. However, one of the rules in the classroom is being respectful of my time and other students' time to ensure that we cover the required material. By asking five or six questions each class period that aren't always related to the subject matter, other students are getting upset and you are taking time away from the exam preparation."

Kim: "I'm ready for the exam already."

Instructor: "That may be the case. But part of getting a good grade in my class is related to participation. By asking questions unrelated to the material, you end up lowering your participation grade. Also, I'm not sure if you realize this, but other students are becoming very frustrated with you."

Kim: "I hear what they say." She lowers her head and looks sad.

Instructor: "I don't think this problem is too difficult to solve. What if you and I come up with an agreement that you limit yourself to one question per class period that is related to the subject matter?"

Kim: "What if I have other questions?"

Instructor: "Well, I suppose we could work out some time during my office hours to talk about those. Maybe you could create a list and hold onto those questions until we have a chance to talk. Or, you could email them to me or post them on the discussion board."

Kim: "I suppose I could do that."

Instructor: "Let's give it a try."

It is important to recognize that part of Kim's behavior may stem from her Autism Spectrum Disorder/Asperger's, and the professor here may want to work through the Disability Support Services Office and/or the BIT to strategize with Kim as well. However, let's say Kim does not have a disability—she just lacks self-awareness. In that case, Kim's reaction may be similar to what is described above, but the causal factors (and thus the response) may be slightly different. But let's say Kim wanted to just behave this way to push your and the other student's buttons. For that, read on.

Contemplation: This is the most common stage of change for students to be in. The student has thought about change and is getting ready for movement in the near future. The student realizes their current behavior is not in their best interest, but is not yet ready to begin their plan to change. The student isn't happy about their current state and wants things to be different, but has not yet explored how to do things differently or take action to make change in their life.

In this stage, faculty or staff can motivate the student and encourage the student to think in more detail about how their behavior is having a negative impact in their life. They should explore ways they might plan for change and what resources could be helpful in implementing change.

Imagine an example where a student, Kevin, is highly opinionated and often "spouts off" in class. He argues with other students about various issues related to the course material. He comes across in a rude and entitled way and has even had several arguments with the professor where he challenged his authority. Kevin knows that his behavior is a problem in the classroom. He has had other students argue with him and then finally stop talking to him altogether. Kevin regrets his behavior toward the professor but gets so passionate about the subject matter that he finds himself getting into similar arguments over and over.

The goal of the instructor here is to assist Kevin further explore his behavior in the classroom and look for ways to implement a more lasting change. Some empathy can be useful for Kevin to better understand how his behavior can be altered. Unlike Kim in the previous scenario, Kevin already knows that his behavior is unacceptable and is working towards change. The role of the professor should focus on ways to help Kevin work toward a more lasting change.

Professor: "I guess you know why I asked you to stay after class today?"

Kevin: "Yes. I just get so focused on the material I lose track of how I'm acting to other people in the class. I'm working on it! I really am."

Professor: "I know you are. Changing behavior like this isn't easy."

Kevin: "You know it. And this isn't even the class where I get into the most problems. Actually, your class is the one where I end up doing the best in terms of controlling my emotions."

Professor: "That's good to hear. I hadn't realized you were having trouble with this in your other classes."

Kevin: "It's really bad. I have to meet with judicial affairs tomorrow because I got so upset in class I shoved another student."

Professor: "Really?"

Kevin, with head down: "I'm not proud of it."

Professor: "Well, have you given any thought to talking to someone on campus about ways you can work harder to change some your 'passionate' responses?"

Kevin: "I'm not sure I can even change it. I've already worked so hard at it. My mom just says that's how we are . . . you know."

Professor: "Well, I'm not sure I buy that. I think people can change their behavior. It just takes some time. You know, it might even help you out with your judicial affairs case if you make an appointment to see someone at counseling about this before your meeting tomorrow."

Kevin: "Wait, you think I'm crazy?"

Professor: "No, that's not what I'm saying. Listen, you go to the gym to get your body in shape, right? Isn't counseling the same thing for your emotions? Wouldn't it make sense to go get some help from a professional before things get out of control again?"

Kevin: "What, like a trainer at the gym?"

Professor: "Sure—I think it's like that. Someone to talk to that can help you be more successful in your efforts to change. If that's really what you want."

Kevin: "You should hear my mom. Getting kicked out of school isn't an option for me. You really think talking to someone could help?"

Professor: "It sure couldn't hurt."

Kevin, laughing: "Ha, yeah. I guess that's true. I'll give it a shot. And I'm sorry about today. I'll keep working on it."

Professor: "Thanks. Don't get discouraged. Changing behavior like this isn't easy."

Preparation for Action: In this stage, the student is aware of a problem and is ready to actively create goals to address the problem behavior in their life. Plans and goals should be focused, short term and designed to be updated and altered to ensure the student's success. Plans should be measureable and something the student can monitor and understand if they are moving forward, static or moving backward. Faculty can help the student brainstorm and update their plans to ensure a better chance of success.

Kelly appears to struggle with not using her cell phone in the classroom. She's had frequent problems using her phone and has been talked to by the instructor about violating the "no texting in class" rule in the syllabus. The instructor has already reduced points for Kelly because of texting and using her phone in the classroom. Her grade has already been reduced an entire letter grade for this behavior. The instructor holds her after class to talk again about the problem.

Instructor: "Kelly, I can't believe I am talking to you again about this."

Kelly: "I know, I know. I can't believe it either. I feel just horrible about it."

Instructor: "Why do you keep checking your phone during class? Is there some kind of emergency going on or something?"

Kelly: "No, that's the sad thing. I just get really, really antsy and feel like I have to check it. Then I just want to send a short text. Really just a 'yes' or 'no' depending on what my friend is asking. Then I checked Facebook. That's what got me caught today."

Instructor: "I just don't know what else to do with you. You've already lost an entire letter grade in the class because of this. I also don't like having to play 'cell-phone cop' with you—it really distracts me from the lecture."

Kelly: "I know, I'm sorry. I've been thinking lately that the only thing I have left is just leaving it in my dorm room when I'm in class."

Instructor: "That's sounds like a really good idea."

Kelly: "I've known this has been a problem for a while. Trust me, I totally know that I lost a letter grade in here because of me being stupid. I want to leave the phone in my room. I'm just building up to it. Kind of psyching myself up for it."

Instructor: "Well, perhaps this incident today can be your 'last straw' and you are finally ready to leave that phone at home."

Kelly: "I think so. I won't bring it to class next week."

Instructor: "Good for you. We'll see how it goes."

Action: This stage of change is where the student puts their plan into action in order to change behavior. The student will attempt to alter their negative behaviors and develop new positive behaviors to replace them. Faculty can support the student in trying out these action steps and encourage them to keep trying, despite setbacks and the potential failures they may encounter.

Nate has schizophrenia and is being seen by a counselor on campus for treatment. He shared with his professor his ADA accommodation note at the start of the semester and talked about his schizophrenia being manageable as long as he keeps on his medications. Nate begins to behave oddly several weeks into the semester. The professor holds him after class.

Professor: "Nate. I'm glad you were able to stay and talk to me today. I have been concerned about you."

Nate: "Yeah, I thought you might be. I haven't been taking my medications as well as I should be."

Professor: "Really? Why did you stop?"

Nate: "It's something I talk about with my counselor all of the time. I kind of like the way I feel when I'm off the medication, even though I know it isn't good for me to stop and I end up getting into trouble."

Professor: "So you are still seeing your counselor?"

Nate: "Oh yes, I like that guy. I meet with him once a week. We actually met yesterday and he talked to me about starting back on my medication again. So that's why I wasn't surprised when you called me in."

Professor: "So, you started up on your medication again?"

Nate:	"Yep, last night. I'll keep taking them this time. Sorry for letting my mind wander in your class. That's a side effect when I stop taking them."
Professor:	"Well, I think it's a good decision to start up again on your medication. I'm glad you kept seeing your counselor."
Nate:	"Yep, I'll keep on my meds this time. Sorry for acting weird today. They should be back in my system by tomorrow."
Professor:	"OK Nate, I just wanted to make sure you were doing OK. I'll talk with you on Wed at our next class."

Maintenance and Relapse Prevention: Here the goal is to continue successful plans and repeat those action steps that work, while adjusting things that don't. Change has occurred for the student, and there has been a reduction in problem behavior. They maintain their successful change and reduce the risk of falling back into bad habits. Faculty can help bolster the student's success and develop awareness of potential obstacles that could lead to relapse.

Delany has had a number of medical problems during her class. One of her problems involved extremely low blood pressure that results in her fainting after being in a seated position for a long time. After several dramatic fainting episodes at the start of class, Delany worked with health services and the campus Behavioral Intervention Team to come up with a plan to walk around about halfway through a 90-minute class to help her circulation. The instructor received a notification from the ADA office about this accommodation and it seemed to work well to alleviate her fainting problem.

Now that it is later in the semester, Delany has not been getting up as often for her stroll around class. She faints again and the instructor has to call the ambulance. This causes a severe disruption to the class and the content of the lecture. Delany returns to the next classes, takes her stroll again. The instructor asks her to stay after to talk.

Instructor:	"I just wanted to check in on you after what happened last week."
Delany:	"Thanks, I'm doing better now. It's just frustrating."
Instructor:	"I can imagine. It seemed like the walking has been helping to keep the fainting from coming back?"
Delany:	"It does. I just feel like such a fool walking around the classroom. I know I have a note and everything, I just wish I didn't have to deal with this anymore." (Note: walking around the classroom during class would be an unusual, but not unbelievable, accommodation.)
Instructor:	"That makes sense. It must be hard having to deal with this as a chronic condition."
Delany:	"I've been dealing with stuff like this my whole life. I just thought I could do without the walk . . . but I guess not."

Instructor: "Well, it can't be easy, but it seems like the walk helps. I'd encourage you to stick with it. Perhaps sitting in the back of the class and just stepping out to walk may help—it may make you less self-conscious about walking around the classroom."

Delany: "Yep, after my epic fail last week . . . I will. Sorry again for all the problems I cause."

Instructor: "You aren't a problem and there isn't anything to apologize for with what happened last week. It's not easy trying to figure out what's going on with your body. Part of getting better is being able to overcome a relapse like this."

Delany: "Yes, I guess so. Thanks again."

QUESTIONS FOR FURTHER DISCUSSION

Here are some additional questions about keeping yourself safe, being prepared and using Change Theory. These questions are useful for self-reflection or to assist in facilitating a group discussion during a faculty training or orientation session.

1. We talk about finding the middle ground stance when working with disruptive students. What are some of the challenges in being able to put this approach into practice? What factors lead professors to fall short (e.g., ignore behavior) or overshoot the mark (e.g., become frustrated and yell at students)?

2. Think of a way to use Prochaska and DiClemente's stages of change in one of your classes? What are the benefits of teaching this approach to your students? Are there any limitations?

3. Think about an example from your life where you tried to change a behavior and were either successful or failed. What stage of change were you at? What factors led to your success? What obstacles led to the failure?

Chapter 4

How to Handle an Emergency

WHAT IS THE NATURE OF AN EMERGENCY?

Imagine you are on fire.

This would be a good example of universal emergency, right? Pretty much everyone, regardless of gender, race or nationality would agree that being on fire would be an emergency. Unless, of coarse, you happen to work for *Walt Disney World's Lights, Camera Action* car chase stunt show and your job is to ride a motorcycle through a fiery oil slick and then run around in a flame retardant suit for the camera.

Talking about emergencies and crisis first requires a discussion about context, individual skills and experience. Take, for example white water rafting. White water rafting is best described as a kind of controlled chaos, as the river itself is never the same any two days you run down it. Varying water levels change the contours of the rapids; as do underwater rocks, holes and tree branches.

Despite the first rule of white water rafting, "do everything you can to stay in the boat," occasionally a participant may fall out of the raft on a particularly knarly hole or after coming over a house-sized wave. This event kicks the rafting guide into emergency mode. If the person who falls out is close to the boat when their bright orange life vest pops them back up to the surface, they are grabbed by the shoulder loops of the vest and yanked back into the raft. They often end up in a wet, panicked lump by the guide's feet. This kind of rescue typically inspires a more personal understanding of the first rule of rafting as well as surprising new loyalty and reverence for their savior, the rafting guide (they don't linger on the fact that it was often the guide's fault for hitting the wave at a slightly wrong angle that caused the person to be ejected like a cork out of a champagne bottle).

Sometimes the ejected person floats a bit further than the guide's arms can reach. In this case, the guide flips over his paddle to reach them. If they are still too far, the guide can throw an emergency bag (which holds 35 feet of rope). If the guide still can't reach them, it's up to the training the participant learned early in the day about the importance of staying in the middle of the river with their feet up away from underwater entrapments until the boat comes closer. The simple act of falling out of a boat has a number of responses based on the severity of the event.

The process of rescue starts with a very important and very active decision on the part of the river guide. This is the moment where they identify that 1) something has gone wrong and 2) this something requires immediate attention. Everything else is secondary to the current emergency or crisis that is unfolding in front of us.

In the same way, *the first step for a professor to handle a crisis or emergency in the classroom is to acknowledge that 1) something has occurred that is outside the normal process of teaching and 2) this something requires immediate attention.*

One of most common and egregious mistakes professors make is failing to acknowledge the behavior in front of them constitutes an emergency. One reason for this may be shock. Another may be that the professor is overly focused on finishing the lecture or worried about getting all the material covered prior to the next test. Another common reason is that they may not be sure what they are supposed to do and they simply ignore the problem. A common reaction is to get upset and overly reactive to the crisis in front of them.

Imagine Mark is a student in your Art Theory class. Mark begins to publicly challenge you about a grade you have given him on his most recent assignments. Mark shouts to you in front of the class, "You don't have any idea what you are talking about, otherwise you would be out there being an artist instead of teaching at this two-bit community college. My work deserved more than a C, given the amount of work I put into it." After calmly telling Mark you would talk with him after class, he stands and continues "I'm not going to stop anything until you change my grade right now or explain to me what the hell you were thinking when you gave me this shit grade!"

A mistake many professors make in this scenario is to further engage Mark in a conversation about his frustration around his grade. This is a mistake for two reasons: one, because the professor is now arguing with Mark—this is never a good idea, as it allows the student to now control the context of the class for the day; and two, the professor has not yet acknowledged that Mark's frustration has shifted from discussing a grade to a conduct violation and threatening behavior. This scenario has shifted from a normal, everyday class discussion to a significant disruption, a potential crisis and emergency.

By not seeing this scenario as a potential or evolving "crisis," a professor may be tempted to engage Mark back and say, "I gave you that grade because . . ."; we trail this sentence off because any explanation of why the grade was given while Mark is escalating and in front of the rest of the class doesn't really matter, and was not on the syllabus as the topic for discussion for the day. The central issue that needs to be addressed is Mark's escalating, disrespectful and rude behavior.

This is the same kind of behavior that parents must address first when their child is having a fit in the clothing store.

This is similar to the situation with Mark. Any intervention with him needs to focus first on ending the disruption and acknowledging the fact that the behavior is unacceptable. In some cases, the safety of the professor, the class and Mark himself would be more paramount—if the outburst gave indications of threat. This is followed with calm and clear directions to Mark to stop his behavior. If he refuses, the class should be dismissed and further steps taken, starting with calling the police/security (if necessary, e.g., the student won't leave or waits outside for the professor), and leaving a voicemail as well as an incident report for the Student Conduct Office.

Before moving on, however, let us be very clear and direct with you. *If a student is escalating (and we will talk more in a moment about what that looks like), everything else needs to be put on hold until the disruptive behavior is addressed.* Faculty must shift their focus from grades, class attendance, the content of the current lecture, etc., to the current disruption and potential crisis unfolding in front of them. All of these other concerns become secondary until the situation in front of you is resolved. This is not any easy process.

Some professors fall into bad habits when faced with a disruption. They automatically meet the student's aggressive, rude or entitled behavior with poor behavior of their own. They may freeze or ignore the behavior with hopes it will disappear. This is perplexing, as we know the behavior will not just "go away" if ignored. They may even overreact and involve the police or Student Conduct Office too soon or as their only response to disruptive behavior. We will discuss the "hows" of responding later in this chapter. But first, we need to insure that we are all on the same page about the importance of identifying the timing for the shift between a normal classroom experience, a disruptive situation, and an evolving crisis situation.

As we've mentioned earlier, we know people like lists. The problem with lists, however, is they rarely can contain all the possibilities. The list below gives you some examples of behaviors that require immediate attention from the professor. This attention requires the professor to shift from everyday lecture and teaching to making an active decision about managing the behavior in front of them. The intervention may require a direct approach or it may require a side (or future) conversation with the student. It may be something that is addressed as soon as it is observed (e.g., bleeding or screaming) or it may require a more subtle approach (observing a weapon in a student's backpack). The common thread for the list is each behavior requires an active decision on the part of the professor on how to handle the situation in front of them.

For example, a student upset with a grade expresses their desire, in no uncertain terms, to discuss this problem on the spot. They are told calmly but directly: "Jon, I understand that you are frustrated with your grade, but this is not what we are going to discuss today. I am happy to discuss this with you after class or during office hours." His response, as he sits back down, dejected and tears welling up: "Fine. But failing this test means I am done here. No scholarship, no job, and no home to go back to." He then puts his head in his hands and is clearly trying to hide his crying. The last part, combined with his demeanor and emotional response, tells us the situation is escalating. This also lets us know that waiting for him to contact me was no longer an option. A professor could take a "recess" and speak to him in the hall or opt to wait and catch him after class. A simple casual and clearly caring statement might work well to keep Jon together and redirect the conversation to a better time, "Jon, can you come up here for a sec before you head out? I have an opportunity for you that I think may help."

FACE TO FACE: SIGNS OF IMMINENT DANGER

Why is it important to focus on this switch from everyday life to the extraordinary situation in front of you? Identifying this point of transition allows the faculty member to more quickly establish the proper mindset in order to quickly respond and properly address the behavior presenting in your classroom. Faculty who are not able to transition from everyday teaching skills into the skills required to intervene with disruptive or dangerous behavior will not be as effective in achieving the desired outcome.

When training faculty across the country, we stress the importance of "being right, but also being punched in the head." These are the times when an instructor says "Well, Dylan . . . I am sorry you are upset, but it clearly says right here in the syllabus—that you have had since the beginning of the semester—that you cannot miss more than four of my classes and expect to still have a passing grade in this course . . ." While the instructor is certainly correct making these statements to the student, they may be missing the subtle changes in the student's behavior such as clenched fists, shifting back and forth and glaring eyes that signal an impending attack.

Likewise, a key to preventing disruptive behavior in the classroom from escalating requires that professors bring their attention and focus to bear on the existing behavioral problem. Too often, classroom management becomes a nuisance and frustration for the instructor and key questions are not considered in deference to getting back to the content lecture ASAP. When confronting disruptive behavior, some questions to ponder include:

- "Why is this student acting out right now? What might be some causes of their inappropriate behavior (talking out of turn, misuse of technology, rude or entitled response)?"

- "What are my goals for an intervention from this student? What is the desired outcome of my intervention?"
- "What kind of intervention with this student will bring about the desired effect?"
- "Is this a behavior I should address now or something I should address after class privately with the student?"

CLASSROOM BEHAVIORS THAT REQUIRE IMMEDIATE ATTENTION

- A student threatens the professor or another student in the class.
- A student brandishes a weapon or threatens to get a weapon.
- A student raises their voice or yells at another student.
- Disrespectful or rude behavior such as misuse of technology (texting, making or taking a cell phone call).
- A student is clearly intoxicated or appears under the influence of drugs in class.
- Writing and displaying to others obscene or inappropriate artwork.
- A student falls asleep in class.
- A student engages in self-injurious behavior such as cutting or punching themselves.
- A student pushes, hits or shoves the professor or another student in class.
- A student exposes himself or herself in class.
- A student engages in an odd, strange, delusional or psychotic rant or action (e.g., standing up and writing on the white board everything the professor says, talking to people who aren't there, etc.).
- A medical emergency such as fainting, a seizure or vomiting.

STUDY HABITS

I have an extensive background in teaching undergraduates. I have taught psychology courses related to abnormal psychology, testing and assessment, and mental health hygiene. I have also taught courses aimed at freshmen to help them make the transition to college life. In many cases, these courses are offered to "at risk" students and focus on adjustment, study skills, stress management, test anxiety and time management.

In my experience, most of the "at risk" students appreciated the tips and coping skills gained in the class. It helped them to successfully manage all the demands of their college experience through learning about campus resources as well as internal resources. Most students left the course with increased academic and personal confidence, including a higher level of maturity. However, some students were overwhelmed by their first year in college and the course provided them with little comfort.

Joel was considered one of these "at-risk" students. Joel was a first generation college student and entered the university after attending an alternative school for students with psychological and behavioral problems. Joel's participation in the class varied.

Sometimes Joel was actively involved, witty and charming, providing the class with much needed insights. Other days Joel was irritable and detached, refusing to participate in class.

While Joel generally got along with his fellow students, there were some very competitive students in the course. While returning exams to students, I put Joel's test on his desk. He had made a low "C" on the test. Being very boisterous, he vocalized his displeasure at the score. I asked him to talk with me after class if he was concerned about his grade. This seemed to appease him. However, one of the more competitive students mumbled something under his breath. While his words could not be understood it was clear that he was responding to Joel's outburst.

"What did you say, asshole?" Joel asked.

The offending student looked around to find everyone staring at him. He responded with, "If you would study for the tests you would make an 'A,' I bet you don't even try."

Joel slammed his book shut. "I did study," he said, adding "how much I study is none of your damn business." The other student escalated the situation by adding a comment suggesting that Joel was not smart enough to attend college.

This comment infuriated Joel and he stood up. "If you don't shut up, I'm gonna kick your ass," he said. The offending student, realizing that he had antagonized an unpredictable person cowered at his desk. The rest of the class sat silent and wide-eyed, watching me for my response.

"Joel," I said. "I can see you're really upset. Let's step out of the room and talk about this." Glaring at the other student, Joel followed me outside the classroom. My goal was to de-escalate the situation by building a sense of rapport with Joel and helping him put the other student's comments in perspective.

I began by informing Joel of the potential consequences of threatening or harming another student. I shared with him that the student made inappropriate comments and that I would discuss this with him. I also reiterated Joel's value to the class and added that I appreciated his participation and perspective. He agreed that he did not want to jeopardize his status with the university.

We then discussed his difficulty with anger. Joel sighed heavily and seemed to calm down. He explained that he did not know how to express anger and was following the example set by his father. I suggested that he see a therapist at counseling services for anger management therapy.

Joel suggested that he was almost too embarrassed to return to the classroom. I told him the issue was resolved and that I would communicate that to the class. My final action was to talk to the offending student after class and remind him that he acted inappropriately and must refrain from denigrating his classmates in the future. He nodded and left the classroom, his face red. I sighed in relief, thankful that the incident did not lead to a physical confrontation.

Eric Manley
Adjunct Professor/Psychologist
Western Kentucky University

SIGNS OF ESCALATING AGGRESSION: WHAT TO LOOK FOR?

Now that we are ready to shift from everyday mode to emergency mode, let's talk about the process when a student moves from being calm, cool and collected to throwing things and punching people. While these behaviors are certainly more rare in the classroom, they do occur. Developing a more detailed understanding of how a student may escalate will provide faculty with a broader foundation to understand crisis events and potential dangerousness.

As a student becomes increasingly upset and escalates, they display a pattern of consistent behaviors and observable characteristics that faculty should develop a familiarity with in order to better identify a potentially violent episode in their classroom. John Byrnes (2002) coined the term Primal Aggression. This is an adrenaline-driven process and occurs as part of a biological reaction to aggression, the production of adrenaline, the increase in the heart rate and the resulting body language, behavior and communication indicators that we can identify and measure. This is similar to the concept of affective (reactive/impulsive) violence outlined by Meloy (2000, 2006).

Dr. Howard (1999) in *The Owner's Manual for The Brain: Everyday Applications from Mind-Brain Research* writes:

> A potential aggressor channels his appraisal into some form of coping. The strength of the reaction is a direct function of the validation of the threat and the degree of certainty that the threat will thwart an objective or a goal. It is the emotion of being threatened and the inability to cope with that threat that initiates aggression. The common thread throughout this process is the release of adrenaline. (pp. 353–354)

Drs. LeDoux and Amaral believe based upon their research that:

> learning and responding to stimuli that warn of danger involves neural pathways that send information about the outside world to the amygdala, an

almond-shaped gray area in the roof of the brain's lateral ventricle. This area, in turn, determines the significance of the stimulus and triggers emotional responses like running, fighting, or freezing, as well as changes in the inner workings of the body's organs and glands such as increased heart rate.

(Laur, 2002, p. 6)

Threat and fear drive Primal Aggression and affective violence—it is the "fight" in "fight or flight."

Grossman and Siddle (2000) have conducted landmark studies, including peer review, on how aggression induces adrenaline's (or Epinephrine's) influence on the heart rate and its resulting body language, behavior and communication indicators. Let's see how this works.

Remember our example of Mark. He has already shouted once at you in front of the class and insulted your choice to teach at this school. You calmly intervene and invite him to talk to you after class. Mark shifts back in his seat and closes his textbook, fidgeting with his pen. He then pushes back from his desk, standing up taking a step forward into the aisle. He yells in a loud and harsh tone, "I'm not going to stop anything until you change my grade right now or explain to me what the hell you were thinking when you gave me this shit grade!" His face is flushed and his neck vein bulges. He clenches his fists as he rocks back and forth. He mutters to himself and his eyes dart around the room looking for other students who may support or challenge him.

Another male student says, "Dude, shut the hell up and sit down."

Mark responds by facing the student and paces back and forth between him and his desk. He swats his book to the floor. He stares fiercely at the other student and growls, "Do you have something to say to me, bitch?"

The other student lowers his head and mutters, "I will if you don't sit down and shut up." Other students in the class shift about nervously. Some nod and express support for the student who challenges Mark.

The adrenaline rushing through Mark's system has been well studied by Hart (1995) who has conducted significant work relating stress and anxiety to adrenaline. He illustrates that when an individual cannot cope with their anxiety, their mind perceives this anxiety as a threat. Coinciding with Dr. Howard's (1999) statement above, Dr. Hart concludes that at this point an individual starts to produce adrenaline, which triggers Primal Aggression.

Primal Aggression, in its extreme state, is a complete loss of control along with an accompanying rage or panic. This violence is fueled by the perception of frustration, threat, anxiety and fear. It is adrenaline driven, predictable and typically represents a progressive loss of control. Imagine a different student, Patti, who is frustrated about a parking ticket, or in conflict with her roommate about how to keep the room organized or what time they should wake up in the morning. She yells at the parking enforcement officer or she smashes the alarm clock against the floor. The resulting violence is reactive, immediate and often not well planned out. She did not plan to yell at the parking officer or smash her roommate's snooze alarm. This is the result of a progressive, biologically driven path towards physical violence. This is Primal Aggression. But, it is still a "path" (albeit a quick one)—one that can be tracked.

Luck, Jackson and Usher (2007) presented some interesting research in this area related to emergency department behavior and patients who subsequently became violent. They created a model, called S.T.A.M.P. that describes some of the same behaviors that accompany the primal aggressor prior to an attack. These include "Staring and eye contact, Tone and volume of voice, Anxiety, Mumbling and Pacing" (p. 14). They found these elements of observable behavior indicated the potential for physical violence. Mark demonstrates almost all of these.

Primal Aggression is based upon the primal instinct of fight or flight, fueled by adrenaline and characterized by someone losing control and ultimately attacking a victim. Caution should be practiced when responding to such an aggressor, since it is likely our own adrenaline will spike when faced with this threat. Faculty should control their own escalation as their aggression rises in response to a threat. A faculty member who simply responds with in-kind aggression will make the situation worse and find it quickly escalating.

Need a first-hand example? At the publication date of this book, there are dozens of videos of college students engaging in disruptive behavior in the classroom. Some of these video clips show students crossing over from disruptive to dangerous as police become involved in subduing the students. On March 18, 2010, Robyn Foster, a 24-year-old student at the University of Wisconsin-Milwaukee, was arrested in class following an argument with a professor about a grade. A student posted a You-Tube™ clip of the disruptive behavior and following arrest in the classroom (Esser, 2010). Jonatha Carr, a 24-year old from Florida Atlantic University, flew into a rage of yelling threats, punches and was eventually tased following a lecture on evolution. The behavior was also recorded and posted on You-Tube™ (Huffington Post, 2012).

HOW DOES THAT MAKE YOU FEEL?

Clara was counseling a male client during her Internship in Counseling that triggered her own experiences with ex-boyfriends. The client demonstrated an angry and defensive demeanor when talking about his romantic relationships with women that Clara responded to in her own defensive way. This response from Clara created an escalating, argumentative dynamic between her and this client that was not helpful or healing for him. I witnessed this dynamic through live supervision, and by viewing her tape in Internship class. I pointed this dynamic out to Clara. She agreed with me that this dynamic was occurring between her and this client, and disclosed that his anger reminded her of ex-boyfriends.

When I gave Clara a suggestion about how to handle this in an experiential, here-and-now way, she gave me reasons why that would not work with this client. I had experienced Clara responding to me this way several times before. She would hear my suggestion, and talk through the suggestion ten steps ahead and figure out a reason why it would not work. I thought the current issue with the male client was critical, so I continued to stress the importance of interrupting this dynamic. Clara became argumentative with me. A parallel process was occurring with the counseling relationship and supervisory relationship. I then felt a need to address the dynamic between me and her, of me giving her suggestions and her coming up with reasons it would not work before she tried it. Clara agreed with my observation of our relationship. The next session she had with that particular client, she addressed the dynamic between them in the experiential, here-and-now way. It went very well, and I believe it released the two of them from continuing in this pattern. I also believe it gave the client some perspective on how someone in a relationship with him may experience his anger. In my mind, a cool, parallel process occurred with not only the unhelpful dynamic, but with the addressing and releasing from it as well in both the counseling and supervisory relationship.

Clara's mid-term evaluation was scheduled for later this same week. Clara broached the relationship between her and me during this evaluation. She verbalized feeling there was a power struggle between us. Although I was surprised to hear her call it a power struggle, I too felt there was something between us that we needed to talk about. She also said she felt that my challenge to her in our last supervision was personal. I explained to her that it was not personal; rather it was part of supervision. I also told her that I tend to be non-hierarchical, and view supervision as a relationship, but that if anyone had the power, it was me who had it. This was a very difficult conversation to have, and Clara spoke to me in a way that I have not had any other student speak to me before. It felt disrespectful, but also felt very raw and honest. As difficult as it was, I was glad that we were able to both be open and honest about how we experienced each other. I felt like it was important for me to simultaneously communicate caring for Clara and establish my own credibility and power, since apparently that was in question with her. I shared with her that in order to successfully complete internship, and ultimately grow as a counselor, she would need to be receptive to feedback from myself, as well as other supervisors and her peers. It turns out Clara has a tendency and a desire to work independently and only ask questions when she feels she needs something. I explained that in the process of becoming a counselor, the feedback is ongoing, honest, and unsolicited, that she will not always know what it is that she needs at this point in her development.

Clara and my relationship improved. She became more open to feedback, and I learned to give her some time to process a session on her own before I would approach her to process it with me and give my feedback. At Clara's end of the semester evaluation, she told me she needed for me to challenge her in the way that I did in order for her to feel safety and respect in our relationship, and for her to grow as a counselor. I realized with Clara that the students I struggle with the most are often the most rewarding and growth producing experiences for them and myself.

Corrine R. Sackett, Ph.D., LMFT
Assistant Professor
Talley Family Counseling Center Director
Western Kentucky University

KEEP YOURSELF SAFE FIRST

Did you ever take a flight on an airplane where the flight attendant gives that little speech at the beginning about what happens if there is a change in cabin pressure? You know the one. It goes like this "In the event of an unexpected change in cabin pressure, an oxygen mask will drop from the ceiling. Attach the mask to yourself by pulling here and here. Then help others with their mask."

One of the first rules of emergency response is to keep yourself safe. No professor is being paid enough to tackle a disruptive student or wrestle a dangerous student to the floor. What's more, these courageous behaviors, while noble and likely altruistic in nature, are not part of a professor's scope of practice or job duties. We are not trained to disarm students or restrain them until the police can respond. Our first goal is to keep ourselves safe. Then we keep the other students safe. Then we keep the student causing the disruption safe. In that order.

A professor may offer up that they have some kind of advanced training in martial arts or self-defense. Perhaps someone reading this book right now has advanced military training in self-defense. Maybe someone has seen enough *Star Trek* episodes to master Mr. Spock's infamous Vulcan neck pinch and feels confident in its application. That is well and good. These skills, training and knowledge have no place in the classroom and are not part of an instructor's job duties. There are many reasons to not touch your students. Keeping yourself physically safe is an important one.

So, how do you keep yourself safe in a potentially dangerous situation? This can be easier to accomplish if faculty develop the proper mindset to manage the situation at hand. This has to be done prior to entering the crisis situation. It is better to approach the crisis in a calm, cool and collected manner. This allows the faculty access to the full range of options to manage the situation. When we allow a student to "push our buttons," we restrict our ability to manage the crisis at hand and limit the kind of interventions we creatively can bring to bear in the situation—a lot of times this starts with faculty taking the disruption or the statements made personally. Remember, even if they are saying personal things about you, they don't mean it. You just happen to represent whatever they are frustrated with at the moment. It may not even have anything to do with you.

John Byrnes (2002) suggests that as we allow ourselves to become escalated by the crisis in front of us, we go through a series of cognitive and biological changes. These changes make it harder to think of creative solutions and potentially lead us to reactive and poorly thought-out responses.

Byrnes suggests the process of cycle breathing to control the biological changes that occur when a student begins to escalate us. This involves breathing in slowly to the count of four, holding your breath for the count of two, breathing out slowly to the count of four and holding your breath for the count of two. The process can then be repeated (or cycled) several times to lower blood pressure, heart rate and allow the faculty member the ability to remain calm, cool and collected to better manage the situation at hand. It can even be done very subtly, so it doesn't look like you are trying not to come unglued (When done "too overtly," it can look—frankly—a little creepy; hence the importance of the next paragraph).

Breathing exercises and calming messages to focus your thoughts will work better if they are practiced prior to dealing with a potentially dangerous situation. These kinds of cognitive rehearsals are practiced by sports players before the big game, by professional speakers before an important presentation and musicians and singers before a performance. These methods are more likely to be successful if they are practiced and incorporated into ritual or tradition. Faculty can practice cognitive rehearsal prior to an emotional interaction with a student by practicing cycle breathing and the introduction of calming thoughts and normalizations.

A student begins a long, off-topic, statement in the guise of a question during one of your lectures. You know you have a lot of material to cover and this student is notorious for making long, off-topic ramblings that frustrate you as well as other students in the class because they prevent you from covering all the material in that day's lecture.

Apply cycle-breathing: You remind yourself that the best way to address this student's off-topic statement is from a position of calmness. You take a minute to let them talk and quietly slow your breathing as you prepare to redirect the student with a relaxed, "I'm sorry to interrupt, but we do have a lot of material to cover today. Let's come back to this point if we have time." It is also better if you have covered this at the beginning of class. We let the students know that they never "have the floor," and that we may need to tell them to stop talking. Not because we disagree with them or don't value what they say, but that we may need to get on with the material, and we are more cognizant of the pace than they are.

Find calming thoughts: This process can involve the interjection of calming or peaceful images into your mind that are unrelated to the topic at hand. These can

47

be images from your latest vacation or something that you are looking forward to in the future. This can also involve the interjection of calming, mantra or habitual phrases that help center your thoughts and allow you to remain calm in the face of adversity ("I should not take this personally . . ."). One of our favorite words is equanimity: the ability to have a sense of calm and patience in the face of adversity and chaos. Simply focusing on the term equanimity and what it means can be helpful in achieving some peace. Take a second to let the student vent, this often allows us to hear what the frustration is, and lasts only about 10–20 seconds (though it might feel longer). While we are listening, we practice cycle breathing, assess the behavior and situation, and tell ourselves what we need to do next. To be honest, we also are assessing escape routes, other "allies" in the room, etc.

Remember to normalize: Another approach to keep calm when facing a disruptive or dangerous student is normalizing their behavior. Imagine the student's behavior within the context of their background or experience. While it is reasonable to expect graduate students to have figured out the basics of common classroom courtesy, first year undergraduate students may have a bit of a learning curve when it comes to acclimating to the college classroom. Perhaps the student in question has just received some upsetting news and their behavior would be more reasonable if you fully understood the context of it occurring. This technique does not excuse the student from responsibility for their poor behavior. It is designed to help the professor understand to help defuse an emotional reaction to the student.

Mark is an example of this behavior when he yells at the professor and begins to escalate. The professor may start from the assumption that there is more in this situation—Mark is upset about or threatened by something besides a grade on an assignment. Perhaps Mark feels this grade is an insult to him as an artist. If that is the case, his reaction can be better understood as a response to an external threat to his ability as an artist, not just a poor grade on another assignment. Mark may, in fact, see this C as a final condemnation on his work and a vote of no confidence in his future career. This does not excuse his poor behavior or remove the need for an appropriate intervention by the professor. However if his behavior can be normalized and seen as a reaction to a direct threat to his ability to have a career in art, the professor will be better prepared to more calmly intervene.

It's easier for the professor to keep himself safe when he can approach the situation calmly with the full range of interventions to draw from. If the faculty member becomes flustered, has "his buttons pushed" and responds emotionally, he limits his ability to address the situation. This is true whether the professor is addressing a student who is speaking out of turn, underprepared for class or a student who is escalating threatening behavior.

48

PORN 101

You read it correctly. Who wants to openly discuss the life of a porn producer as an opening exercise (may be the opposite of "ice" breaker for sure) in the very first meeting of a graduate class? Not me, and perhaps not the rest of the class as well.

I have been teaching graduate school for over 25 years, encountering just about everything that happens to students while juggling the roles of student, worker, family member and, yes, now an aspiring porn producer.

Typically an easy exercise in which students identify their occupational "daydream" without the cumbersome restrictions of having the money or talent to do so, many aspire to acting, dancing, becoming athletes, curing cancer, being entirely philanthropic. And the list went on for a smooth 20 plus years until my porn producer showed up. Ouch.

"Does anyone in here watch porn, and how great would it be to be a producer of films? That's what I would be, think about it." All eyes rolling or now looking at the floor, and I can do neither . . . it's my class. Ignore? Engage? Challenge? Most likely, at that moment, it would be like stepping in quicksand, sinking slowly, and no one's around with a branch to pull me out.

Enter in all my savvy training in crisis response (stay calm); how to work with disruptive and offensive students in class (alleviate any escalation of topic that incites or creates danger); and assess the reality of the situation.

OK—it deserves a reality check—two word answer "for real?" I ask Mike (not his real name). "Yeah, for real, and I just wanted to get a rise from the class, get it?" Quicksand, I jumped in. Silence in the class.

Utilizing all my skill sets in teaching, I made direct eye contact (we are sitting in a round circle) with him and profoundly said "Thanks Mike" and moved to his neighbor and asked, "what's your daydream?" Disaster averted, but you had to know not for long.

Indeed, I could have confronted the issue of it being inappropriate, sexist, degrading to women and the danger that lurks for relationships—but a vacant look and challenge let me know it simply was not "to get a rise" but to satiate some other need.

It was the beginning of a long, arduous relationship for Mike, the class, and I. The consistent off-beat comments, inappropriate discussion in small group work and generally bizarre behavior are clearly not acceptable in class. Beginning with the very first class, I connected with Mike to meet with me during office hours. I engaged the department chair to join us as well. Trying to help educate Mike as to acceptable classroom decorum went nowhere—so the paper trail began after the second meeting, ultimately having Mike removed from the class and eventually the program in which he was enrolled.

49

It's clear we have to at least attempt to support any student's quest to complete their education. Assist with what we can, and then the issue becomes, in the end, a matter for student conduct, and sometimes with police involvement on your campus.

That being said, we need to remain prudent in how to manage classroom activities and protect the integrity of all students, at times at the expense of their fellow students. It was important for me to remember that; and to engage others (faculty colleagues, chair, dean, student conduct, etc.) so the road I take with students will be well traveled.

David J. Denino, LPC, NCC
Director Emeritus, Counseling Services
Adjunct Professor, Clinical Mental Health Program
Southern Connecticut State University

PREPAREDNESS, SELF PRESERVATION, BACKUP

It's the Scout motto. Be prepared. Don't wait until the crisis is happening to make sure you have the basics down when it comes to being prepared. To that end, here are some merit badges instructors should have lined up before facing an emergency in the classroom:

1. *Location, Location, Location*: While helpful in selling real estate, finding a good location within the classroom is also essential to handling an emergency. Don't get yourself blocked into a corner with no exit. Be aware of the exit to the classroom and avoid creating a conflict in front of the exit. Know where the "geographic center" of the room is. Know where the exits are—all of them—to the room and the building.

2. *Know Your Backup*: Know who you need to call for backup. If a situation goes chaotic in your classroom; who are you going to call? Do you have the number for campus safety on your phone? Is your phone charged? Does calling 911 reach campus safety or the state police dispatch 30 miles away? Are police on campus the same for a class at 2 p.m. on a Tuesday afternoon when compared to 8 p.m. during a Wednesday night class? Is there another classroom or instructor close to assist in the situation? Do you know how to reach your Student Conduct Office? Do you know how the BIT and/or Threat Assessment Teams (TAT) work and how to best report to them?

3. *Mental Health Resources*: Who can you call on campus for advice or consultation related to mental health problems—and not on your campus do you know the community resource? The community emergency access points? What is the phone number(s)? When are they available? Can you walk a student over to their office or will they come to you? As with any

emergency situation, these are things you need to know prior to the crisis event. Take the time to get to know your local mental health resources, either on campus or in the larger community.

4. *Enlist a Confederate*: Early in your class, choose a student or two to assist you in the event of an emergency. This conversation should take about five minutes after your first or second class. It could go something like this:

> Given all of the worry about campus violence, I wanted to pick you two students in my class to leave and call the police in the event an emergency situation occurs. If I need you to do that, I will give you a nod or ask you to bring this file out to my car. Either of these is a sign to go get some help. Are you OK doing this for me?

This may be difficult and take more than the first class to choose two responsible students—be sure you connect with someone trustworthy.

5. *Who Will Make This Worse?* Assuming you have had some time to get to know your class, assess who may make a crisis situation worse. This could be a student who is prone to overreaction and hysteria. It could be a student with mental health problems who doesn't deal well with stress. It could be a student athlete who challenges the disruptive student back that escalates the situation violently. Identify these factors in your classroom and attend to them as you address the disruptive/dangerous behavior. And remember, prevention, prevention, prevention: lay out expectations and how to manage frustration at the beginning of the term. This is critical, and will serve you well.

6. *Who Will Make This Better?* What students in the classroom will have a positive impact on others during a crisis? Who can you lean on for support, agreement and to move the situation toward a more positive outcome? This may be a student who you can engage in a conversation to calm down the disruptive/dangerous student. This could be someone you could leave in charge of the discussion while you talk with the disruptive/dangerous student alone in the hallway (assuming you are able to do this safely). This may also be someone you know to be the student's friend or colleague; all the more reason to get to know your class.

"Being prepared" means thinking about crisis response and emergencies in the classroom prior to their occurrence. The best time to find the counseling center phone number isn't when you are sitting across from a suicidal student after class. Faculty should find emergency numbers and give thought about whom they would call or contact before the problem behavior occurs. While this may seem like common sense, many faculty become overwhelmed with course preparation and getting ready for a new semester and may neglect this. We encourage faculty to spend time checking in with the student conduct officer, campus police, health or counseling services to make sure they have the emergency numbers entered into their cell phones. We encourage instructors to have the campus or community resources listed on the syllabus.

This concept of being prepared is even more important for faculty who are teaching after-hours, in an adjunct capacity or at a community college. Resources may be even more limited in these scenarios, requiring more investigation and research to determine who to call and how to access help in an emergency.

At the risk of preaching to the choir, another useful aspect of being prepared is both thinking and reading about classroom crisis, disruption and dangerousness before you encounter these events in your classroom. Luckily, you have an excellent resource in your hands right now. Another approach may be faculty development workshops, conferences or simply having conversations with an experienced faculty member who may have advice for newer faculty when addressing disruptive or dangerous behavior.

Consider developing tabletop exercises and discussion topics to be included in faculty orientation and in-service trainings. These scenarios and exercises need not be long or wordy. Some examples of discussion topics are provided at the end of the chapter.

WHAT MAKES THEM TICK? MOTIVATION AND CRISIS

We alluded to this concept a bit in the previous sections on normalization, but wanted to clearly stress the importance of understanding the motivation of a student who engages in disruptive or dangerous behavior as a central tool in the selection of an intervention technique to address the behavior.

DON'T EAT THAT

I was in a master's level class with a professor who taught in an adjunct capacity for Salem State College. The professor also happened to work in the local high school guidance department. One night, as I rushed from work to my 6:30 pm class, I stopped to grab a salad and bring it to class. I remember about fifteen minutes into class the professor become increasingly upset at me, glaring at me (with what Mr. Potato head from the movie *Toy Story* might call his "angry eyes") and then proceeded to embarrass me, saying "I can't believe you are eating in this classroom. How dare you." Everyone was silent and you could hear a pin drop.

My response was one of immediate shock and shame. I threw away the rest of the salad and sulked back into my chair. Others whispered under their breath about the professor, "What's his problem?" This occurred early in the semester and the incident contributed to the entire class losing faith in the instructor. This led to many students writing letters to the department head and the complete breakdown in the usefulness of this class.

While this is an extreme example of what can happen when a professor publicly embarrasses or is seen attacking a student, I think there are several lessons that can be learned from this. The first is his overreaction to me eating in class. This most likely comes from some expectations that he feels extremely strongly about but had not clearly expressed. He undoubtedly saw me eating in his class as an extremely disrespectful action. From my perspective, most night professors in this non-traditional master's program allow food in their class. They understood students were often leaving working and coming to class without first stopping at their homes. In my case, this incident occurred early in the course and his rules about eating in class were not mentioned in the syllabus or during any of our class meetings.

Regardless of my intentions, I can imagine his initial reaction was "I shouldn't have to tell students not to bring food into the classroom. It is common sense." He might think this way since his primary job working with high school students had firmer boundaries in terms of where and when food was allowed in the classroom, what could be worn in class or that people need to raise their hands to ask questions.

Brian Van Brunt
Director of Counseling and Testing
Western Kentucky University

The professor in Van Brunt's From the Trenches story would have been much more effective if he had simply talked to him at break or asked him to stay after class to discuss his feelings about food in class. It is likely the event would still have been upsetting for Van Brunt, but he likely would have felt less embarrassed and attacked and responded with apologies or perhaps attempted to explain why he had brought the food (e.g., rushing from work to class, assuming it was allowed because it had been in other classes). He would have respected his approach and the situation could have led to a closer relationship in the future.

The problem is twofold on the part of the professor. First, he had a clear and strong belief about classroom etiquette that he had not communicated to the class. Whatever his feelings about food in the classroom, wearing of hats in the high school or raising your hand if you had a question, they are better explained in the syllabus. The second problem was an assumption that the student was intentionally disrespecting him and made this choice in direct opposition to his expectations. Neither of these assumptions was correct.

TECHNIQUES OF MOTIVATIONAL INTERVIEWING

Motivational Interviewing, or Motivational Enhancement Therapy (MET) was developed by Miller and Rollnick (2002) and used primarily with mandated alcohol treatment to help people change addictive behavior. Their approach is useful when there is disconnect between the goals of the therapist and client, or in our case, between the professor and the student. It is an adaptable approach to working with those who haven't yet recognized their behavior needs to change. Five key concepts make up the foundation of motivational interviewing.

We will discuss five techniques that exist within the MI toolbox. These are meant to be used based on need and do not have a hierarchical application.

The *expression of empathy* involves a conversation with the student that attempts to both understand his perspective (empathy) and communicate an understanding of that perspective (expression of empathy). This expression of empathy respects the student's point of view, freedom of choice and ability to determine his own self-direction. Suggestions for change are subtle from the instructor and the ultimate change is left up to the student.

Imagine a student, Marceline; frustrated with a grade in class, she stays after to talk with the professor about her experience.

Marceline [rageful]: "There is no WAY that I answered this question wrong. I clearly answered this based on the material YOU told us to study in class. I am so angry I could spit!"

Professor: "I can see you are upset. I remember how frustrating that can be, studying really hard and not getting the answer correct. What part of the grade do you feel was inaccurate?"

Marceline [shaking the paper]: "Right here!"

Professor: "Oh, I see. You answered this without correcting for the error. That was covered during a previous test. I know for me, I sometimes become so focused on the new material, I can overlook something I learned before."

Marceline [sullen]: "You said this exam would only cover the material in current chapters."

Professor: "Well, like I said, I can certainly remember what it was like to have to juggle all of these things. It's early in the semester for you and you'll have a chance to pull your grade back up. In fact, this one section you got wrong really didn't pull your grade down very much at all."

Marceline [defeated]: "I suppose."

Professor: "Well, how about this. Take your test home with you over the week. Explain which answers you got wrong and what the correct answer was. If you do that, I'll give you some extra points to help make the hole you are in not as deep."

Marceline [hopeful]: "Really? That would sure help. Thanks."

Developmental of discrepancy is the process by which a professor helps a student understand that their current behavior won't help them achieve their desired goal. The professor explores with the student the consequences of their actions in a neutral manner avoiding sarcasm or a condescending tone. The student should become aware of their choices and begin to explore the advantages to choosing a different way to interact.

Imagine Jake, who looks upset. The instructor asks him to step into the hallway during a group study session and asks what is wrong.

Jake [explosive]: "I can't even tell you how freakin' pissed off I am right now at you! My resident advisor just caught me for underage drinking . . . which is total bullshit, by the way . . . why can I go off to war and kill someone for my country and I can't freakin' have a beer is beyond me. But then I just got this letter telling me I have to go to an eight o'clock alcohol and drug class for six hours each day this Saturday and Sunday? Are you kidding me? How am I going to study for your exam and deal with all of this?"

Instructor: "Well, let me see if I understand what's going on first so I can try to help? OK? Can I see the letter you have there?"

Jake [still upset]: "Here. I just don't get this place. Half my friends are from England and they can drink when they are eighteen. It just makes no sense to me. And this class! [*escalating again*] There is no way I'm going to that. No freakin way!"

Instructor [takes the letter and pauses]: "Listen, I want to help you. I hear what you are saying about the drinking age in this country. I really do. But it's hard for me to read this and take the time to try to help if you keep yelling at me. Also, I have the whole class going on in the other room. Can you let me try to help you?"

Jake [looks down]: "Yeah, I'm sorry. I just have so much to do and I don't know where to start."

Instructor: "No problem, I just want to try to help you out. From this, it looks like from this the process was pretty quick and they aren't giving you a lot of notice about the class. While I don't have much I can do about you having to take the class—it should be pretty easy to request another date since you only had two days' notice. Maybe they thought they were doing you some kind of favor getting the class out of the way sooner, I'm not sure. Another option for you is to appeal the class altogether if you think it isn't fair or an overreaction for what happened. I can help you with that and the request for the date change if you want."

Jake [less angry, more optimistic]: "Well, that would sure help. I didn't know I could appeal this. I mean, I was drinking, so I get that I broke the rule. I just thought it was too quick to force me into the class. I have so much going on right now."

Instructor: "I get that. It makes sense."

Jake [grateful]: "Yeah, that would be great. Thanks. Sorry I lost my cool with you."

Instructor: "No worries, why don't you call their office or send the Dean an email and ask them for an appointment and explain your situation and that you want to take the next available class. I am happy to go there with you if you would like or you can copy me on the email in case they have questions about how this might affect your work in my class. Until then, why don't you settle back into your study group and I'll be right back in."

The third technique of motivational interviewing is called *avoiding argumentation*. This is probably the easiest technique to understand, but the most difficult to put into practice. When you argue back to the student who is arguing with you, neither of you are listening to each other. Let's say that again, if a student is arguing with you and you argue back, they are not listening to you. They are thinking of a retort to what you are arguing. So, don't do that. It doesn't help. Be clear about your expectations and follow through with consequences of the student's behavior.

A student, Ward, uses his cell phone in class. The professor confronts him after class.

Ward [defiant]: "I needed to check my cell phone in class. I'm sorry about that. I didn't have any choice. It went off and I had to check the text message. It's not like I could do anything else."

Professor [BAD RESPONSE]: "What? Are you serious? There are so many other options you had to avoid this problem from happening. First you could have turned off your phone, as I require in the syllabus you received during the first day of class. If it did go off and you had some kind of emergency like someone was in the hospital, you could have excused yourself from class and checked the phone in the hall so you didn't disturb everyone! And given that you didn't get up and leave class after you texted back to whoever it was that called you, I'm guessing there wasn't some kind of earth-shattering event you had to attend to, right?"

Professor [GOOD RESPONSE]: "I'm sorry, Ward. But I'm pretty clear on my cell phone policy in class. I don't want to argue with you about it. If you have your phone go off in class, I deduct ten points off your next quiz. If there is an emergency, you should let me know about the possibility if you can and, after I know, you can leave your phone on so you could see it, and then, if you needed to, check it in the hall."

The fourth technique is called *roll with resistance*. Faculty are encouraged to avoid meeting a student's resistance to change head-on. Instead, they should try to engage the student in new ways of thinking about the situation. Perhaps trying to evoke new solutions to the conflict from the student. Lack of motivation or an unwillingness to change and be positive are understood as normal developmental responses and interventions are designed to avoid becoming mired down in the students' lack of developmental growth and personal responsibility to change.

Finn [demanding, yelling]: "I need to talk to you about your viewpoints. I am furious that you shared your political views with the class. I think that is total bull. You used your influence to share your views with the class. [*bangs hand on desk*] And I'm here to hold you accountable!"

Instructor: "Well, I'm glad you came in to talk with me today about it. Many times students get upset or frustrated about a problem with something I said in class and end up just keeping it to themselves. I'm glad you came in and are giving me a chance to deal with it. I want to be able to help you today. Can you calm down and let me do that for you? If you need to take a moment to step outside and calm down, I would understand completely. I will still be here when you get back."

Finn [mad, but slightly calmer]: "I don't need to go outside. You can't do anything to fix it. The election is over and you already spread your thoughts out and changed how students thought about this. I'm not OK with that and I don't see what you are going to do to fix it."

Instructor: "Well, for what it's worth, I hear what you are saying. You feel like the cat is already out of the bag. And you are right. I can't do anything to change the course of the election; that is over. But what I can do is listen and try to understand your point of view. Perhaps that will help me see things the way you do and I can change my behavior in the future."

Finn [quieter, embarrassed]: "Yes. Sorry . . . I just got upset."

Instructor: "That's OK. I've been upset before and I understand. Now why don't you tell me more about what I said that got you upset?"

Once Finn calmed down it would be advisable for the staff to continue the conversation privately—even in email—with Finn about his behavior, raising his voice and banging his hand. This behavior could be forwarded to the conduct office if it was a concern or Finn began to escalate more. In an ideal situation, Finn would apologize again for his behavior and perhaps express some remorse and consider ways to behave differently when upset in the future. If Finn begins to escalate again, it would be advisable for the staff to end the conversation quickly to avert another crisis and report the incident to the conduct office or BIT/TAT. Here there may be some kind of further meeting or intervention with Finn around his behavior.

The final technique of motivational interviewing we will discuss is *supporting self-efficacy*. This involves helping the student understand that change is possible and there is the opportunity for a better outcome in the future. Staff and faculty encourage and nurture growth in the student, finding times and opportunities to "catch them doing well" and praising this behavior with hopes of shaping future positive behavior.

Professor: "Pendelton, can you stay after and speak with me for a moment."

Pendelton [worried, he stays]: "I'm sorry I was talking to Jessica again, she just started dating a guy in a Fraternity and wanted to talk to me about it. I know you've talked to me before about my attention in class."

Professor: "Actually, I didn't notice you talking to Jessica. So you must be hiding that better than you think. [*both smile*] What I wanted to say was that I appreciated you getting to class on time all this week. I know I talked to you last week about coming in late and interrupting the lecture and I wanted to thank you for taking my concerns to heart and making an effort to be here on time. I appreciate it."

Pendelton [a bit surprised]: "Oh, well . . . oh. Thanks. I mean you're welcome. Thanks. I'll keep it up."

Professor: "Thank you. I'll see you at our next class."

QUESTIONS FOR FURTHER DISCUSSION

Here are some additional questions about keeping yourself safe, being prepared and using motivational interviewing techniques. These questions are useful for self-reflection or to assist in facilitating a group discussion during a faculty training or orientation session.

1. Think about a time you felt threatened or unsafe around a student. What kind of steps did you take to ensure your safety? The safety of other students in the classroom? What could you have done differently given the advice in this chapter?

2. We mention five techniques useful in the application of motivational interviewing. Which do you find most helpful in your day-to-day interactions with students? What are some ways you have persuaded students to behave differently in your classroom?

3. It can be helpful for professors to understand their own motivations as well as assumptions they may make about a student's behavior. What are some of the misconceptions you have had about students? What kind of past behavior from other students impacted your thoughts on the student you had misconceptions about?

4. Consider using some of the following scenarios to begin a discussion with your fellow faculty and brainstorm how you might handle the situation at your campus.

    • A student continues to use their cell phone for text messaging in class despite several requests over the past weeks for them to stop. How might you handle the situation? What are the benefits to having a private conversation with the student after class? What kinds of technology rules are included in the syllabus at the start of class to get out ahead of this problem?

    • Several students engage in cross talk during your lectures in the back of the classroom. They are not talking about the lecture material and continue to engage in this behavior despite being asked to stop. The course is in introductory psychology and about half the students in the class will not take another psychology course in the future. What are some ways to engage the students who might not be interested in psychology? How could the entire class discuss this kind of crosstalk at the start of the semester?

    • A student in your class shares some upsetting comments related to race and/or gender. The comments enrage others in the class. The scheduled topic is left behind and several in the class are escalating their behavior. How would you handle (e.g., clam down) the acute crisis unfolding?

    • A student shows up to class smelling strongly of alcohol, trips as they sit down at a desk and then pulls a hoodie jacket over their head as you begin your lecture. How might you handle this behavior in the classroom?

    • A student shares during a class discussion that they frequently cut themselves to deal with their anxiety, take several anti-depression and mood medications and have suicidal thoughts everyday. How do you handle this disclosure made to the entire class? What steps might you take to ensure their safety in terms of talking to them after class and potential referral?

- A student decides to share their HIV positive status in classroom introductions. How do you handle this disclosure made to the entire class? How may this impact your next class lecture? What if other students no longer want to remain in the class? How will you manage parents' inquiries?

Chapter 5

Threat Assessment
Core Principals

THREAT ASSESSMENT AND DANGEROUSNESS

People are more likely to buy into a concept if they understand the greater purpose behind their participation. Have you ever gotten those little messages on your computer after something crashes that say, "We would like to send an error report. Continue or Cancel?" We never send it. We don't understand where it goes or what is done with the information that is sent. We don't have any buy-in to the process. We assume our message doesn't mean anything. We think it is added to some great digital pile of messages from around the world. Like the messages sent in tubes on the island from the TV show *Lost*. They are a big pile of wasted messages with no clear purpose.

We want to share a little bit about the concepts of threat assessment and violence. We've already shared what it's not (e.g., predicting future attacks or best done by profiling students based on some list of characteristics). So what is involved in assessing threatening behavior that a faculty reports from their classroom? What happens next after your referral/report? It's important you know because we think faculty having this knowledge helps you better understand the referral process.

Threat or risk assessments can be performed by clinical or non-clinical staff who work in the areas of human resources, workplace violence, law enforcement and executive protection. Threat and risk assessment techniques examine the individual to determine their risk to the greater community through asking contextual questions about the nature of the threat and risk, using computer-aided models and assessing risk factors used to determine a level of potential dangerousness. Threat assessments generally take place when a communicated threat has been made.

Determining whether or not an individual is organized or disorganized in his behavior or communication allows the evaluator to determine the relative level of risk for an impending attack. Turner and Gelles (2003) write:

In cases where the level of organization of behavior and communication is rated as high, the author has stuck to a single theme that is continuous, linear and logical. . . . disorganized communication with a multitude of messages jumbled together . . . from a risk point of view . . . such ideas usually represent a decreased risk for a planned, effective attack.

(p. 96)

ORGANIZED OR DISORGANIZED

In a college setting, the difference between an *organized and disorganized* threat profile may be seen in Nathan, who has frequent arguments about the uselessness of liberal education and how the administration forces students to take classes they don't need and will never use. He targets his arguments only to professors who teach courses he doesn't see value in, such as remedial math. He argues against having to take the class multiple times and expresses frustration at being cornered by the administration to complete this class to graduate. Nathan's thoughts are organized, linear and follow a logical pattern. Contrast this to another student who believes her professors and administrators are "out to get her" and who might be just as likely to be upset with a professor as she will be with her dentist, the police who pull her over for speeding or her parents who think she should change majors from education to business. Her outrage and potential threats lack any kind of continuous or linear direction.

Jared Loughner (Von Drehle et al., 2011) demonstrated some organization and logic in his plan to attack the government based on his delusions around the need for a new currency in the government and posted a video of himself burning a flag prior to his shooting of U.S. Representative Gabrielle Giffords. There was an organization to his delusional and paranoid thoughts. There was a fixation and a focus that moved him forward in his attack. There was also an extended period where his delusion was allowed to fester and "settle in"—where he went unreferred and "unattended." (This is certainly not an indictment of Pima CC—where he was when his odd, but not dangerous, behaviors began—or the community mental health system, but instead a pointing out of the potential dangers of cutting the funding of the latter, and arguably the former.)

FIXATION AND FOCUS

Turner and Gelles (2003) also suggest individuals with a *fixation and focus* to their threats present a higher risk than those who lack these traits. Fixation relates the degree of blame and how it is attributed. Imagine Grace (our guillotine wielding student) begins to blame all of social problems on her drunkard, narrow-minded, idiotic peers who don't understand her. If Grace also blames her social problems on her high school friends who just didn't care enough to know her, her rural geographic location and the limited travel opportunities she had because of her parents' limited finances, there is little evidence of a fixation.

Focus occurs when an individual with a particular fixation, such as Grace, who blames others for her social problems, begins to zero in on a single professor who confronted her after class about her "off-topic" questions. She might brood about the encounter, making notes and planning ways to get back at her professor. The focus of her fixation would increase as she ruminates about cutting off their head with a guillotine. This professor becomes responsible for all of her troubles, perhaps beginning to establish the irrational thought process of "if I can only get rid of her, all my problems will be solved. I'll stand up for myself and show everyone they can't walk on me."

Jason Hamilton displayed this level of fixation and focus in 2009 when he blamed his mathematics professor for a failing grade and took two shots at him with a .30–06 rifle (Martine, 2009). George Sodini became fixated on the idea that over 30 million women in the world had rejected him and brought his frustrations into focus on the seven women he shot, killing three at an aerobics class in an LA Fitness club (King Greenwood, 2009). One also will recognize these behaviors in assassins such Hinckley (Reagan), Fromme (Ford), Chapman (Lennon), and Charles Manson.

ACTION AND TIME IMPERATIVE

The *action and time imperative* relate to the impending nature of a potential attack. The action imperative, according to Turner and Gelles (2003), "refers to the need on the part of the person to take personal action to resolve the situation . . . the person has determined that all other avenues (administrative, legal, criminal, etc.) are not going to help with the resolution" (p. 97). Carlos knows he isn't doing well in the class, given his anxiety during the dissection lab and failing the first exam. He knows he has to do something or he will end up being kicked out of the nursing program. Things can't continue the way they have been. His performance so far in class gives him an imperative to take action.

The time imperative gives a sense of urgency to the action imperative. Will something occur today, several days from now, a week or a month in the future? Turner and Gelles (2003) write, "Here, the person has not only determined that he or she needs to act to harm the company, but that this action must be taken soon or within a near time frame." Carlos may begin to feel this time pressure as he misses the study session for his second exam. He knows that if he misses the exam itself he will not be able to complete his class and will not fulfill the requirements for the nursing program. He begins to see all of his dreams and desires fall apart around him. This drives him to a sense of desperation and hopelessness that results in his email and potential suicide threat. The time imperative is Carlos' belief that missing the second exam is a critical juncture.

63

He has both an imperative to take action (do something) and a pressing time event (second exam) that may drive him to a suicide attempt.

In 2002, Robert Steinhäuser killed sixteen and injured seven before committing suicide during the Gutenberg-Gymnasium shooting (Hooper, 2002). He was expelled from school and had concealed his expulsion from his parents for six months. His ruse would have been discovered as soon as the exam results were published. These pending exams created both the action and time imperative.

The 1996 rejection of Frederick Davidson's second thesis defense and the requirement to pass his thesis to secure a job created a pressure to act immediately to punish his committee and then kill himself at San Diego State University (Burd, 1996). After a decade of study, academic failure also drove James Kelly to shoot his advisor and then kill himself in 2000 at University of Arkansas (Wilson, 2000). Kelly brought an attaché case to the shooting with the five letters addressed to him explaining that he no longer could take courses at the University.

WHO WILL BE THE NEXT CAMPUS SHOOTER?

There is an education occurring at college and universities about the nature of assessing threat and dangerousness among their students, faculty and staff. In an effort to help crystallize the process of threat assessment, we have included some of the foundational questions that teams consider when attempting to answer the question alluded to at the beginning of this chapter, "Is this kid going to come back into the classroom with a gun and start shooting people?" We can't predict future violence with any degree of certainty. However, we can look for risk factors that indicate a potential escalation. These are some questions designed to ferret out some of the more common risk factors.

Question 1: Is there is a direct communicated threat to a person, place or system? (ASIS & SHRM, 2011; ATAP, 2006; Drysdale et al., 2010; Meloy et al., 2011; O'Toole, 2002; Randazzo & Plummer, 2009; Turner & Gelles, 2003).

Examples of this type of behavior might include statements such as, "I'm going to blow up this school." or "I'm going to kill my four professors" or "This is why places like this get pipe bombed." Though direct communicated threats need immediate evaluation, Vossekuil, Fein, Reddy, Borum and Modzeleski (2002) found most attackers don't threaten their targets directly before an attack.

If there is a direct communicated threat, there are certain follow-up questions that are important to consider. Understanding these questions may assist faculty in focusing their observations and making connections they could otherwise overlook. These include:

- *Question 1.1: Do they have the plans, tools, weapons, schematics and materials to carry out an attack on a potential target?* (US Post Office, 2007; ATAP, 2006;

Turner & Gelles, 2003) Has the student begun to acquire weapons, make lists of weapons or objectives? While this may be outside the range of a faculty member's perception, a faculty member may see the student writing a list of names or weapons during class.

- *Question 1.2: Is there an increase in their perseveration on the person or object they are targeting?* (Meloy et al., 2011; ASIS & SHRM, 2011; ATAP, 2006; Turner & Gelles, 2003) For example, do they talk incessantly about the person or place they are interested in harming? Does their talk border on ranting?
- *Question 1.3: Is there an action and time imperative to complete an attack on a target?* (Meloy et al., 2011; ATAP, 2006; Turner & Gelles, 2003) As mentioned above, is there an indication of impending action such as: "They are going to be sorry if they give me a poor evaluation next week." or "I'm going to take care of them this weekend."?
- *Question 1.4: Are they fixated and focused on their target in their actions and threatening statements?* (Meloy et al., 2011; O'Toole & Bowman, 2011; ASIS & SHRM, 2011; US Post Office, 2007; Turner & Gelles, 2003) While the general accusation causes some concern, "Everyone is causing me to fail at college", we would be more concerned with the more focused and fixated comment, "It's Becky, that bitch, from the Kappa Gamma Sorority that is going to pay."
- *Question 1.5: Is the target described negatively in writing or artistic expression?* (Meloy et al., 2011; O'Neill, Fox, Depue & Englander, 2008) For example, has the student created a webpage about the target? Do they write about their frustrations and negative attacks in a blog or other social media site? Does the student write negative or critical stories in class about a particular target?

While outwardly concerning and in need of student conduct or law enforcement follow-up, a direct communicated threat cannot be the stopping point for threat assessment. Unfortunately, many colleges approach threat in this manner. Separating a student who makes a direct communicated threat (e.g., students who say "I am going to blow up this school" and "This professor needs a bullet in his brain") does not solve the larger problem of assessing the validity of this threat. In addition to direct communicated threats, threat and risk assessment needs to be focused on the more subtle questions related to violence escalation.

As you read through the additional risk factors listed below be aware that single affirmations of the questions are of a lesser interest than the development of a broad pattern of endorsements throughout these questions. The old illustration by Aristotle, "One swallow does not a summer make, nor one fine day; similarly one day or brief time of happiness does not make a person entirely happy," could be applied here. We will be more concerned with a student who has feelings of persecution, a hardened point of view and has little remorse for his actions than

65

we may be for a student who simply shows an interest in paramilitary organizations. It is the combined weight of these questions that lead the threat assessment to indicate a higher level of risk.

Question 2: Do they talk about being persecuted or being treated unjustly? (ASIS & SHRM, 2011; ATAP, 2006; Meloy et al., 2011; O'Toole & Bowman, 2011; Turner & Gelles, 2003; US Post Office, 2007).

This would include a student who feels singled out in the classroom and often complains about being teased or picked on by other students. Faculty are in a unique position to detect these kind of students who voice concern about "everyone being against me" and "the unfairness of the university system."

Jared Loughner voiced these complaints about Pima college months before his shooting spree. He talked about the university participating in genocide against him, professors seeking to censor his free speech and the bookstore and U.S. government stealing his money through an illegal scam (Von Drehle et al., 2011).

Question 3: Do they display a hardened point of view or strident, argumentative opinions? (ASIS & SHRM, 2011; ATAP, 2006; Byrnes, 2002; Meloy et al., 2011; O'Toole, 2002; Randazzo & Plummer, 2009; Turner & Gelles, 2003).

This can be difficult to assess, since one of the main goals of college is to encourage discourse, debate and critical thought. A hardened or strident point of view, however, is a bit different than simply disagreeing or debating in class. There is a lack of tolerance for other viewpoints and emotional explosions when challenged. Students are not able to allow for discussion or compromise, and may take the role of the martyr to reinforce their viewpoint. An example may be, "I'm not going to change my opinion about abortion. It is God's law and you are going to hell for your beliefs. And you will get what you deserve."

A dilemma has recently developed in detecting some of these behaviors. This may be attributed to the media's (and politicians) fatalistic approach to all "debates." For example, on one show, if a guest disagrees with the host, he cuts off their microphone since they are "not patriotic" or "are ignorant." The ads and rhetoric from the recent campaigns resulted in a "you either agree with me or you are contributing to the end of society!" This hyperbolizing and lack of principled respectful debate has—in our opinion—made it more difficult at times to recognize "hardened" points of view as opposed to just disrespectful (and at times overly simplistic or uneducated—which is contra to our educational mission) debating.

Question 4: Do they have a lack of options and/or a sense of hopelessness and desperation? (ASIS & SHRM, 2011; ATAP, 2006; O'Toole, 2002; Randazzo & Plummer, 2009; Turner & Gelles, 2003; US Post Office, 2007).

Does the student see a certainty to the future that leaves them hopeless and overwhelmed? Do they say things like, "I can't see a way out of this. I feel like my life is over" or "I want other people to feel as bad as I feel. I want to make them hurt." Do they see next steps as inevitable? Is there any hope for a new outcome or novel or creative solutions?

Question 5: Have they had a recent breakup or failure of an intimate relationship? Have they become obsessed in stalking or being fixated on another person romantically? (ASIS & SHRM, 2011; ATAP, 2006; Drysdale et al., 2010; Randazzo & Plummer, 2009; Turner & Gelles, 2003; Vossekuil et al., 2002).

This risk factor is best seen as a contributing or escalating factor that should be a concern when other risk factors are also endorsed. The adjustment and perceived trauma of losing someone romantically close to them can be overwhelming to their coping mechanisms. This may lead to unwanted conversations or stalking behavior. This may also occur in unrequited love where they engage in repeated attempts to connect with another despite requests to stop.

Question 6: Have they have engaged in "last acts" behaviors? (ATAP, 2006; Meloy et al., 2011; Turner & Gelles, 2003).

This may involve giving away personal property, writing a suicide note/or making a video, destroying property or engaging in ritualistic acts. Faculty could directly witness this behavior if a student bequeaths things to the faculty member or if they indirectly witness the creation of a suicide note or final video post. Other examples include: "Facebook suicide" (killing one's Facebook profile but leaving no forwarding information), erasing their computer's hard drive, deleting all contacts in their cell phone or giving it away, etc.

Question 7: Do they have a weapon (or access to a weapon), specialized training in weapon handling, interest in paramilitary organizations or veteran status? (ASIS & SHRM, 2011; ATAP, 2006; Meloy et al., 2011; Turner & Gelles, 2003; US Post Office, 2007; Vossekuil et al., 2002).

Simply owning a weapon or being a veteran does not make someone more likely to engage in rampage school violence. In fact, we each own several guns and have concealed deadly weapons permits. We don't consider ourselves at risk to go on a shooting rampage. However, the presence of weapons along with the skill to use them is a risk factor. For example, while someone may not have any travel plans to drive across the country, the likelihood of this would be increased if the person in question happens to own a Recreational Vehicle (RV), has access to funds to pay for such a trip and the knowledge and ability to successfully plan the trip. Possessing these attributes does not make a trip a sure thing, but if a trip does occur, it can be accomplished more quickly and easily given these elements. Professors may overhear talk or read in essays about weapons, bragging about specialized training or experiences of killing from past military service.

Question 8: Do they glorify and revel in publicized violence such as school shootings, serial killers, war or display an unusual interest in sensational violence? Do they use weapons for emotional release and venerate destruction? (ASIS & SHRM, 2011; ATAP, 2006; Meloy et al., 2011; O'Toole, 2002; Turner & Gelles, 2003; US Post Office, 2007; Vossekuil et al., 2002).

Violence is all around us in American society, whether it be *Call of Duty*™ or *Grand Theft Auto*™ video game series or the latest explosion-riddled action movie or gritty NYC crime drama. Fascination and obsession with violent themes is identified as a risk factor for violence. While it is not true that all those students who talk about their latest killstreak in *Modern Warfare*™ or how much they enjoyed the torture scene in the most recent *Saw* movie will go on to shoot up the college, we will pay increasing attention to those students who are obsessed with glorified violence, possess a weapon collection, see others as persecuting them and then start drawing up hypothetical plans of how they would ever carry out an attack if they "snapped." This can be a matter of subtle distinction in some cases of threat assessment that requires careful questioning throughout the assessment.

Question 9: Do they carry deep grudges and resentments? Do they "collect injustices" when they were hurt, frustrated with someone, annoyed, or had trouble "letting things go?" (ASIS & SHRM, 2011; ATAP 2006; O'Toole, 2002; O'Toole & Bowman, 2011; Randazzo & Plummer, 2009; Turner & Gelles, 2003).

Does a student in your class talk about minor incidents that upset him from years ago? Does he lack empathy to understand others' perspective? Does he seem overly self-focused and collect past wrongs done to him? The concern here is a pervasive attitude of "the world owes me" that leads to emotional outbursts, poor empathy and the carrying of deep and powerful grudges long beyond what would be considered a normal period of frustration.

Question 10: Do they externalize blame for their behaviors and problems onto other people? (ATAP, 2006; O'Toole, 2002; O'Toole & Bowman, 2011; Turner & Gelles, 2003; US Post Office, 2007).

This can be seen as a normal developmental hurdle for many college students. A late paper is blamed on a lost syllabus. A poor group grade is blamed on the lack of a clear assignment from the professor. The behavior here escalates to a level of concern if a student displays a pervasive pattern of blaming others and avoids taking responsibility for more serious infractions. A student blows up during a discussion and insults the heritage and gender of another student in the class. He then blames the student for starting the argument. A student rants against the professor who failed to fully detail the material on the test after he earns a poor grade rather than taking ownership for his lack of effort in studying.

Question 11: Do they have a sense of entitlement, intimidation or act superior to others? Do they display intolerance to individual differences? (ATAP, 2006; Meloy et al., 2011; O'Toole, 2002; O'Toole & Bowman, 2011; Turner & Gelles, 2003).

Professors witness this behavior from students in the classroom. A student may intimidate others through rants and diatribes about his beliefs on a subject while he ignores anyone else's input on the matter. This may be a learned behavior from being raised in an environment where individual differences, tolerance and diversity were limited learning opportunities. A student may see himself as having a special viewpoint or place in the world that trumps other students' rights or beliefs. This is commonly born from religion or politics.

Question 12: Do they have a past history of impulsive, erratic or risk taking behavior? (ASIS & SHRM, 2011; O'Toole & Bowman, 2011; Randazzo & Plummer, 2009; Turner & Gelles, 2003; US Post Office, 2007).

We learn from the past. If there is any chance of predicting future violent behavior, one strong indicator is to understand how the student behaved in similar situations in the past. If a student in your class has a long history of impulsive acting out behaviors that involve yelling, intimidation and threats, it's reasonable to assume future stressful events such as a poor grade, difficult feedback session or a scenario that might embarrass the student in front of others would lead to a similar explosive action. Similarly, if a student engages in extreme risk-taking behavior, he may not have as much investment about following traditional rules or respond well to limits placed in syllabi or codes of conduct (a good example would be riding a motorcycle at high speed at night with the headlight off— however, drinking copious amounts of liquor to the point of illness, drinking power drinks to stay up for days at a time, or engaging in unprotected sex with multiple partners are not good examples, but are still risky behaviors).

Question 13: Do they have a past history of problems with authority? Do they have a pattern of intense work conflicts with supervisors and other authorities such as a Resident Advisor, Conduct Officer, Professor or Dean of Students (ASIS & SHRM, 2011; ATAP, 2006; O'Toole, 2002; O'Toole & Bowman, 2011; Turner & Gelles, 2003; US Post Office, 2007).

How does a student manage their frustration with a professor during times where the professor has to enforce authority (for example, with grading an assignment, requiring compliance with a behavior in the classroom such as talking out of turn or texting while in class)? While none of us likely enjoy the idea of an authority figure enforcing a rule or holding us responsible for our poor conduct, our response to such a corrective action is typically fairly restrained. A student who explodes, threatens, manipulates, yells or curses at an authority figure may lack the ability to stop an escalation toward violently acting out toward others. At times, they may challenge the authority of the professor or administrator merely for the sake of doing so. This could be the precursor to the other acts.

Question 14: Do they have difficulty connecting with other people? Do they lack the ability to form intimate relationships? Do they lack the ability to form trust? (O'Toole, 2002; Randazzo & Plummer, 2009; US Post Office, 2007).

A student who isolates himself from others in the classroom may be feeling overwhelmed, hopeless, frustrated or out of touch with others. This isolation creates in the student a feeling of separation and detachment from the rest of the class (potentially the rest of the college community, town, country and planet). This isolation feeds distrust and creates negative feedback loops for the student to have his thoughts reinforced over time ("I hate everyone," "I am different and feel things more intensely than others," "Everyone else is stupid," "They don't deserve to live"). Faculty often observe these students drifting away from social connection like a boat untied from its mooring.

Question 15: Do they objectify others (perhaps in social media or writings)? Has there been a shift from non-objectified writing to objectified? (Byrnes, 2002; O'Toole, 2002; O'Toole & Bowman, 2011)

A significant step down the pathway to violence is the distancing and, finally, objectification of others. Byrnes (2002) argues that harming others or committing violence requires an objectification of the target. Many military training programs highlight this concept of seeing the enemy as "Charlie" or a "Tango" to help depersonalize the potential target and the impending violence. The same trends exist for domestic/intimate partner violence, child abuse and animal abuse. Those who see people as objects in their path to be dealt with rather than as fellow human beings with the same thoughts, feelings, hopes and dreams they have move closer to violent action. Another element of this phenomenon is the shift from writings or social media posts from non-objectified to objectified writings. There is a shift when writings move from "you are my friend, I love you, you are beautiful" or "I don't like this school" [non-objectified] to writings such as: "you are a dirty whore" or "the maggots in this school need exterminating" [objectified]. There is a level of depersonalization that occurs as the target begins to be seen not as a person but instead as an object. This may be an object of lust, anger, disdain, hatred, pity, love or obsession.

The object may be possessed as well. One student sent messages ranging from "I love you." to "You must be mine!" to "You belong to me," (possessive) to messages that contained solely the passage from the Bible 1 Corinthians 13 (often read at weddings). These were clear indications that she moved from a person he loves to an object he must possess. These texts all take a back seat to his delusion of their relationship (they had gone out a couple of times). This is also a good example of how these topics can be overlapping. These assessments are not performed in a vacuum, not unlike the behaviors.

70

Question 16: Do they display a confused or deteriorating thought process? Do they hear voices or hallucinations that command them to action? (ASIS & SHRM, 2011; ATAP, 2006; Drysdale et al., 2010; Dunkle, Silverstein & Warner, 2008; Turner & Gelles, 2003; US Post Office, 2007).

Those with mental illness are not more likely to be violent. Students with mental illness are more likely to hurt themselves or be the victim of a violent crime than they are to commit such an assault (Choe, Teplin & Abram, 2008). The symptoms of mental illness can, however, be a contributing factor to violence. The paranoia, impulsivity and psychotic or deteriorating thought process could exacerbate and amplify an individual already predisposed to take out their frustrations and anger towards others. While students with mental health difficulties do not pose a greater risk to the campus population, ensuring proper care through adequate therapeutic support and services (Harvard Mental Health Letter, 2011) can help reduce any potential risk. Faculty is in an ideal situation to refer at-risk students with untreated (or undertreated) mental health problems to receive proper care and treatment.

Question 17: Do they have poor support and connection from faculty, administration and staff? Do they have an unsupportive family system and peers who exacerbate bad decisions and offer low quality advice or caring? Are they experiencing evaporating social inhibitors? (ATAP, 2006; Randazzo & Plummer, 2009; US Post Office, 2007; Vossekuil et al., 2002).

A student without proper support to manage the stress they are struggling with can be at risk to move further down the pathway to violence. Likewise, if other students and adults encourage poor decision making and inspire the student to engage in depressed, isolated and negative thoughts and behaviors, the risk grows. Like a suspension bridge suffering under the weight of neglect, wind, rain and rust, a catastrophic failure may occur because the previous supportive, risk-mitigating factors have been removed. The cables of the bridge snap from rust and a storm; the student loses a girlfriend, incurs a criminal charge or gets fired from a job and the results are the same—an explosive crash. Remember, Loughner was home with family while he deteriorated—but it appears that was not a supportive environment (Von Drehle et al., 2011).

Question 18: Have they experienced a drastic, unexplained change in behavior? (ASIS & SHRM, 2011; ATAP, 2006; Randazzo & Plummer, 2009; US Post Office, 2007).

Drastic and unexplained behavior changes require concern and further investigation. They are suddenly much more happy, less social, spiritual (having no interest before), manic and/or verbal. It may be the student has finally chosen to change their bad behavior and adapt a more positive and healthy lifestyle. It may also be that they have chosen to put their plan of attack in place and the things that previously frustrated them no longer do because everything will be fixed next

71

Tuesday when they show up to class with a gun. Faculty are in a position to observe patterns of student behavior over the course of a semester. If there is a drastic behavior change, this should be seen as a potential risk factor and a subject for further exploration. But even minor shifts in behaviors—what we call moves away from "baseline" behaviors—are important as well. This is another reason why getting to know your students and being observant are important.

Faculty should have an awareness of the threat assessment process in order to better understand what kind of behaviors they should be keeping an eye out for in the classroom. Again, it's not our intent to have faculty conduct threat assessments and take this information as a "how to" guide to determine a student's risk level. It's not our intent to turn faculty into some kind of Big Brother monitoring system for the university administration.

Instead, we wish to help educate faculty concerning the behavioral, cognitive, social and personality changes they should look to identify as risk factors in the classroom.

QUESTIONS FOR FURTHER DISCUSSION

Here are some additional questions concerning the threat assessment process. These questions are useful for self-reflection or to assist in facilitating a group discussion during a faculty training or orientation session.

1. Describe what is meant by action and time imperative. How might you assess this in a student you are concerned with in your classroom?

2. Think of an example in your life where the organization (or disorganization) of someone's thoughts either made a situation more serious in your mind or less serious.

3. After reviewing the threat assessment questions, which stood out the most to you? Discuss a student behavior that came to mind when reviewing these questions.

Part II

Individual Behavior in Context

Chapter 6

Non-Traditional and Veteran Students

Many of us have been taught we are all unique, special snowflakes—and that is somewhat true. We are all unique; however, we also share many commonalities. This book would triple in size if we attempted to discuss each special and unique student faculty may come in contact with during their teaching career.

In an effort to address some of the broader categories of students who may present a challenge, we've dedicated this chapter to discussing non-traditional and returning active duty veterans.

NON-TRADITIONAL STUDENTS

When offering training on non-traditional students, a woman in the back of the room joked, "you mean old, right?" And yes, older students are one of the many categories of non-traditional students who find their way into the classroom. But there are others who take "the path less traveled" into college, and this, more than solely age, is a better way to think "non-traditional."

These other students include those who:

- don't enter college directly from high school;
- attend college part-time;
- work full-time while enrolled at college;
- are financially independent;
- have dependants other than a spouse (usually children, but sometimes others);
- are single parents;
- do not have a high school diploma;
- may be coming back from military service or involved in ROTC.

There are a myriad of reasons a student may take a non-traditional route through the college. Some of these reasons are within the student's control, such as the benefits of asynchronous education and the flexibility of distance learning. Other reasons are related to external factors, such as current economic conditions or changes in the work force that require different skills. As a result of economic constriction and a desire to offer education to a wide range of individuals, schools have broadened their admission standards during the past few years (including community colleges and, of course, open-enrollment institutions). This has resulted in increased enrollment.

So what are some of the differences and challenges non-traditional students pose for college and universities? Non-traditional students may require more personal connection and understanding of their life circumstances in order to move forward and achieve academic success (Dill & Henley, 1998; Gearon, 2008). While many non-traditional students come into college highly motivated with the technical skills needed for success, others struggle with basic technology such as sending an email with an attachment or using the cut-and-paste option in Microsoft Word. These differences require individual assistance and care from the professor to ensure the student doesn't fall behind. They may become easily discouraged and begin to think, "I can't do this. This is more than I signed on for. I'm not cut out for this" (Keith, 2007).

Disruptive behaviors may manifest with the non-traditional student, related to a variety of reasons. A student might become frustrated by the speed at which material is being presented and frustrated with the instructor for not providing them a way to obtain the material they need. They may be frustrated with the lack of deadlines or structure when they need structure to manage school with their lives. They may struggle balancing the roles of family and student life (Chao & Good, 2004; Greenhaus & Beutell, 1985).

Imagine Sylvia, a non-traditional student coming back to school after years in the workforce. Sylvia feels overwhelmed by the technology in the classroom and lacks the basic skills to email, edit text in a word processing software program or post on the online classroom discussion threads. Sylvia falls out of step with other students in her classroom and consequently becomes increasingly upset and frustrated by her performance. She begins to focus her anger on the instructor who moves quickly through his PowerPoint slides and rarely pauses in the lecture to entertain questions or clarify the material.

Her anger grows and she begins to give off passive aggressive non-verbal behaviors to the instructor such as frowning, grumbling under her breath and loud sighs each time the professor advances a PowerPoint slide during a lecture. These disruptive behaviors have the potential of frustrating other students, interfering with the learning environment or escalating into more direct expressions of dissatisfaction.

The instructor notices this behavior and engages in a conversation with Sylvia to see what she is upset about. The professor offers to help Sylvia during office hours to clarify the material and help her with some of the technology issues she is having in class. Sylvia flies into another rage. This time she raises her voice and yells, "That's just it! You don't understand. I have to work, when I'm not here. I can't stop by your office because I'm either at work or watching my kids. That is why I'm so frustrated in class when you move through the material so quickly!"

Stress, both in terms of balancing work schedules and family life, can contribute to non-traditional students feeling hopeless when trying to access support services (Kohler-Giancola, Grawitch & Borchert, 2009). Many professors post office hours strictly during the 9–5, M–F block of time. Tutoring and academic support, financial aid and counseling services are often limited to traditional hours during the week. This can make it difficult for non-traditional working students to come to campus for meetings or support. These students receive little empathy about the challenges of balancing school, work, family and commuting (Gearon, 2008).

Hans Selye first defined stress in 1936 as "the non-specific response of the body to any demand for change." Stress is a broad term, impacting the physical, social, cognitive and psychological parts of who we are. He introduced the term Eustress in 1975. Eustress is a positive form of stress, usually related to desirable events in a person's life. This may include planning a wedding, studying well for a hard final, or feeling good about a difficult workout. While stressful, the end result reduces the overall stress level for an individual.

These "stress reactions" experienced by non-traditional students are the signs and symptoms that should be received as a "heads up" from their body in times of turmoil. Instructors should look for the various signs of stress that may affect non-traditional students in their classroom. These can include both cognitive symptoms (exhaustion, negative ruminating thoughts, inability to focus on a task, reduction in joy, mental fatigue, feelings of futility and devaluing of others) as well as physical symptoms (headaches, teeth-grinding, insomnia, irritability, muscle tension, gastric disturbance, high blood pressure, rapid heartbeat).

During trainings, we often remind faculty that being fair doesn't always mean equal. Policy and procedure are important, but non-traditional students thrive from a personal connection with faculty. They do understand that you have a life too, so even a well-crafted email can suffice, as can a phone call. Identifying early signs of stress and expressing care and concern can go a long way in preventing disruptive and dangerous behavior in the classroom.

SARA'S STORY: FINDING BALANCE

Sara is 38 years old and coming to college to study nursing after raising her family of three children. Her husband has mixed feelings about her going to college and has worked in a blue-collar factory job for most of his adult life and doesn't see the benefit. It has always been Sara's dream to be a nurse, but family and other commitments have kept her from going to college. She was a good student in high school, but has missed the technology revolution and is having trouble keeping track of online assignments and the great deal of memorization that is required for the chemistry section of the course. She's falling behind and her professor, Carol, has asked her to stay after class to talk about her latest assignments and difficulty on the last test.

Carol: "I wanted to talk to you today about your performance in class. I've noticed you haven't submitted the online assignments on current events in nursing and your last grade on the organic chemistry exam wasn't very good. What's been going on? How can we get you back on track?"

Sara: "I don't know. [*tearful*] All this isn't like I thought it would be. I was anticipating the hard work, but I've never been very good with computers and feel lost with the online assignments. As for the chemistry . . . well that comes down to the time I was able to put in studying. The final came when I had to take my oldest in for the state all-star basketball finals. I was hoping my husband was going to be able to help out so I could study more, but he had some extra shifts at the factory and I just didn't get the time I needed to put into studying."

Carol: "It sounds like there are two issues here. One is getting you up to speed in technology. The other is looking at trying to set up some time to be able to study the amount you need in order to get a decent grade on the tests."

Sara: "I know, I know . . . I just can't even think about what my first step would be. I feel like I'm wasting your time. You have 40 other students to work with and I should have found a way to do better on the test. I've never failed anything before. I really thought about just dropping out of school when I got that back. I know it would make my husband happy."

Carol: "I'm happy to talk to you Sara. That's why I do what I do. It also sounds like you aren't getting the kind of support you need from home."

Sara: "He's supportive and loves me, that isn't it. He just hasn't gone to college and has trouble understanding why this is important to me."

Carol: "You said in the first class you've always dreamed of being a nurse. You've been a kind of nurse to your three children for almost two decades. It seemed like something you were very excited about."

Sara: "It still is. I am just discouraged about how hard it has been so far."

Carol: "Well, it is an adjustment. Let's break it down into these two pieces: technology and study time. Have you gotten any extra help with the online assignment to find a current article about nursing and post a summary on the discussion board?"

Sara: "I wasn't sure where to do that. Is there someone who can help?"

Carol: "Yes. The academic support center has office hours just for this reason. If you can set up a time with them, maybe right before or after our class, I'm sure they can help you learn to find an article, print it and post a response on the class discussion board. Have you logged into our course shell yet?"

Sara: "That's the Blackboard, right? I did sign up for that the first week of class. I just wasn't sure what to do next. I am really lost. Then I feel more and more behind and it is so hard to even think about where to start."

Carol: "Let's do this. I'll give you the number of the academic support center and you call them to set up an hour-long tutor session for Blackboard before class next week. In the mean time, you've missed what? Three postings?"

Sara [looking down]: "It's been four counting this week."

Carol: "OK. How about you go to the library and take out the latest issues of *Nursing Today*. They will have articles you can read, summarize and bring to hand out to the whole class. Read four articles, write four brief summaries and then bring them to hand out in class."

Sara [brightening]: "Really? I could do that. Will that be OK?"

Carol: "Sure. Not a problem. How about the studying time? What do you need to get a better handle on that for the next test?"

Sara: "I think the main trouble was the weekend before the Monday test. I don't have anything else like that coming up before the next test. So I can just study twice as hard."

Carol: "OK, how about this? Take the last test and write up where you went wrong on the answers you put down. I'll bring your grade up to a D on the test if you put that work in. That will help you when you do the next test."

Sara: "That would be amazing. Thank you so much."

Carol: "Well, the thanks will come if you make that appointment with academic support and get over to the library and bring those article summaries to the next class. Do you think you can pull all that off?"

Sara: "Yes. I can do that. It'll take some work, but I finally feel like I'm headed in the right direction and can see a light at the end of the tunnel."

Carol: "Good. I understand it can be hard to reach for your dreams, particularly when other supportive people don't understand why they are so important to you. I know you will make a great nurse, Sara. I believe in you and think you can do this."

Sara: "That means a lot to me. I'll make you proud."

Carol: "Good. Here is the number for academic support. I'll expect those articles for the class next week. If you can get your summary to me before class, I can make the copies for you."

Sara: "I'll do that. Thanks again."

RETURNING ACTIVE DUTY VETERANS

Veterans are, and will be, returning from active duty to the classroom in record numbers (Wallis, 2012). Faculty will be seeing more veteran students in their classroom, and in some of these cases, they will be struggling to create a learning environment for these returning soldiers. Many vets make the transition into the classroom very well. One distinct advantage to a veteran is that they, unlike many students, understand bureaucracy at a very high level. They've lived it like no other student. Thus, they transition easily into the structured requirements of assignments, class attendance and discussions (as well as financial aid, advising, etc.). Others struggle greatly with Post Traumatic Stress Disorder (PTSD) or with the adjustment following the traumatic experiences of fighting for their lives to worrying about completing a math assignment. According to the Department of Defense and *Time* Magazine (Haiken, 2013), when compared to their peer groups, they (especially combat veterans) struggle at a higher level with depression, substance use, suicidal ideation, etc. This is not to say that all veterans are suffering from mental health issues, but that we should be attuned to their needs.

We should also remember that while these men and women have had experiences that their fellow students and we have not, they will share them as they see fit. Do not call on them and ask them to speak of their experiences. Do not ask them to speak for "all vets." Pay attention to anniversaries and events that may bring certain emotions (Veteran's Day, 9/11, Deployment anniversary—which you will likely not know the date of—and other days, etc.).

AMANDA'S STORY: WOUNDED SOLDIER

An example of these struggles is included within this rather stunning email shared by a student with an online professor.

Instructor,

I know this is unorthodox, but I hope you can understand. I was recently diagnosed with PTSD. My mental health advisor at my command made me go see, told me to talk to someone. I don't have anyone to talk to. My sister is dealing with her own issues from her deployments and my father disowned me the last time I talked to her about my deployments. I am having trouble focusing and haven't been sleeping very much. I see so many things when I close my eyes. I see my friends, myself, the people I killed, the people I failed; the people that I buried. I remember my friend Rev. That was his nickname. I remember doing so many things with him, then I remember him crying in my arms as he bled to death, due to the lower half of his body being blown off. The other Marines around me were yelling and screaming, I didn't hear anything except him saying "I'm sorry." I just got angry and started yelling at him "FOR WHAT?" I was hoping he would respond but he didn't.

Another in my unit died by a sniper shot. The bastard shot him right in the head and his brain hit me. I remember getting back to base and scrubbing myself so hard I began to bleed. I remember Omar, he was an 11-year-old boy that I shot because insurgents captured his family and killed his mother and said if you don't take this bomb to those Americans, they will kill his entire family. He was walking towards our post and I saw him carrying a box. He was crying harder and harder with each step. Our translator was yelling at him to stop and put down the box, but he didn't. I got the order and executed the order. After I shot him, as he began to fall to the ground, the bomb exploded. All that I could find of the boy was his arm. I remember seeing an entire family captured by terrorists. We were on an observation post and we could see inside of a building 50 yards away. Our mission was to report everything we see. Well the terrorists forced their entry and immediately shot the oldest boy, restrained the mother, father, and two children. As they raped the woman and daughter, we requested permission to enter and eliminate the enemy personnel. We were ordered not to interfere.

We had to watch as they raped and killed the mother and daughter. They then told the father if he didn't take a bomb to a checkpoint Houston, they would kill his youngest son. As soon as they took the man out of the house, they cut the boys throat. I had to fight my Marines just to restrain them from advancing and killing the enemy. I believe we never forgave ourselves for that.

So last night I was tossing and turning and couldn't really sleep, because every time I fell asleep I would have dreams from my deployments. I would wake up feeling scared and alone and very angry. Around 0500, I swear I heard, as clear as if you were standing in front of me talking to me, someone say, "You are not in the right place, MOVE!!!" and I jumped out of bed screaming. I think I scared my neighbors, cause I could hear them talking about calling the cops. I had to go explain everything was fine and that I just had a bad dream. I laid my head down again and my 0530 alarm went off. After I turned off the alarm I pushed the screen lock button and swear I saw a skull or demonic figure on my phone, I jumped back and fell off the bed. I said fuck it and took a shower and I started crying. I couldn't stop crying.

By the time I finally came back to reality, I was in the fetal position in ice-cold water. On the drive in this morning I couldn't focus. I was driving 30 MPH on the highway, which is odd, because normally I speed and I got pulled over. The cop said he was following me for five min and he thought something was wrong with my car. I explained to him I didn't even realize I was driving and apologized. He told me he wasn't going to give me a ticket, and to be safe. My partner is worried, cause I picked him up from the campus parking lot and I didn't talk the entire trip to the unit. I feel like I'm losing my mind. I can't focus.

I think I am just telling you everything because I need a vent. Please be understanding.

—Amanda.

I believe we find a few things in this extreme example of the horror a student witnessed and shared with her professor. First, we see the harrowing courage a young woman has in the face of trying to reorganize her life in the United States following the horrors of what she witnessed while deployed. One can barely contemplate the strength of character and determination it takes to simply get out of bed each day, let alone try to balance course syllabi, assignments and class discussion.

The instructor's response follows:

I would like to begin by saying how sorry I am for all you have been through and the losses you have suffered. I cannot imagine the horrific events and the sadness you had to encounter daily both in Iraq and now here at home. I hope you don't mind, but I have reached out to our university's crisis management team in hopes that you will receive the support you need to help you with all that you have endured and continue to endure. I would also like to pass along their information if you would like to contact them directly. You can email them at email@school.edu or phone them at 866–555–5555.

My heart goes out to you, Amanda. By reaching out to me, I think you are taking the first step in helping yourself get a handle on something that may be too overwhelming for you to handle alone. My thoughts and prayers are with you.

We have an opportunity to witness the grace and mercy an instructor shares with her student. This level of response from a professor to this email demonstrates the level of caring and empathy that sets an aspirational standard for all who work in higher education. We are particularly impressed with the instructor's willingness to express her emotions and offer prayers of support while also referring this kind of serious interaction to her school's office of disability support and crisis management team.

Another approach to help students who are struggling with a return to campus from combat or active duty can be found in Albert Ellis' (2001) work in Rational Emotive Behavioral Therapy (REBT). REBT was developed by Albert Ellis and is useful to assist students in identifying irrational thoughts that the student has in reaction to activating events. The REBT approach can be described in terms of A–B–Cs: these are Activating events, Beliefs about these events and the Consequences of these beliefs.

Activating events can be anything from a relationship argument, getting cut-off in traffic, spilling coffee on your favorite shirt or having your computer crash. These events cannot be prevented, they just occur throughout our lives. It's our "beliefs" about the activating events that lead to increased anxiety, panic and negative consequences. We cannot change the activating events in our lives, but we can change our beliefs about the activating events and the resulting consequences of our behavior.

When working with a student such as Amanda, faculty can teach this approach by discussing several A–B–C examples and have the student come up with some of their own examples, to highlight both the negative and positive outcomes from the beliefs we each choose to have.

For Amanda, we cannot change her experiences in the war. These activating events will remain with her after she returns from the war. Helping her find some kind of meaning or new belief about these events may help her find some peace and lead to a more positive consequence.

Perhaps a caring professor helps her understand her fellow soldier's sacrifice had some greater meaning for our country's freedom. Perhaps the professor helps her to see that part of going on with her life and assignments can be its own honor or memorial for her fallen brother.

Likewise, if Amanda chooses to believe her friend's life was a waste and there is no real point in pursuing education when so many in the world are living in violence and poverty, it is likely her consequences will also be negative. The result would be Amanda failing her class or dropping out of school.

Helping students control and alter their negative beliefs about activating events can lead to more positive consequences for their future. This can be a powerful tool in a faculty member's collection of intervention techniques.

DEALING WITH DARRYL

I have taught graduate classes for over 20 years. During that time, I can count on one hand the number of times I encountered a potentially violent student or felt personally threatened by the behavior of someone in one of my classes.

The helping professions attract a wide range of individuals. In my experience, counseling students constitute a fairly diverse and unique group. Most have a deep commitment to serving others that drives their passion for entering the field. Occasionally, however, I've run across students who have enrolled in the program seemingly for reasons more related to personal development. Certainly, some students bring more baggage with them as they enter the academic arena.

Such was the case with Darryl. Darryl had decided to continue his education after serving two tours in the military. As an undergraduate, he had majored in philosophy and religious studies at a small, liberal arts college in the southeast. In his mid thirties, Darryl was older than most of the other students in my testing and assessment class. He seemed to get along with everyone; some of his classmates even admired him. After all, he had done and seen things few of them had ever been exposed to—except vicariously.

It was during one particularly engaging class that a side of Darryl emerged we had not seen before. I was explaining how factors such as race, ethnicity, socioeconomic status and religious heritage can influence a person's performance on standardized tests. To make a particularly important point, I drew a comparison between test scores Christians and Muslims had achieved on a test designed to measure the degree of devotion to core beliefs associated with the two religions. I noted one study found that Muslims exhibited significantly higher levels of commitment to their religious convictions than did Christians.

Before I could proceed with a discussion of why this might be the case, Darryl slammed his notebook closed and yelled "Bullshit!" This caught me, as well as most of the class, completely off guard. There was the proverbial moment when you literally could have heard a pin drop. I could tell Darryl's temperament was continuing to escalate; he was becoming visibly more agitated with each passing second. Eventually he added, "Fuck the Muslims," but in a slightly softer voice.

Realizing the subject matter had obviously triggered some deep and potentially explosive feelings within him, I immediately recognized the potential for class not to end well. The other students sat motionless, glancing at each other passively. I knew they were waiting to see how I would handle the situation.

I turned toward Darryl, but I did not move in his direction. In these situations, I knew maintaining some distance from him was probably the best course of action. I was especially relieved when none of the students sitting close to Darryl reached out to him or tried to—heaven forbid—put their arm around him or give him a hug as I knew some of them were inclined to do in this kind of emotionally charged situation.

Mindful of Darryl's body language and nonverbals, I looked at him directly but in an empathetic manner. I tried to maintain eye contact with him as I said "Darryl, I need you to calm down," in a serious but normal tone. I purposefully tried not to raise my voice or do anything that could be interpreted as challenging or threatening. "I can tell you are upset, and that's OK," I continued. "Take a deep breath."

At first, I did not know what Darryl's response was going to be. He glared at me for a couple of seconds and then looked down at the floor. Without looking away from him, I then added, "I realize today's topic obviously hit a nerve with you, and that's OK, too. We can talk about it, if you want."

Within a few moments, Darryl seemed to regain his composure. He looked around the room. I noticed he was still clenching his fists; his knuckles were white. I was a little relieved when I saw him unclench them and relax a bit. He let out a long sigh, closed his eyes for a minute, and then kind of half-smiled at everyone.

"Sorry about that," he said apologetically. He then went on to explain how a good friend of his was seriously wounded in Iraq a few years ago. He has seen the "commitment" I had mentioned earlier first hand and he had been jolted by a momentary flashback to the awful moment when his friend—who was standing right next to him at the time—had his right leg blown off.

With that admission, we spent the rest of the class discussing his experience in some detail. He became quite animated as he described what had happened and how it affected him. I figured we could always come back to testing and assessment at the next class session. What initially seemed like a dangerous situation eventually evolved into a powerful learning opportunity for everyone—including myself.

Again, although the incidence of these episodes seems to be pretty rare, when they do occur it is imperative that the instructor know how to respond appropriately. Staying calm, accurately reading the situation, and responding with just the right combination of concern and self-control in a confident and reassuring manner seems to be the key to de-escalating a potentially violent student.

Aaron W. Hughey, Ed.D.
Professor and Program Coordinator
Department of Counseling and Student Affairs
Western Kentucky University

QUESTIONS FOR FURTHER DISCUSSION

Here are some additional questions about non-traditional and veteran students in the classroom. These questions are useful for self-reflection or to assist in facilitating a group discussion during a faculty training or orientation session.

1. What are some of the challenges student veterans bring to the classroom environment? If you have worked with student veterans in the classroom before, what are some approaches that worked with them? What are some approaches that were less successful?

2. Discuss some of the difficulties you have experienced in working with students who have served in the military in your classroom. Have you had difficulty referring veterans to campus services? Why or why not?

3. What are some of the hardest challenges when working with a non-traditional student? What buttons do they push in you (if any)? What has worked in the past to move through these frustrations?

Chapter 7

Millennial and African American Students

THE MILLENNIAL GENERATION

They have been called Generation Y, Echo Boomer, Generation Next and, of course, Millennials. Entire books have been dedicated to understanding the needs of these students (Bonner, Marbley & Hamilton, 2011; Coomes & DeBard, 2004; Elam, Stratton & Gibson, 2007; Price, 2009; Strauss & Howe, 2007). Millennials are defined as being born between 1981 and 1999 (or thereabouts).

While we must be cautious about stereotyping behavior onto an entire generation of college students, there are some common observations concerning Millennial students. They have been described as more relational and enjoy a personal connection with professors. This goes hand in hand with a more relaxed and non-authoritarian learning environment. They are more likely to follow the course rules and expectations if they have an understanding of why these exist. Millennials also respond better to lectures that focus on multimedia, collaborating with classmates and connecting to the course material in terms of practical application rather than just information to be consumed. Having grown up being able to find most information at their fingertips through the Internet, they value the utility and connection of this information beyond its simple intrinsic value.

One approach that works well with Millennial students is walking them through a clear and well-thought-out plan to best illuminate their path moving forward. I have found William Glasser's (1999) work in Reality therapy particularly helpful when working with Millennial students. He offers a system based on the Wants, Direction and Doing, Evaluation, Planning (WDEP).

W = exploring the student's wants and needs: Here we look for the desires and direction the student wants to head in. It's no good developing a plan to move forward with a student to reduce disruptive behavior in the classroom without first ensuring that they have an interest in changing the behavior. Help the student understand that by changing their behavior, they can improve grades, reduce stress about passing the class and can move closer to completing their degree program.

$D = direction\ and\ doing$: Assess what the student is doing and the direction these behaviors are taking them. Students who act out in class, misuse technology by texting in class or engaging in cross-talk with other students are not engaging in behaviors that will help their long-term academic success. Help the student understand that their current behavior is going to result in a failing grade in the class and keep them from reaching their goals.

$E = evaluation$: Make an evaluation of the student's total behavior. Is the behavior taking them closer to their wants and needs? Have they implemented change in their behavior? Is that change successful?

$P = planning\ and\ commitment$: Assist the student in formulating realistic plans and make a commitment to carry them out. As with most change in life, this will often be a "two steps forward, one step back" process.

So, what does a plan end up looking like? What are some of the qualities of a successful plan with a student that is designed to change behavior and reduce classroom disruption? Again, Glasser (1999) shares some thoughts on the qualities needed for a successful plan with a student. These are:

- Simple: plans are broken into small, easy pieces
- Attainable: plans are realistic and can be accomplished
- Measurable: plans can be assessed and evaluated
- Immediate: short term goals that occur soon
- Controlled by the planner: ensuring adjustments
- Consistently practiced: repeat until habits form
- Committed to: buy-in and investment.

When developing a plan for corrective action with a student, focus on these aspects of the plan to ensure a higher rate of success in the students' follow through. A student who does not buy into the plan, or who cannot see the immediate progress of their behavior related to the plan's success will likely fail to achieve the goals.

AFRICAN AMERICAN STUDENTS

At Western Kentucky University, several parents and White students complain about groups of African American students who gather around the entrance to one of the residence halls on campus as well as groups that hang out around the southern end of the campus. The concern is not just limited to students and their parents. Some staff and faculty express concern about these kinds of "gangs of Black youth" that seem to gather, talk and listen to their music.

Upon reflection and some efforts by the university, it is determined that most of these African American students are simply waiting to go to the dining hall, waiting until their next class or spending time with friends. There is some music occasionally, but nothing against any college sound regulations. The problem, it seems, is several White students and faculty are bothered by any gatherings of African American students on campus.

When addressing disruptive behavior in the classroom, it is essential to be aware of our personal biases and past history with interacting with those who may be different than we are. While it is understandable to be cautious around something unfamiliar or someone new, there is a difference between simple discomfort and reading potential threat into a gathering of students. There's a difference between being cautious in a new city and a White person locking their car door as a Black person walks by.

Gosset, Cuyjet and Cockriel (1998) found that African American students perceived significantly more discrimination from the administration, their peers and faculty when compared to White students. While not always intentional, prejudice and discrimination may come from students who've had limited contact with those different from themselves or those who make snap judgments about risk when witnessing African Americans hanging out in a group or dressing differently than they are accustomed to. Ancis, Sedlacek and Mohr (2000) found that African American students perceived significantly more racial tensions and separation than did White and Asian American Students.

DIVERSITY IN THE CLASSROOM

Teaching a course that focuses on diversity is often like walking through a minefield: you must be careful of each step you take. The topic of diversity is complex and dynamic. As the instructor, I often ask my students to engage in introspective self-analysis while simultaneously challenging their worldviews, ideologies, belief systems and perceptions. For some students, it is the first time that they have had to reflect on dimensions of their lives that have not been subject to much scrutiny up to this point. As such, I always look forward to engaging with my students and listening to their viewpoints.

As an African American woman, I am acutely aware of the resistance I often experience and its manifestation as a challenge—either direct or more covert—to my instructional responsibility. I have come to understand that resistance and challenge are important parts of the educational journey as I work to teach my students about the influence and impact diversity has on the lives of individuals. The skills required in order to work productively with individuals and groups who come from varying cultural backgrounds can be difficult to acquire.

Diversity is a sensitive topic for many students; it can precipitate considerable discomfort and anxiety. There is often a fine line between challenging my authority as an educator and being antagonistic toward me as a human being. I recently encountered one student who crossed that line. Alicia is a middle-aged, White female from a fairly diverse community. During our initial introductions during the first class meeting, she made it abundantly clear that she already knew enough about diversity to continue being successful in her current position. Consequently, she did not feel the course would be of benefit to her either personally or professionally—and this attitude characterized her interactions with me and the rest of the class for the entire semester.

At several instances throughout the course, she voiced her discontent and irritation with the ideas and concepts covered in the class, principally related to race and ethnicity, as well as with the pedagogical approach taken to dissect that content. One of the stories Alicia shared with the class was a narrative outlining how she lost a scholarship to an African American female. Apparently this was an institution that she really wanted to attend. From her vantage point, the desire for a more diverse student body outweighed her individual aspirations. She interpreted this as a clear-cut case of reverse discrimination as well as a textbook example of how minorities in the United States are routinely "given handouts" simply because of the color of their skin.

It often appeared as if Alicia was holding the classroom hostage. She was definitely stifling honest discussion and critical discourse. Needless to say, her constant diatribe created an atmosphere of uneasiness in the classroom and prompted several of her classmates, all of whom were White, to openly challenge her views. As an instructor, I used these times to explore the different perspectives that are commonly held about diversity and why it is considered such a prickly issue by many in our society. Balancing Alicia's microaggression with the need to maintain an open, comfortable learning environment became a primary goal.

I received a steady supply of emails from Alicia outlining her ongoing displeasure with me and the class. After numerous attempts to work with her both inside and outside the classroom, I finally realized that Alicia's subtext and constructed meanings related to diversity were impeding our relationship. Coming to this realization was initially difficult for me, but I soon understood that I should not take her failure to engage with me or the resultant accusations from that failure personally. This insight was subsequently reinforced through the advice and counsel offered by colleagues and the department head.

The experience with Alicia taught me that appropriately addressing students' acts of insularity and resistance related to diversity takes determination, the ability to be comfortable with discomfort, and the humility to ask for insight and support from those who have traveled the same road. When dealing with another person's long-held beliefs, particularly about diversity-related topics, not every opportunity will present itself as a teachable moment. It takes perseverance to build rapport and engage in meaningful dialogue to recognize how our views about diversity impact how we work with others. The bottom line is that you should always be prepared for resistance—it is a constant in the universe.

Monica Burke, Ph.D.
Assistant Professor
Western Kentucky University

UNDERSTANDING MICROAGGRESSIONS

A central challenge for professors working with African American students in the classroom is the importance of understanding and responding to microaggressions. Microaggressions are defined by Sue (2010) as "brief, everyday exchanges that send denigrating messages to certain individuals because of their group membership" (xvi). Sue and colleagues (2007a) further divide microaggressions into three categories: microassaults, microinsults and microinvalidations. By definition, these are often unintended slights that have serious implications and impact on African American students in the classroom.

Imagine an instructor asks the class to break up into groups and a group of White students proceeds to ignore an African American student who requests to join their group as they have a number of things in common related to the assignment. This would be an example of a *microassault*. The slight might not have been intended, but the failure to include a classmate in a group based on the color of their skin sends an unacceptable message in the classroom. This kind of action is closely related to discrimination and may also involve a direct verbal assault (Boysen, 2012).

Microinsults are actions that disrespect or demean a person based on their group status (Boysen, 2012; Sue, Lin, Torino, Capodilupo & Rivera, 2009; Sue et al., 2007a; Sue, Bucceri, Kin, Nadal & Torino, 2007b). An example of this could be a student who makes generalizations about African American women and their level of intelligence or that all African Americans are only at your college because of an overly generous affirmative action policy. Again, these comments may come out of ignorance, poor access to teaching or information about ethnicity and culture or simple stupidity. In any case, the instructor has a responsibility to address these microinsults as they have a strong impact on African American students.

A student in a public speaking class who congratulates an African American student on a presentation by saying, "I'm really surprised at how well that went. You were very well spoken today," is an example of a *microinvalidation*. A microinvalidation undermines or denies the experiences of a person of color (Boysen, 2012). This kind of comment sends the message to the African American student that "I didn't expect you to be so well spoken today in class" (Sue et al., 2007a; 2007b). Another example of a microinvalidation may be a student who says, "I don't really see color—racism is a problem of the past." While probably unintentionally, this conveys the message that the African American student's experiences are not valid.

So, what is a professor to do? The challenge here is addressing a potentially insulting, invalidating or assaultive comment or action by a student or group of students who may not have an awareness that the behavior or what they said has been taken poorly. One approach to addressing this conflict is to engage students early on in the class with examples of microaggressions and then create an opportunity for a discussion and remediation.

Sue and his colleagues (2009; 2010) offer research that demonstrates that students of color want professors to engage in these kinds of discussions and for instructors to facilitate an open dialog that validates their experiences of bias and racism. Professors should be involved in this process and not let the students dominate the discussion and take it away from the lessons of microaggressions. Instructors who are not trained or prepared to discuss these issues with their students might lean on the college or university office of diversity programming, counseling or ask a psychology professor versed in microaggressions to discuss the topic. Boysen (2012) suggests brief minute-long response essays after the presentation in an attempt to gauge how students receive the information.

The issue of microaggressions in the classroom is not easy to address for instructors. Increased training to identify, intervene and manage these behaviors and comments is needed. Sue (2010) suggests that knowledge and awareness are key to recognizing and effectively handling microaggressions. It is unlikely that all professors will become experts in diversity issues or multiculturalism, but with increased exposure to the importance of this topic it may be an area in which instructors can learn more around how to successfully engage students in these kinds of discussions.

QUESTIONS FOR FURTHER DISCUSSION

Here are some additional questions related to working with Millennial or African American students. These questions are useful for self-reflection or to assist in facilitating a group discussion during a faculty training or orientation session.

1. Discuss your personal past experiences with either Millennial or African American students and reflect on how they shape your expectations for future behavior? How accurate are your expectations?

2. Talk about a time where you witnessed a microaggression toward a student of color or experienced a microaggression yourself because of some trait you possess.

3. Discuss how you would respond to a parent who calls and reports a large number of African American students are gathering outside of a residence hall and it is upsetting their daughter. What might you *want* to say compared to what you *should* say to help bring about potential change?

Chapter 8

International and GLBTQ Students

INTERNATIONAL STUDENTS

Over 600,000 international students come to the United States each year to study (Hyun, Quinn, Madon & Lustig, 2007). More than half of the international students come from Asia, with the largest representation from China and India (Rothstein & Rajapaksa, 2004). International students have trouble adjusting to their new surroundings primarily because of culture shock (Poyrazli & Lopez, 2007).

When working with students who are in the minority population at your college or university, it will pay to educate yourself about the services (International Student Programs Office, etc.) offered by your college. While you do not need to be versed in "all things visa," you should know what topics they have had covered in orientation (and whether they were able to attend)—the ISP should be able to help you with this.

Also, remember not to isolate them and/or ask them to "speak for all [insert race/culture/ethnicity/religion here]." Too often, after 9/11 and during the wars, we heard from Middle Eastern and/or Muslim students who were asked to "educate the class" about their culture or religion. Can you imagine asking a Southern Baptist Student to speak for all Protestants? Asking a White student to speak for all Caucasians or Americans of European descent? We would never do that to them, why to an international student?

Recently in a class, there was a Palestinian student who learned that one of the other students in the class was Egyptian. He insisted to the professor that he could not be in the same small group with the Egyptian, as they "support the Israelis through their peace treaty, while my people are killed." The professor's response was, "I'm sorry, the groups are set, and you need to learn to work with others you may disagree with. It will serve you well later in the business world." This resulted in the student storming from the class, threatening to sue the school, and also saying, "You can't make me do this! I will report you!"

Clearly, this was not the most compassionate way to manage this situation, and it escalated a situation that could have been de-escalated from the start.

That being said, we do need to recognize that the cultural norms and mores of their home country are different than ours. Attitudes towards women, dating, clothing, and individuals of other cultures and religions are just a sampling of the issues. Even attitudes toward academic integrity (citation, collusion, etc.) are different in different regions in the world. Thus, it is imperative that professors are clear about the expectations in these areas. But it must be made clear in a fashion that indicates that the professor is just clarifying behavioral and academic expectations for *all* students, not just for the international students in his/her class.

International students face a range of adjustment problems in addition to culture shock including homesickness and understanding the requirements of a new academic environment. The effects of homesickness are often negative and can include loneliness, sadness and adjustment issues (Poyrazli & Lopez, 2007). Tseng and Newton (2002) outline four major areas of adjustment for students. These include 1) general living adjustments such as food, housing, financial transactions and transportation, 2) academic adjustment to the University system and developing the skills they need to be successful, 3) adjusting to the cultural norms and behaviors and 4) personal psychological adjustments such as dealing with feelings of homesickness, loneliness and feelings of isolation (Hyun et al., 2007).

These problems can easily drift into the classroom and create challenges for managing behaviors that may be disruptive to the academic learning environment. One of the biggest challenges for professors may be overcoming the language barrier in order to communicate with students about classroom policies and norms. International students may have differing expectations for what is considered normal within the classroom and language differences may make it difficult to communicate these expectations.

When international students struggle with mental health problems such as homesickness, depression and anxiety, they may be less likely to seek assistance. Hyun et al. (2007) suggest a host of factors for this resistance for accessing services. These factors include a lack of awareness of their needs for mental health services, the retention of health-related beliefs and practices from their home country and the cultural stigma associated with emotional expression.

Instructors who help international students with their transition will be more successful if they work with international support service departments, friends and advisors. Hyun et al. (2007) find international students rely more heavily on their peers, rather than professionals, for both social support and information about resources. Professors can assist international students to connect with their advisor. International students who have better relationships with their advisors are less likely to report having stress-related or emotional problems and are more likely to utilize counseling services (Heggins & Jackson, 2003; Rai, 2002).

When approaching internationals students in the classroom, instructors should first attend to any language barriers that may exist. This may require enlisting a supportive staff or peer who can assist with translation. This kind of communication can be even more difficult when trying to communicate subtle social norms around classroom behavior. Instructors will be more successful in their interactions if they have a working knowledge of the international student resources on campus. There is typically a staff person or department tasked with helping international students through problems that may occur on campus.

STUDY ABROAD

A professor contacted me not knowing what to do about an international student who was disruptive in their class. This was an open access public community college setting. The professor stated that the student would occasionally get up and leave the class at random times without asking for permission or making any statements. The student would return again after random intervals and return to their seat. The professor found this very odd and had never experienced this before; they wondered whether the student was psychotic and/or was on any drugs. I suggested that the professor send the student to me to assess this behavior and determine whether any intervention was necessary. The student was compliant and came to speak with me in my role as a counselor at the college.

The student explained to me that he had moved to this country a few years ago from the Republic of Georgia (in the former Soviet Union). He was surprised when I explained to him that his behavior was seen as "problematic and disruptive." He further informed me that in his country and culture it was common practice for students to leave class at any time without permission for a "cigarette break." He explained this is what he was doing. The student gave me no indication of being either psychotic or on drugs. I used this opportunity to explain to him the expectations in American colleges and why the professor was concerned. He stated that he understood and accepted my recommendation that he speak with the professor and apologize. Clearly, this case was an excellent reminder to me not to make assumptions or forget the potential impact of cultural norms regarding disruptive behavior.

Mitchell A. Levy
Dean of Students
Atlantic Cape Community College

AWAY FROM HOME

I lived as an expatriate in Europe and Asia for a third of my adult life, and now I teach English to expatriates from more than a dozen cultures, languages and countries studying on a college campus in order to gain admission to university-level classes. This job provides some unique challenges, but combined with my prior experience, it has also provided a double-sided understanding of culture stress.

Cultural adaptation depends on several factors: previous amount of time spent away from home, learned coping strategies, felt connection to home, and meaningful relationships with the expatriate community—all play a role in someone's ability to adjust, adapt, and thrive in their new environs.

Many instructors may not feel they have time to evaluate all of these factors in determining the level of stress experienced by the student, but even a cursory understanding of these issues might prove helpful in tailoring the approach an instructor takes in dealing with students by getting to know a little about the different interpersonal differences in their respective classrooms. One thing I have found and experienced personally is that while cultural assimilation can be progressive, in many of my students, as in many Western expatriates living in other cultures, culture stress is progressive. A student can sit in classes all semester and seem fine, but the stress and discomfort is bearing down on him or her increasingly. Many of the students studying in American schools come from cultures wherein complaining carries serious social stigma, especially complaining about school. Being aware of this progressive nature of culture stress can be helpful in dealing with international students, as can allowing accommodation as incrementally as possible.

Many young men and women that come to our school from the Kingdom of Saudi Arabia possess serious misgivings about speaking to a person of another gender in public. The reasons have been explained in several different ways to me, but the end result is that men and women, unless married or related, don't speak to each other in public. They also do not attend schools together. Usually, the more advanced students come to the conclusion that this one cultural aspect of American life becomes one they cannot live without, that to do their jobs, to graduate, to do well in school, they need to speak to the other gender, and that it means something almost completely different here than in their homeland.

A young male Saudi student (let's call him "Motaib"—note: not his name) had sat slumped in a chair for most of the semester one fall in an introductory English class. After seeing Motaib speak to a young woman outside school one day, I assumed he was one of the Saudi men who had less reluctance about speaking to Saudi women. Seeking a chance to spur Motaib into doing something, anything in my class, I asked him to partner with the sole woman in the class. He refused. I saw it as another sign of recalcitrance on his part. I gave him a zero, and then he came to me after class and explained to me that in his family, men aren't allowed to speak to Saudi women unless they are family or their wives. I asked him about the woman I saw him with earlier. He said it was his sister. I relented, and explained to him that at the university, men and women must work together. He may even be forced to work with another Saudi woman. He nodded, and said "I know, Teacher." He went on to explain that he just couldn't bring himself to do it, and described the sleeplessness he was experiencing, the loneliness, and the longing for home he had. "Everything here is so uncomfortable. I want to go back home, just to relax for a while."

I completely understood his feelings. Being away from home brings a not-fully conscious discomfort that an expatriate often doesn't even recognize until it is lifted, and bearing up under the weight of it can lead to depression, anxiety and destructive behavior. My best take on this issue after consulting with the other teachers was to tell students in the introductory classes that they didn't have to do this now, but when they reached the upper levels, they must partner with the opposite gender. It seems to give them some relief from the "everything is so uncomfortable" feeling that Motaib expressed to me outside the classroom that day, and as the students transition through school they largely grow in acceptance of this as just another new part of the culture in which they live.

Jack Cobb
English Professor
English as a Second Language Institute (ESLI)
Western Kentucky University

GLBTQ STUDENTS

Conservatively speaking, there are over 8.8 million gay males, lesbians or bi-sexuals in the United States (Chonody, Rutledge & Siebert, 2009). When working with students who are in this minority population at your college or university, there can be challenges that occur in the classroom that can make managing disruptive or dangerous behavior difficult. Students who are gay, lesbian, bi-sexual, transgendered, queer or questioning often come to class with a history of being bullied, teased and treated poorly by others. This is certainly not the case for everyone, but these students may report lower levels of perceived social acceptance, lower levels of psychological well-being and lower levels of physical well-being (Woodford, Howell, Silverschanz & Yu, 2012).

Faculty should be aware of the impact of certain stigmatizing language and how this language impacts GLBTQ students in the classroom. While the professor would certainly be expected to avoid using phrases such as "That's so gay," they should be aware that the use of this phrase and the negative impact is common on college campuses (Woodford et al., 2012). The word "gay" is frequently used to describe something as stupid, weird or undesirable. Students who hear or are exposed to this language experience negative effects. Even the term "homo-sexuals" has moved into a questionable realm of propriety and has been replaced by "gay or lesbian" (Chonody et al., 2009).

There may even be the potential for some students to defend the phrase "that's so gay" by downplaying their intent and offering that this phrase isn't meant to be hateful for the GLBT population. Certainly, some argue, it is not as hateful as terms such as "fag" or "dyke." It may be that the research supports a continuum of negative experiences following these different phrases; however, none have a place in the classroom. Faculty are encouraged to develop some language to respond to these arguments before they occur; perhaps including a statement in the syllabus about expectations around community, supporting each other and being aware of how language may affect different people different ways. As with sexual harassment language, the issues here are not so much the intent of the statement, but the impact.

Faculty should be aware of potential conflicts among groups of different students in their classes. Research supports a number of groups that are more frequently correlated with high levels of anti-gay biases. These include: religiosity, persons who are from the Midwest or South, those from more rural childhood settings, and those who have little contact with gay and lesbian individuals (Chonody et al., 2009). We would suggest these as starting places for awareness and education, rather than blindly assuming anyone from the rural south who is religious hates gay students. That would be an unsupported extrapolation.

When offering education and support to those around GLBTQ issues, Ben-Ari (1998) suggests a threefold education process. This includes "exploring one's own history, learning the facts and getting to know lesbians or gay men" (p. 62). This could involve class assignments around understanding early beliefs and messages from family, panel discussions with GLBTQ students and addressing any myths or incorrect information (e.g., all people who are gay have AIDS and were molested as children). Obviously, these kinds of assignments lend themselves more to general education, sociology and psychology classes rather than math, economics or Spanish.

One approach to addressing the experiences of GLBTQ students prior to conflict in the classroom could be inviting a campus speaker to discuss these issues to the classroom. This could involve a program such as Safe Zones. Safe Zones is described at one college as the process where:

A number of faculty and administrators set out to create a network of faculty, support staff, and students who, after receiving training, would display a pink triangle outside their doors as a representation that a member of the LGBTQ community could find therein a resource for information, support, and, if needed, safety.

(Alvarez & Schneider, 2008, p. 71)

The use of inclusive language in the classroom can also have a positive impact on those students who may feel marginalized or left out in discussions. This can be as simple as using inclusive language such as "partner" instead of boyfriend/ girlfriend and using domestic partner or significant other. When developing case studies, consider using relationships that also reflect the gay GLBTQ community.

QUESTIONS FOR FURTHER DISCUSSION

Here are some additional questions about international and GLBTQ students. These questions are useful for self-reflection or to assist in facilitating a group discussion during a faculty training or orientation session.

1. What has been your experience with international students? What have been some of the greatest challenges for them to study in the United States? What has been helpful for them with the adjustment based on your experience?

2. Discuss some of the challenges you have experienced in working with students from other countries in your classroom. Have you had difficulty referring students to services?

3. What kind of experiences have you had with GLBTQ students in your classroom? How would you address a student who says, "that is gay" in the classroom?

Chapter 9

Distance Learning Students

DISTANCE AND BLENDED LEARNING: EMAIL AND DISCUSSION BOARDS

Ah, the joys of technology. We were completing a training at Bridgepoint Education in San Diego, CA and noticed their new slogan "Technology changes everything." The text of the ad slogan is set against an old library wall with nice leather-bound books. As nostalgic as some good leather books might be for some of us gracefully aging generation Xers, technology is here to stay.

Technology, in all of its glory, has the potential to make education a wonderful experience. Asynchronous classes allow students to access course material at a time that works best around their work and family schedules. Online chat and message boards allow students to interact with each other and share comments after thought and reflection. Internet links, video and live streaming technology provide specific content delivery that allows students to learn content material in various modalities, improving knowledge retention and practical application of theory. Email allows for direct conversations with the instructor to clarify misunderstood information and turn in assignments.

However, "with great power comes great responsibility" and some of our students aren't quite up to that level of responsibility. Forum discussion boards become overrun with ignorant, racist and insulting language. Email correspondence can be rude, disrespectful and entitled. How should one approach online disruptive behaviors? What kind of behaviors should be forwarded to the Campus Conduct Office or Behavioral Intervention Team?

Examples of Disruptive Online Communication

- Student posts non-relevant spam or unrelated personal advertising material in the forum discussion board.
- Frequent interruption of the professors questions, threaded discussion posts with non-relevant comments or off topic personal discussions.

- Inappropriate or overly revealing pictures shared with members of the online community through the profile.
- Choosing a screen name or profile name that is offensive to others such as Smokingthedope420@university.edu or assman69@university.edu.
- Posting or making comments while drunk or intoxicated. Attending online class discussions or lectures while under the influence of alcohol or other drugs.
- Arrogant, entitled, rude or disrespectful emails or messages to the professor or other students.
- Arguing grades or "grade grubbing" for extra points after the professor requests the student to stop.
- Inciting other students to argue with the professor over grades or other assessment related expectations.

Examples of Dangerous Online Communication

- Racist or otherwise fixated thoughts such as "Gays should be stoned like back in bible times," "Men should go back to playing football and stop thinking so hard. Leave the mental heavy lifting to the ladies in the class," "Muslims and Mormons are cults and should be wiped off the planet," and others posted to the discussion boards to troll for a response or to incite an electronic "riot."
- Bullying and teasing behavior through messages, emails or online hazing.
- Direct communicated threat to the professor or another student such as: "I am going to kick your ass" or "If you say that again, I will end you."
- Prolonged passive aggressive behavior such as constant disagreement with everyone and everything in class, challenging the professor's credentials, refusal to respond to questions or directives.
- Mentioning of self-injurious behavior such as cutting or burning self or suicidal thoughts or intentions in online posts.
- Threats of physical assault such as pushing, shoving or punching.
- Threats of online assaults such as hacking a website, sharing personal information or pictures online without permission.
- Conversations that are designed to upset other students such as descriptions of weapons, killing or death.
- Psychotic, delusional or rambling speech in posts.
- Arrogant, entitled, rude or disrespectful messages to the professor or other students.
- Objectifying language that depersonalizes the professor or other students.

So, given the wide range of behaviors that can be encountered by an instructor, what should be our approach to working with students? Let's start with what not

101

to do. Professor Galloway is known in NYC as the professor who gives his students a bit of tongue lashing when it comes to email correspondence. The following is an email exchange between professor Galloway and a perspective student (Daulerio, 2010).

Prof. Galloway,

I would like to discuss a matter with you that bothered me. Yesterday evening I entered your 6 p.m. Brand Strategy class approximately 1 hour late. As I entered the room, you quickly dismissed me, saying that I would need to leave and come back to the next class. After speaking with several students who are taking your class, they explained that you have a policy stating that students who arrive more than 15 minutes late will not be admitted to class.

As of yesterday evening, I was interested in three different Monday night classes that all occurred simultaneously. In order to decide which class to select, my plan for the evening was to sample all three and see which one I like most.

Since I had never taken your class, I was unaware of your class policy. I was disappointed that you dismissed me from class considering (1) there is no way I could have been aware of your policy and (2) considering that it was the first day of evening classes and I arrived 1 hour late (not a few minutes), it was more probable that my tardiness was due to my desire to sample different classes rather than sheer complacency.

I have already registered for another class but I just wanted to be open and provide my opinion on the matter.

Regards,
xxxx

––––––––––

Thanks for the feedback. I, too, would like to offer some feedback. Just so I've got this straight . . . you started in one class, left 15–20 minutes into it (stood up, walked out mid-lecture), went to another class (walked in 20 minutes late), left that class (again, presumably, in the middle of the lecture), and then came to my class. At that point (walking in an hour late) I asked you to come to the next class which "bothered" you. Correct? You state that, having not taken my class, it would be impossible to know our policy of not allowing people to walk in an hour late.

Most risk analysis offers that in the face of substantial uncertainty, you opt for the more conservative path or hedge your bet (e.g., do not show up an hour late until you know the professor has an explicit policy for tolerating disrespectful behavior, check with the TA before class, etc.). I hope the lottery winner that is your recently crowned Monday evening Professor is teaching Judgment and Decision Making or Critical Thinking.

In addition, your logic effectively means you cannot be held accountable for any code of conduct before taking a class. For the record, we also have no stated policy against bursting into show tunes in the middle of class, urinating on desks or taking that revolutionary hair removal system for a spin.

However, xxxx, there is a baseline level of decorum (i.e., manners) that we expect of grown men and women who the admissions department have deemed tomorrow's business leaders.

xxxx, let me be more serious for a moment. I do not know you, will not know you and have no real affinity or animosity for you. You are an anonymous student who is now regretting the send button on his laptop. It's with this context I hope you register pause . . . REAL pause xxxx and take to heart what I am about to tell you:

xxxx, get your shit together.

Getting a good job, working long hours, keeping your skills relevant, navigating the politics of an organization, finding a live/work balance . . . these are all really hard, xxxx.

In contrast, respecting institutions, having manners, demonstrating a level of humility . . . these are all (relatively) easy. Get the easy stuff right xxxx. In and of themselves they will not make you successful. However, not possessing them will hold you back and you will not achieve your potential which, by virtue of you being admitted to Stern, you must have in spades. It's not too late xxxx . . . Again, thanks for the feedback.

Professor Galloway

Funny? Sure. We'll give that to you. Probably something many of us wished we could have said to a student. It feels good to "send one back across the bow" to students who behave in this rude, entitled and ultimately, unprofessional way.

However, we think Professor Galloway lost an opportunity to teach the student in question some valuable lessons. The message he has is a good one. Take responsibility. Be professional. Don't assume things. The message is lost, we think, in the sarcasm of his response. This disruptive email that appeared in his inbox from this student resulted in a sarcastic response from the Professor: a response that probably gave him some joy to write and one that has certainly given many other instructors a cathartic release and perhaps some laughter at the student's expense.

Sarcasm is a poor form of communication when trying to correct behavior, given the fine line between sarcasm and humor. Since electronic communication lacks inflection, tone, etc., this has the potential to make a bad situation even worse. While it can be used well in lighthearted exchanges with friends, more often than not the sarcastic response comes off as cruel or rude. This form of passive aggression often sneaks out of an instructor's mouth without much forethought, screening or balanced consideration. A better approach is to recognize that any disruptive behavior is a change from the everyday content teaching and requires a thoughtful, planned intervention.

When responding to student emails, bulletin board posts or online comments remember to keep your message clear and concise. Lengthy, rambling responses open up the possibility of misunderstanding. In a calm, cool and collected manner present a clear and concise reply. Avoid preaching to the students; instead, look for ways to expand the discussion or bring it from the theoretical to the practical.

Likewise, when addressing student behavior, keep your message consistent over the course of the class. While moderating an online discussion, have clear expectations about the tenor and content of the dialogue. Hold students accountable and moderate the discussions closely. It is much easier to start with a hard and fast set of rules at the beginning of the class that are repeatedly stated and enforced then to foster an "anything goes" mentality followed by an instructor attempting to regain control of a discussion.

Have a developmental stance when responding to students. This applies whether you are communicating online on a forum, over the phone or through email. Set clear expectations and explain to the student why these are the standards that have been established for your course. Engage in dialogue and make attempts to see the student's mistakes, slip-ups and failures as opportunities for corrective action, rather than a time to pounce and punish.

If the disruption or dangerous behavior occurs in a public forum online, an instructor should avoid embarrassing the offending student as a method of corrective action. Embarrassment is one of the lowest forms of behavioral control. *A professor who achieves compliance through embarrassment is achieving compliance through fear rather than through respect.* Similarly, responding in kind to inappropriate behavior (as with Professor Galloway), lowers the instructor to the student's level and loses the opportunity for a developmentally focused teachable moment.

In the event that a more serious disruption occurs in the online classroom, the instructor should report this information to the campus conduct office, his or her department head and/or behavioral intervention team. The message should be clear and concise, based on objective facts and clear of subjective opinion (e.g., giving your thoughts on potential mental health diagnosis) and exaggeration. Clearly describe your actions and the student's actions accurately. Forward any saved messages or screen captures.

HOW TO HANDLE DISRUPTIVE AND DANGEROUS ONLINE COMMUNICATION

Email communication, specifically, is fraught with opportunities to get a faculty member into hot water. You can make a quick response to students who are demanding and entitled in their email. You can get into lengthy debate on a listserve or with other faculty or staff around campus. Given the potential for problems, here are some suggestions to avoid the minefield that can be email communication gaffs and mistakes.

Don't email angry; they won't like you when you are angry. One of the most common email regrets is an email that is sent when upset or frustrated with a situation. You may receive a message and assume the other person had a particular tone or attitude attached to what they wrote (and they may very well have) that leads to a quick, knee-jerk response. Instead of emailing angry, make a rule that you will take at least an hour to respond to an email. And after the hour, read your draft response . . . aloud . . . to a colleague. It may sound worse than you think. Ask yourself: can this wait until tomorrow?

Don't ever email negatives, don't. No. Bad. A good rule of thumb is to avoid sending emails that involve negative, critical or other general "no" answers. You may need to tell the person no; however, people generally take this kind of information better either on the phone or in person. This approach also minimizes the potential for misunderstanding and gives them a chance to respond.

Avoid the same paterns of mistakes. Avoid the same paterns of mistakes. I'm always a little surprised to find the same people getting into the same problems over and over again with their email communication. Sometimes they come off as too abrupt and annoy people. Sometimes they come off as angry and uncaring. Sometimes they don't fully understand the question or situation and respond to the wrong thing, making everything worse. Ask yourself whether you are caught in one of these loops and try something different.

Take the time to re-read your message before hitting send. Despite the desire to have the technology to "recall" any email; this is just wishful thinking (like good tasting low calorie mayonnaise). Once you hit send, the email is out there. Forever. Fight the desire to clear your inbox and deal quickly with an email response without taking the time to edit. A simple re-read of an email may make all the difference between "I think all of us could benefit from looking at the situations once again" and "I think all of us could benefit from liking at the sittings once again."

Examples of Behaviors and How to Respond

Online behavior	What not to do	What to do
A student sends the instructor an email about a late paper "I need to turn this in late, I have a lot going on and can't do this on time. OK?"	Professor responds, "Umm, no. It's not 'OK' and I also don't care for the way you are addressing me. Late papers will not be accepted and you are already doing quite poorly in this class. Another late paper will likely result in you failing."	Professor responds, "I would be happy to talk with you about this in more detail. I may consider a late paper but I would need more details about the type of emergency you are experiencing."
A student argues with another classmate in the online discussion board, "You are a freaking idiot. It's hard to believe that you got into this college to begin with. Try reading a book once in a while, dumbass."	Instructor responds, "This kind of post is not allowed in my class. Do it again and you'll be the one who needs to go the library to get a book—because you won't be enrolled at this institution any longer."	Instructor reposts the standards for a respectful online community. He removes the student's post and then sets up a call with him to discuss the insults and language used. The professor freezes the student's account until the conversation happens.
A student posts messages about his drinking escapades online as an example. He writes about drinking in excess, disrespecting women and blackouts.	The instructor embarrasses the student and says, "Hey, Drinky McGee. This is college writing 102, not 'Hangover Care 420. Stop writing about your drunken escapades and don't post again unless it's an apology to the class.	The instructor asks the student respectfully to talk with him. He explains that the student cannot write what he is writing about alcohol. The instructor follows up with a call to counseling service to talk with a referral to BIT or Student Conduct.

Examples of Behaviors and How to Respond (*continued*)

Online behavior	What not to do	What to do
An online student shares with the class on an open discussion thread that he is thinking of killing himself this weekend. "I just can't handle school anymore. It's time for me to take my gun, put it in my mouth and say 'sayonara'."	The instructor doesn't see this as part of her job to deal with. She forwards an email to the campus police and leaves for the weekend.	The instructor contacts the BIT Chair and/or campus PD with the email. She then looks up the student's contact information and gives him a phone call expressing concern. She refers the student to counseling.
A student disrupts other students with off-topic posts. The professor has previously talked about this with her and it clearly states in the syllabus there is a zero-tolerance policy on this behavior.	The professor embarrasses the student by posting "hey, ding-a-ling, I thought I set you straight on this already. Do it again and you are dropped from my class."	The professor reminds the student of the importance of staying on topic during posts. The professor talks to the student after class, penalizes her attendance and participation grade and explains about what will happen next time if it happens again.
An online student posts "You know, this isn't just my opinion. Gays are an abomination and should be killed to ensure the survival of the human race."	The instructor posts back, "Welcome to 2013. This kind of narrow-minded bigotry is not acceptable in my class." The instructor deletes the post, suspends the student's posting ability and requires him to write an apology email to the class.	The instructor removes the post and suspends the student's account. The instructor then emails the student to set up a time to talk about the post. The instructor sets clear limits about this kind of threatening post and shares the information with the campus BIT.

Don't respond or send sensitive information via email. Email is a very useful tool to confirm dates, find out about a conference, check up on a project or ask a simple question to a team member. It's a very bad tool to discuss a student's mental health history, describe a threatening situation or respond sarcastically to someone who annoys you.

If it's more than a few sentences, stop, step away from the computer, and call the person. Don't write lengthy missives via email, no matter how good a writer you may believe yourself to be. If you have that much to say to another person, take the time to talk with them face to face or over the phone. Like a car with tires out of alignment; the longer you write, the more likely the email will start to swerve to the side of the road. Keep it clear, concise and to the point.

STANDARDS FOR A RESPECTFUL ONLINE COMMUNITY

Online learning provides students with the opportunity to share ideas and receive feedback as part of a respectful community. To this end, the following are three standards central to the growth and nurturance of a supportive online community with the goal of creating thoughtful and interactive conversations among students and faculty. Please copy these and share them as you like with your students.

Respect: Respect is needed to build any learning community. This must be respect for fellow students as well as respect for faculty and the learning process. Respect does not imply blind obedience and conformity to standards, but instead infusing all interactions with a sense of grace and tact. Students should avoid rude interactions, name-calling, teasing, bullying or posting simply to cause a reaction (trolling).

Integrity: The work you submit should be your own. If it is not, you need to provide a proper citation for the author in question. In the information age, there are a large number of resource websites and depositories of writing and commentary. It is helpful to remember that there are also an equal number of well-designed software packages available for faculty to scan suspect text and determine whether it has been "lifted" from another source.

Tolerance: Care for and support others who may not share your point of view. A core aspect of higher education is being exposed to divergent viewpoints to better shape your own personal worldview. Simply closing off your mind to other perspectives because they do not match up with your currently held beliefs robs you of the opportunity to learn and grow. Practice active listening and work on developing empathy for those in your online community.

Failure to adhere to these standards or any of the policies of the college may result in temporary removal from the discussion group, access to the class or a class session, and/or any other sanctions as determined by the appropriate institutional official.

QUESTIONS FOR FURTHER DISCUSSION

Here are some additional questions about distance learning, email communication and online interactions with students. These questions are useful for self-reflection or to assist in facilitating a group discussion during a faculty training or orientation session.

1. Have you ever sent an email like Professor Galloway? What motivated you to do so? After reading this chapter, reflect on how effective you think your email was. What might have been another approach that would have had a positive impact on the student?

2. What kind of examples have you experienced from your online interactions with students that you would classify as disruptive? Have you experienced any that would be classified as dangerous? These could be online chats, forum message board threaded discussions, emails or phone calls.

3. What are your personal warning signs or "lessons learned" from dealing with technology? We list several including: don't email when angry, avoid lengthy missives and make sure you use email for the proper kind of information. What advice do you have for new faculty when they approach technology?

Chapter 10

Mental Health in the Classroom

There is a wide a range of mental health disorders that keep college students from performing at their optimal potential. Having an understanding of the common mental health disorders experienced by college students may allow faculty to better understand and intervene during crisis events.

This chapter is dedicated to sharing some basic information with faculty to better understand some common mental health behavioral difficulties they may encounter while teaching. Examples include suicidal behavior, off-topic questions related to a personality or Autism disorder, manic behavior, delusions and hallucinations, eating disorders and substance abuse. The chapter focuses on practical advice on how to approach student behavior. To that end, we include a basic overview of the topic at hand; advice on how to approach students and a brief summary of frequently asked questions.

Each of the six major topics (Depression and Suicide, Alcohol and Addiction, Eating Disorders, Anxiety, Bipolar Disorder, Autism Spectrum Disorder/ Asperger's Disorder and Thought Disorders) also include a text box that summarizes "What to Do" and "What Not to Do" for faculty.

The chapter is not meant to provide a comprehensive summary of all mental health concerns, just the most common issues experienced by faculty. Likewise, the chapter does not set out to offer a complete review of these six mental health concerns. Other texts offer this kind of substantive review of mental health symptomology, pathology and treatment. The goal is to provide instructors and faculty an abbreviated field guide to addressing common mental health difficulties that may arise in their classroom.

DEPRESSION AND SUICIDE

Students who experience suicidal thoughts often experience depressive symptoms. These symptoms can include difficulty sleeping or eating (either more or less than normal), a lack of interest in activities that they used to enjoy (going to the movies, hanging out with friends) and general feelings of unhappiness and hopelessness for a better future. While students can be depressed without feelings of suicide (often described as a more lethargic unhappiness or dysthymia), it is rare for a student to experience suicidal thoughts without depression.

The degree to which a student experiences suicide is important to understand for faculty. For those with *low suicide experiences*, students experience fleeting thoughts of wanting their pain and the frustrations of everyday life to end. These feelings and thoughts may not contain any plan for the student to kill him or herself or, if there is a plan, the plan is vague (*someday I may just start walking at night and never come back*), non-lethal (*I'm going to take 5 or 6 aspirin and go to sleep*) or far in the future (*sometimes I think about just ending my life when I finish college*). Students who experience low suicide experiences need to talk with a professional counselor before these thoughts increase. Faculty are often in a position to refer these students for help at the on-campus counseling center or other community resources.

Other students may have *moderate suicidal experiences.* These students spend time thinking, dreaming and planning about how they will kill themselves. There is a more serious content and tone to their suicidal talk. There are often feelings of hopelessness and sadness about their current life and the direction it is heading. While there is not a current date and method expressed for when they will take their life, they are putting together plans to narrow down this information. A student may say, "*I am sad all the time and I don't see things changing. I've been thinking more about stepping in front of a train when I am out walking at night. I don't know what to do.*" Faculty should report this kind of talk or ideation immediately, ideally with the student available for a follow-up meeting with a counselor or other mental health professional.

Students with *severe suicidal experiences* have a plan, date and time for when they are going to kill themselves. They are not safe to leave alone and have often become so hopeless and full of pain the only relief from their predicament is through suicide. They have struggled with their pain for quite some time and now have a sense of inevitability about their decision to kill themselves. Many times, they write goodbye notes to their friends, give away their personal belongings and reduce any obstacles that might get in the way of their choice to die (hoarding pills, obtaining a firearm, collecting a rope and finding a place to hang themselves). Instructors may be in a position to witness these exchanges. A student may say, "*I'm done. I won't be here tomorrow. I just wanted to let you know.*" Faculty are required to take immediate action with these students to refer them to help. This may involve calling the police or emergency services.

The only way to know how depressed or suicidal a student may be is to engage them in conversation about what they are feeling. Faculty need to ask questions in order to learn how students view their current situation. This requires faculty to engage students in a conversation about their thoughts of depression, suicide and self-harm.

Depression can have both an environmental component and a biological component. Treatment often involves talk-therapy as well as having a medication evaluation. Any student who struggles with depression is at a higher risk for suicide. Faculty need to ask direct questions about suicide to any depressed student.

It's not just a bad day. We all can relate to having a bad day, even a series of bad days. Depression is more serious than this. It's as if a weight falls down on the student and they will become lethargic, apathetic and struggle to see any hope that things will improve. Depression is beyond a bad day or series of bad days. It is an overwhelming burden and all-encompassing sense of dread and hopelessness that surrounds the student.

It's not my problem. Don't assume that someone else is taking care of the student with depression. Depression can feel like a difficult topic to discuss, so faculty avoid talking to students about it because they don't feel qualified or don't have any easy answers for the depressed student. If you notice a student who is depressed, reach out to them and try to help. Work with your counseling center, department head or campus BIT to keep them informed and seek out ways you can be most helpful to the student.

Physical problems. Some of the key diagnostic criteria for depression are related to sleep and appetite disturbances. Others relate to lethargy and an upset stomach. Sometimes the only outward signs of depression we have to work with are those physical disturbances. Many times, students in college have sleep and appetite problems as well as homesickness, stomach problems adjusting to the food and feelings of tiredness. The only sure way to know what is depression and what are normal adjustment issues is to talk to the student in question.

Stick with it. Getting help for someone with depression can be a daunting task. Students with depression often lack the energy needed to follow through with the healthy steps laid out in front of them (e.g., getting to therapy, attending class, seeking support from friends, exercising and staying on medication). One way an instructor can help is to offer extra support during the early stages of treatment. Once a student begins to recover, it is likely he or she will need less and less support. Faculty should also seek support from their department head, counseling center or campus BIT in order to remain positive and effective with the student they are trying to assist.

Verbal / Non-verbal. Some students are very clear about their suicidal statements: "I am going to kill myself" and "I can't live any more. I am going to do something to end my life." More frequently, students make vague statements that provide only a hint of their true intentions, "I don't want to be here anymore" and "I can't live this way. I'm too exhausted to go on." Instructors need to have keen detective ears when it comes to listening to students who are depressed and potentially sharing suicidal thoughts.

Are you suicidal again? There are times when students express suicidal thoughts frequently. Faculty are tempted to see the situation like the boy who cried wolf. It can be frustrating when a student continually voices a desire to die. However, a suicide-training program emphasizes the importance of taking each suicidal statement seriously. No faculty wants to be in a position of ignoring the one serious suicidal statement in a sea of false statements. Take every conversation about suicide with a student seriously. Ask yourself, "If the student kills himself tonight, have I done all I need to do in order help?"

DEPRESSION AND SUICIDE

What to Do

- Engage the student in questions about their depressive thoughts.
- Keep in contact with your department head, counseling center and campus BIT when you are concerned about a student.
- Check in with the at-risk student's peers, family and staff who know the student.
- Help the student understand how medication and therapy may be helpful in the treatment of depression and suicide.
- Provide hope and support for the student (even if you don't feel as hopeful about their future).

What Not to Do

- Ignore suicidal statements with the hope that they will go away.
- Challenge depressed students by saying things such as "you just need to get over this!" or "God only gives us what we can handle."
- Avoid talking to students about depression or suicide because that's best left for the professionals.
- Assume that medication is the solution. It can help with some kinds of depression, but the best treatment is a combination of medication, exercise and talk therapy.

Frequently Asked Questions (FAQ) about Depression and Suicide

I feel like helping someone who is suicidal is beyond my training. Am I wrong? You are right to be concerned about the seriousness of the situation. However, talking to someone about suicide is not going to make them more suicidal. Someone who is having suicidal thoughts is already in a bad place. It's important to talk to them to better understand the depth and severity of their thoughts. This is the first step towards help.

Sometimes students seem to talk about suicide a lot for attention, but don't really seem like they would ever do anything. What's the best way to work with them? The problem is you never quite know when they really mean it. It may be that a student talks about feeling suicidal for weeks as a "cry for help," but there comes a time where it is less a cry for help and more something they are getting ready to do. The best approach when dealing with a student who continually expresses suicidal ideations is to talk with them directly about what they are saying, take what they say at face value (believe them), and respond with care and concern. It may be that over time their verbal comments about suicide become a factor in their leaving the program, so it is also important to document their behavior and your conversations with them.

Does medication fix depression? Not very often. Medication should be used as an augment to talk therapy. Harvard Medical School (2003) shared in their paper *Understanding Depression* that regular exercise can improve mood in people with mild to moderate depression. Medication alone may be used when a student completes their therapy. In these cases, medication can help support a student's long-term recovery. The best use of medication is in combination with talk-therapy for a combined effect.

Why are students with depression even in college? Shouldn't they get well before enrolling in college? Sometimes. It would be helpful for students to have their mental health issues stable prior to studying in a high-stress environment. There are times when the depression has been under control for a long period of time and the stress of college causes it to flare up. Stress is often associated with an increase in depressive symptoms. There are other times when a student hasn't experienced any type of depression and the adjustment to the academic requirements can cause a depressive episode.

I've heard that when some people get depressed, they cut themselves. Should this be handled like a suicide attempt? Self-injury involves a student who cuts themself with razors, straight pins or other sharp objects. These cuts can be superficial or deep and

114

dangerous, depending on what their intentions are. Some students also hurt themselves with fire, or by punching themselves or hitting themselves with a stick or other object. Students hurt themselves for a variety of reasons. Some students hurt themselves because it helps them feel better about their internal pain for a short time. Others engage in this behavior as a cry for help with the hope that others can talk to them about how they are feeling.

Self-injury is not always related to suicide or depression. It can become an obsession for some students, a bad habit or a coping mechanism they developed in high school. It is understandable that other students become concerned a student is thinking of killing herself when she cuts her arm with a razor. However, suicide is rarely the desired outcome for those who self-injure. In either case, it is difficult to determine what might be one student's self-injury and another student's potential suicidal gesture. In the absence of information, it is best for the faculty to assume the more concerning of the two and treat self-injury as a behavior that may include suicidal thoughts. In this case, reporting the student behavior to the campus counseling center or BIT is the best course of action.

ALCOHOL AND ADDICTION

Addiction is a compulsion that perpetuates itself. It can pertain to a substance or an activity. Some of the substances and/or activities that lead to addiction are alcohol, drugs, shopping, gambling, sex, overeating and smoking. A common addiction students struggle with is alcohol addiction.

How do you know if a student in your class has an addiction? Addicts are trapped in their behaviors and cannot always simply quit on their own. People often assume that because addiction begins with a voluntary behavior and is expressed in the form of excess behavior, an addict should just be able to quit by force of will alone. However, it is essential to understand when dealing with addicts, we are dealing with individuals whose brains have been altered by alcohol, drugs or behavioral abuse.

While there is no absolute scientific formula for identifying when an individual's use or behavior has developed into a full-blown addiction problem, most drug and alcohol or rehabilitation counselors agree that for drug use, alcohol use or behavioral misuse there are four distinct stages that may lead to addiction.

The four stages are generally acknowledged as:

1. Overuse or experimentation of a drug, alcohol, or behavior.
2. The misuse of a substance or behavior.
3. The abuse of drugs, alcohol or behavior.
4. A drug, alcohol or behavior dependency or addiction.

115

While individuals in the first or second stages of use and misuse may not necessarily progress into addicts, individuals in the third stage of abuse are likely to develop full-blown addiction problems.

How to Help. There are many places that a person can find help with their addictions, starting with helping them understand the impact of their use in regard to their life, work, friends and family. Those who are developing drinking problems may defend themselves by saying "I don't have a problem, look how good this aspect of my life is . . .." Another way to help is to point them toward the resources that might be useful for when they are ready to change their behavior.

When in college, students can become overwhelmed with the choices they have in terms of alcohol. Other times, there can be rather severe restrictions on alcohol. Developing educational programs and discussions about alcohol use and typical experiences may help get ahead of the problems students may encounter.

Helping those who don't want help. This can be a central challenge to working with students who are struggling with their drinking, but are not ready to change. The approach of motivational interviewing (Miller & Rollnick, 2002) offers some suggestions to help students who don't want help. These include expressing empathy for their situation and frustrations, rolling with their resistance and, instead of challenging them directly, finding other ways to talk to them about change and supporting them when they make good decisions about their drinking.

Bi-Phasic Curve. Faculty with a strong relationship with a student might seek to engage them in a conversation about his or her motivation for drinking. It is generally accepted in the harm reduction community that students who drink to get drunk (obtaining a blood alcohol level of over .10) ensure that they have all of the worst side effects that come from drinking. Students who drink with the goal of getting drunk end up having stronger hangovers, since alcohol is basically a poison, and the body needs some time to clear the alcohol from your system. Faculty could engage students in this example:

> Think of a big funnel underneath a water faucet. Turn that faucet on full blast and the funnel fills up quickly and overspills the sides. The funnel allows the water to pass through the same way our liver processes alcohol. The more we consume quickly, the harder it is for the liver/funnel to keep up.

Maintaining a Blood Alcohol Level. Another lesson from harm reduction education that faculty can share is the importance of students attempting to maintain a certain BAC when they choose to drink: A blood alcohol level that hovers around .02–.04 and makes the student feel good while they can still maintain control of their fine motor skills and cognition. A caring faculty can encourage a student to shift their drinking goal from "getting drunk" to just keeping enough alcohol in their system to maintain this balance. For the student, this means understanding how quickly his or her body processes alcohol and how much it takes for them to begin to feel intoxicated. The only way they can determine this is through practice.

Self-Awareness. Students can't control their drinking unless they know how much they have had to drink. Without knowing how much they have been drinking, they cannot measure how quickly alcohol affects them. Faculty could share that women take longer to process alcohol. The more they weigh, the more they need to drink to raise their blood alcohol level. The less they weigh, the more quickly their blood alcohol level rises. These kinds of facts can be helpful for students to understand. While it is not a prime function of faculty to educate students on the effects of alcohol on the body, there can be opportunities to share this information when instructors have a concern for a student with whom they have a rapport.

All drinks are not created equal. Students have frequently been exposed to slide shows and public service announcements where they learn that one shot = one glass of wine = one beer. Faculty may be in a position to help educate students that the big red party cup full of shots and fruit punch probably is closer to 5–6 drinks rather than a single drink or two. Students need to understand that giant margaritas at the restaurant served in those party glasses as big as their head are really 3–4 drinks, not just "one drink." Students can benefit from understanding that it's not just how much they are drinking, but what percentage of alcohol is in the drink they are consuming. While this information may not fit neatly into an instructor's weekly lesson plans, there may be some opportunities to share with students the difference among drinks.

Eat something and mix in non-alcoholic drinks. A core teaching lesson from harm reduction alcohol education programs teaches that our bodies process alcohol more efficiently when an individual has some food in their stomach. A student's liver can process about one drink an hour. Teaching students to simply have some pizza before the party can help absorb some of the alcohol they are consuming. Faculty can share the importance of alternating alcohol drinks with non-alcohol drinks or encouraging students to have a glass of water with that glass of beer. This will help the student stay hydrated and keep them from getting too drunk, too fast. Finally, share with students simply having more non-alcoholic drinks or drinking things such as coffee won't counter the effects of the alcohol already consumed. They often believe these myths about alcohol consumption and only will think differently when a trusted adult shares new information.

Get some help. Students should be taught to identify the risk of drinking to escape an emotion such as sadness or anger. If they need more and more alcohol to reach the same level of intoxication (building tolerance) or if their friends and family have talked to them about their drinking causing problems, they may be at risk for alcohol dependence or abuse. A caring faculty member can be very helpful in offering a referral to the counseling center in these cases.

If a student frequently misses class or falls behind in assignments due to their drinking, it's probably time for them to talk to someone about their drinking. If a student has tried to cut back and failed or finds him or herself thinking about drinking and getting drunk most of the day, they should talk to someone about their drinking. This can involve a conversation with the faculty member after class, walking the student over to the counseling center or even inviting a counselor to do a presentation in the classroom to help raise awareness about substance dependency.

ALCOHOL AND ADDICTION

What to Do

- Develop a relationship with the student you are trying to help. Students listen more to those they trust and those who care about them.
- Help them understand how their drinking may be impacting their school or social life.
- Look at ways to slowly reduce drinking by cutting back a small amount at a time.
- Know your resources (both online and local) to refer the student to when they are ready.

What Not to Do

- Lecture the student about their drinking and call them an alcoholic.
- Call the student's parents and report the student without talking to him or her first.
- Tell the student all about your own personal exploits with alcohol and warn them not to make the same mistakes.
- Tell the student the only way he or she can stop drinking is to join Alcoholics Anonymous (AA).

EATING DISORDERS

Eating disorders are notoriously difficult to treat. They often begin in early childhood or middle school years and are often created by powerful, harmful messages that are difficult for students to fight against. These statements may come from society through media and toys, from parents and/or from peers.

Students may experience an eating disorder that can be diagnosed as a mental illness or they may experience disordered eating behavior. A full eating disorder diagnosis involves a more severe level of impairment that begins to impact the student's academic, social or personal life. They often put themselves at physical risk by reducing food intake to a dangerous level or engaging in a binging/purging process that can also cause serious physical risks.

Other students may experience periods of intense exercise, extreme dieting and difficulty maintaining a healthy weight. While these problems are typically not life-threatening, they also can be very upsetting and have a strong psychological and emotional impact on a student's mental health.

Faculty should understand some common problems related to eating disorders and disordered eating to better help the student address these problems. Faculty should be looking for the following signs and symptoms in students:

- Spends most of their day thinking about food, calories and exercise.
- Counts calories obsessively and worries about any deviations from the plan.
- Avoids eating or eats very little food (under 500 calories) a day.
- Has unrealistic body image and always feels "fat," even when they are drastically underweight.
- Exercises excessively on a daily basis when not in training or on a sports team.
- Eats very large amounts of food (binge) followed by vomiting (purge).
- Food or food thoughts dominate decisions they make in terms of social activities or exercises.

Helping a student with eating problems is often an uphill battle. Eating difficulties and disorders often have deep roots and students are resistant to change their behavior. When they are able to change the behavior, the change is often brief and the student becomes upset at their apparent lack of progress.

Changing this behavior is complicated and will require a team approach to address the medical, social and psychological issues. Staff should adopt a caring approach and be aware that their support is helpful to the student even if the student is not in a position to acknowledge their help.

Ask the Question. One of the hardest things for an instructor to overcome is beginning the conversation with a student they believe has an eating disorder. It is a difficult conversation to have and most faculty are uncomfortable approaching a student about binging, purging or not eating enough. When talking with the student, it is important to avoid using accusing or labeling language or taking a stance where the instructor is the detective trying to figure out what is going on. This will lead to defensiveness from the student. Instead, approach the student from a caring, concerned perspective and see if there are ways for you to assist.

Often a Larger Problem. Treating an eating disorder successfully typically involves a group of medical professionals including counseling/psychology, nutrition and a primary care doctor. This is because eating disorders are hard to treat and it is difficult to maintain a lasting change. Students may become defensive, evasive or treatment resistant and lasting change requires a connection to a treatment team. It is important for the instructor to avoid becoming disheartened when working with a student with an eating disorder. It is common to see a relapse when the student is away from his or her support and under new stress.

Community Impact. Eating disorders have a strong impact on a college campus. The individual clearly suffers and feels the impact of the disorder. Community members become concerned and are unsure how to address the problem. It's important that eating disorder prevention is addressed through prevention programming, on-campus eating disorder screenings, and further education and training. Instructors should remember they are not alone when trying to help a student with eating problems. They should connect the student to existing community supports (counseling, health services, local mental health resources) to gain additional perspective and improve the chances they will receive the help they need.

Frequently Asked Questions (FAQ) about Eating Disorders

What should I say to a student with an eating disorder? Simple statements such as, "Jeez, you've lost way too much weight" and "Wow, you really need to eat more" are not effective or helpful for those struggling with eating disorders. More helpful statements might include saying something such as, "I know you aren't happy with the way you look, but I think you look really nice in that outfit today" or "I like it when you come out during our class field trips to restaurants to talk, even if you aren't too hungry."

Is this really a "mental illness"? How serious is this issue? Yes, the Diagnostic and Statistical Manual IV, which defines mental illnesses, includes eating disorders.

EATING DISORDERS

What to Do

- Encourage the student to talk openly about their relationship to food, exercise and appearance.
- Have a realistic understanding about how behavior (particularly eating disorder behavior) can take a number of attempts to change. Relapse is common.
- Help the student build a support network of friends, family and clinical staff that give the student positive, encouraging and hopeful advice. Minimize their contact with those who make the situation worse.
- Realize eating disorders and disordered eating habits fall on a wide spectrum of behavior—some very serious and some not as serious. Consult with your department head, counseling center or campus BIT early to help determine what the student may be experiencing and how you can help.

What Not to Do

Set hard and fast rules that have no flexibility and require complete compliance from the student.

- Talk freely about the student's problems with other students, professors and their family without concern for the student's privacy.
- Make it your personal vendetta to solve the student's eating problem and try to do it all yourself. For example, eat with the student at every meal and listen outside of the bathroom for sounds of purging.
- Downplay the seriousness of eating problems. For example, "Well, everyone has trouble now and then learning how to lose weight. Just eat healthy and exercise a little more."

Eating disorders can lead students to life threatening behaviors such as starving themselves, seriously disrupting blood chemistry and damaging the esophagus lining through frequent purging. There is also serious psychological impact and emotional pain experienced by those with eating disorders. This often extends to their family, friends and community. Faculty should avoid adopting a stance that an eating disorder isn't "a real problem, like cancer" and that the student should simply "get over it and have a sandwich."

ANXIETY

What is anxiety? Well, for starters, anxiety is a very useful part of who we are as people. Without anxiety, college students wouldn't study for their tests, talk to their parents, drink in moderation or even be able to safely cross the street. Anxiety, at its core, helps us set limits on our behavior. Without this limit-setting anxiety, people would say and do whatever they want. That would lead to chaos.

Anxiety provides some important safety limits to our behavior. It keeps us wearing coats in the winter to keep from freezing to death, washing our hands to protect from germs, not yelling at the mixed-martial arts fighter who cut in front of us in line. Anxiety is a safety mechanism hard-wired into our brains.

Anxiety becomes problematic when it expands beyond the normal range. Students who experience anxiety disorders may become anxious about a classroom presentation the same way others normally would become anxious if a tiger ran across campus. Imagine the panic, sweating, tunnel vision, difficulty breathing and feeling of impending dread. Fight or Flight!

This level of reaction over a class presentation is out of step with the perceived threat. It is exactly appropriate given a tiger on campus. The problem then becomes one of understanding why some students become so anxious and experience panic attacks at the thought of class presentations, at the prospect of asking someone out or worrying about getting a perfect 4.0 GPA when a 3.3 GPA would suffice.

Anxiety can occur as a result of early trauma or early expectations about behavior. The anxious reaction (panic attack, continuous worry, paranoia) becomes linked to an idea or event that doesn't need that kind of reaction. Perhaps there was a physical beating that came with talking out of turn when a student was growing up as a young child. This then becomes a connection they bring to college with them.

Another school of thought regarding anxiety is some people are just wired differently. Anxiety is also understood as having a hereditary basis. Regardless of how someone was raised, some people are just more prone to worry about things around them, out of step with everyone else. In extreme circumstances, this hard-wired neurological problem can form a mental illness such as schizophrenia or bipolar disorder. Here the anxiety shows up as paranoia that keeps the student worried and overwhelmed, frightened at every possibility of life-threatening attack.

There is some good news regarding anxiety, whether it is related to a mental illness, learned environmental behavior or a more subtle worry about tests, performance anxiety or talking to people. Anxiety and panic attacks are very treatable with talk-therapy and/or medications.

CALM AND CARING

Teaching Law and Psychiatry at a law school can be fun, daunting, rewarding, intellectually stimulating, but also challenging when a student signs up for the class believing that part of the curriculum includes counseling and/or medication therapy. Such was the case last semester. I have now learned to offer full informed consent to my class the very first day, including a discussion about this being a law school not medical school and my class is about legal not clinical interventions and solutions.

Daniel Psychman was a second year law student. He sat in the front row of the class (unusual for students in any class). He was always well prepared, but had difficulty sitting still or not shouting out during discussions and he became visibly agitated when we had detailed discussions about psychiatric symptoms or decompensations, while reading a case or statute, and raised the volume of his voice each week as the minutes of each class passed. The other students in my class tolerated his behavior and responded reasonably well the first couple of weeks, but began to lose patience as the semester went on. One month into the class, Daniel's fellow students became increasingly agitated and worried looking. Many stayed after class to voice their concerns about Daniel's potential for violence to either himself or others.

As a mental health attorney and consultant on higher education campuses I have had training in watching for "red flag" behaviors or students "at risk." All of the warning bells I had been taught and teach to others began to go off in my head. I came back to my office after class and began to review my own notes, books on the subject and lecture outlines. What I read alarmed me and I could well understand why my students were alarmed as well. So what to do? I could speak to the head of the Department, the Dean of Students, the Dean of Academic Affairs or others. But, this was a law school class and I was concerned about my student's academic records following him on into his career as an Officer of the Court, practicing attorney.

Although I was concerned about the risk, I was willing, at least for another couple of classes, to speak privately with the student, and read the first of his two papers required for the class requirements. Speaking to him calmly and with insight into his behavior worked: he calmed down during class. Reading his mid-term paper, which was well written, well organized, well researched and ended with an intelligent and thoughtful as well as legally sound conclusion worked also to allay my fears. I did suggest he seek help as needed, treading lightly on the issue of "professional" help and I did offer to make recommendations to him for such assistance if he wanted these. The rest of the semester went smoothly: he finished with a grade of B and seemed genuinely appreciative of my efforts, the subject matter covered, and my willingness to stay the course (so to speak) to keep him in the class.

Carolyn Reinach Wolf
Senior Partner
Abrams and Fensterman

Treating Panic Attacks. A central concept in working with students experiencing a panic attack requires the instructor to take control of the situation in a firm and confident manner. They need to be seen as Mr. Solution with answers at the ready. A panic attack is essentially a spiraling out of control of both physical symptoms (blood pressure, heart rate, breathing) and cognitions (irrational beliefs and catastrophic thoughts). When dealing with a student having a panic attack:

Help them breathe. Walk the student through the cycle breathing approach. The process of cycle breathing involves breathing in to a slow count of four, holding your breath for a slow count of two, breathing out for a slow count of four and holding your breath for a slow count of two. Then repeat for five or six cycles. This process lowers blood pressure and heart rate, allowing you to regain calm and manage the student who is challenging you.

Distract Them. Help the student focus on something else. This may involve talking to them about something different or trying a technique to distract them such as getting them to read a book or brochure upside down. This cognitive distraction will help stop the panic cycle from increasing.

Help Normalize Anxiety. Help the student understand anxiety in the overall context of their lives. People who experience anxiety also have a tendency to think the worst in a given situation. An instructor can assist by helping the student see different options and other (often more plausible) outcomes to their situation. For example, a student who is panicking if they fail a test might jump to the idea that they will get expelled from the program. In reality, they may just need to study a bit harder on the next test.

Reduce Stress. Like many problems, anxiety becomes worse under stressful situations. When a student is worried about their family, adjusting to a new culture and academic stress, it can all be too much. When a new stressor, such as a family illness or other unexpected bad news hits a student, it can be the tipping point. Think of stress like a glass of water. When keeping the water from overflowing, there are two options: find a bigger glass (e.g., work on ways to be able to handle and manage more stress) or reduce the amount of water in the glass (find ways to feel less upset and stressed or work on finding a better balance to your life).

Frequently Asked Questions (FAQ) about Anxiety

How can you talk a student into going to counseling? Getting help for an anxiety diagnosis often requires a visit to a psychologist or counselor. As you can imagine, this is difficult since the student who needs therapy is already very anxious. The added stress of coming into a therapy office, filling out paperwork and telling their

ANXIETY

What to Do

- Help the student keep things in perspective and realize it will not always be this bad.
- Offer support and normalization for the things that are stressing them out. Help them keep the things they are concerned about in proper perspective.
- Find ways to help the student "de-stress" and work breaks and fun activities in when they are feeling overwhelmed. This may also include the use of journaling or reading about ways to deal with stress.
- Encourage the student to exercise and redirect their nervous and worried energy.

What Not to Do

- Tell the student they "are being overly dramatic and just need to get over it."
- Ignore their anxiety and hope they find some way to deal with their problems as they grow up and learn how to take care of themselves.
- Simply refer them to therapy because this isn't part of what you should have to talk about with them.
- Report anything they say directly back to their parents, professors and peers without regard for how this might impact the student.

story to a stranger often prevents students from seeking help for their problems. This is sad, since many who come into therapy for anxiety feel better almost immediately after their first session.

The process of connecting a student to a therapist can be a challenging one. Some things that help are:

1. Make the intake/start process easier by helping research where the office is located, what the cost is and other obstacles.
2. Help the student understand therapy and counseling are not just for weak students who can't "make it on their own," but a place to receive help and training. Counseling is similar to going to the gym, but in therapy you work to strengthen your mind instead of your body.

I heard medication may help with anxiety. Is that true? Anxiety disorders respond very well to medication. The medications can either be a short-acting calming agent (such as Ativan or Xanax) to address panic attack symptoms or a longer-acting medication (such as Zoloft or Paxil) to address more long-term worry. While the short-acting medications work wonders in reducing panic, it is important to remember the Goldilocks' principle: don't use too much (this medication can be addicting when used over several months) and don't use too little (some students won't use any out of fear of addiction). It is important to use the short-acting medication somewhere in the middle—to find a dose that is just right. The longer-acting medication takes a bit longer to reach a full effect, requiring students who start on the medication to be patient for several weeks as they reach a therapeutic level.

BIPOLAR DISORDER

Bipolar disorder can be a devastating illness for a young person to struggle with while in college. Bipolar disorder involves periods of manic moods that lead to poorly planned activities, a lack of impulse control and increased risk-taking behaviors. These manic moods may include overspending on credit cards, starting various business ventures, collecting multiple speeding tickets and a lack of overall stability.

These manic episodes are often alternated with severe depression that can include a lack of energy, hopelessness for a better future, isolation from friends and family, and suicidal thoughts. These manic and depressive periods can occur over relatively short periods of time (days) or can extend over long periods of time (months or years).

Medication often helps those who struggle with bipolar disorder. Medications include mood stabilizers to reduce the rapid cycling between the manic and depressive states as well as anti-depressants to prevent the student from becoming so depressed they commit suicide. Bipolar disorder typically manifests in late-teenage years through the early twenties. Stress often exacerbates the disorder and the stress of adjusting to college life could make the disorder worse.

Many who experience bipolar symptoms are misdiagnosed as only having major depression since the main concern with their behavior centers on their depression and potential suicide. In contrast, some students use the energy during their manic phase to work ahead on their assignments and may seem to be very productive in their academics. Accurate diagnosis and treatment of bipolar disorder depends on clear and objective information from the student.

Bipolar disorder symptoms increase with stress and often the stress of academic programs combined with the freedom of exploring and learning at a new college or university may be the "tipping point" for a student to have their first crisis. Other times, students with bipolar disorder have been successfully treated for years in high school and hope that a fresh start at college will help them break free from their past behaviors.

Family and friends who offer support to those students with bipolar disorder are a crucial element in treatment. While professional therapists, psychologists and psychiatrists are important in diagnosis and providing treatment, it is the friends, peers and family that help ensure the bipolar student remains well and in treatment. One central role for an instructor is to serve to connect the student to these supports and to help the student avoid isolation from those who care about them.

Seek help. One of the biggest challenges of helping students with bipolar disorder is keeping them connected to treatment. Students often function well (in their minds, better than well) during manic phases of the disorder. They don't see the need for help because everything is going so well in their eyes. When students are depressed and overwhelmed, they will struggle to have the energy in order to take care of themselves and may be thinking about suicide. A caring faculty member can help them remain connected to their therapists and doctors, during both the up and the down times.

Don't wait. Likewise, faculty should try to stay ahead of problems they see with students before the problem reaches the height of its difficulty. If a student has bipolar disorder, it's best not to wait until they are so depressed they have worked out the details of a suicide plan to begin an intervention. If a student is manic, they may have already set problems in motion such as legal difficulties, financial over-commitments and dangerous social relationships. In either case, it's best for the instructor not to wait until the peak of the manic phase or the lowest point of the depressive phase to encourage the student to seek treatment.

It takes a village. As the saying goes, don't try to address this problem alone. The most important way an instructor can help a student with bipolar disorder is to ensure that the student is connected to treatment and the people in the student's life (e.g., family, peers, professors) are aware and communicating about how best to help the student when they start to struggle. While bipolar is a very treatable disorder with medication, the part of the disorder that is hardest to treat is getting the student to accurately report their symptoms, show up for appointments and to take their medications. Keeping them connected to a larger network of support is the best way faculty can assist a student with bipolar disorder.

Frequently Asked Questions (FAQ) about Bipolar Disorder

Isn't bipolar another name for artistic people? Don't the medications just dull their creativity and passion for life? The best approach is to find a way for the bipolar student to continue to express their passion and creativity, but in a manner that is safe and brings them long-lasting fulfillment. The "tortured artist" is a romantic notion for some, but the reality of depression and the risk of suicide becomes all

127

too clear when the "tortured artist" isolates themself and takes their life. Likewise, the cost of the mania in terms of social relationships, academic progress and financial safety also becomes a concern over time.

How can you keep someone on their medication and stable when they don't want to be? The best way to address this is through connecting the student to a supportive network of friends and family who are concerned and willing to help. A parent or sibling may have a way of talking to a student suffering from bipolar disorder where they can impact his or her decisions and help them make a more stable choice. It may also be helpful to engage the student in a discussion about the pros and cons that occur when they are off their medication as well as on their medication. Bipolar students may have a tendency to focus on the good (e.g., productivity, creation) and minimize the bad (e.g., lost friends, financial instability).

BI-POLAR DISORDER

What to Do

- Form a personal connection with the student during the better times so that you have "money in the bank" when things become more problematic.
- Work with the student to develop a support network of friends and family to be involved when they are struggling.
- Understand the up-and-down's of bipolar disorder and that each person who has the disorder is unique. Each person with bi-polar has different experiences with their cycling ups and downs.
- Work with the student to explain to others how they can help when the student is manic or depressed.

What Not to Do

- Believe the student should just go home and work out their mental illness before trying to go to college.
- Assume that they are doing just fine despite evidence to the contrary.
- Allow the student to talk you out of involving other people in their care or to "call for help" when the problems become more intense.
- Accept that medications can't help someone with bipolar disorder and they would be best left to find their own way to live their life medication-free.

AUTISM SPECTRUM DISORDER/ASPERGER'S DISORDER

Autism Spectrum Disorder (ASD, formally known as Asperger's Disorder) is a developmental spectrum disorder that impacts an individual's ability to read subtle social cues (such as flirting, sarcasm), function in social situations and experience distractions in the classroom setting. This may include sensitivity to stimuli such as florescent lights or loud noises. Students with an Autism Spectrum Disorder may have very intense, very idiosyncratic interests such as collecting items or obsessive interests in particular subject areas. They may also display odd movements, ways of interacting or unusual speech tones as they talk.

Students with an Autism Spectrum Disorder and those with social behavior problems are increasingly finding success in colleges and universities. Students are having better success with the additional support they are receiving in college through the Americans with Disabilities Act (ADA) and counseling support.

It's important to understand that all students with ASD are not the same. Asperger's is a spectrum disorder, which means that some have very few disruptions and others have extreme difficulty functioning. While a general understanding of the traits and characteristics of Asperger's disorder can be helpful to better work with the student, these should not be used to "box in" the student and limit their potential.

Faculty is not expected to be mental health professionals who determine the exact nature and type of problems a student experiences. Some students may meet the diagnosis of ASD, while others may have social problems, attention problems or a personality disorder. The purpose of this section is to help staff work more effectively with students who may exhibit behavior that disrupts the classroom.

Students with these social difficulties, whatever their diagnosis, experience difficulty and teasing from other students. They may find themselves manipulated in social relationships or being teased because of their interests, questions or social difficulties. Again, as a spectrum disorder, some ASD students may do very well in college either because their level of symptoms is not particularly severe or they have invested in therapy and social skills training to overcome these differences.

An instructor working with a student who has ASD should seek to have their communications be calm, clear, concise and consistent. The student with ASD struggles with subtle communications or inconsistent rules or instructions. They may be sad or depressed about how others are treating them and need some added explanation or support to avoid teasing. They may also not notice others teasing them and have difficulty weighing the social costs of their odd or unusual questions or interests.

A LESSON IN ASPERGER'S

Several years ago, I was teaching a developmental psychology course to masters' level students studying to be teachers at a public institution as I typically did. This was, however, no typical semester! There were 30 students in the class—one of them with

Asperger's syndrome. Neither the student nor college administration warned me or the class what to expect or how to handle the inevitable disruption. After some quick research, I informally determined that this was indeed Asperger's syndrome—as identified by the Diagnostic and Statistical Manual. In his case, the disorder was characterized with frequent inappropriate comments in class, difficulty catching social cues of other students and a sensitivity to both loud noises and the florescent lights in the classroom. Although I was a psychology major and an assistant professor, I was shocked and at a loss for how to properly (both legally and ethically), handle this situation.

I immediately informed and consulted with my chairperson about how to best handle this issue. She gave me great advice: speak with him in private. I indeed (anxiously) approached him by the second class meeting in private. He acknowledged his disorder (later providing me with official paperwork), but admitted that he was too embarrassed to inform me beforehand. After we both settled our nerves discussing the issue we began to confer a feasible plan on how to best "damage control" the disruption. With his permission, I informed the class very early on of his condition and how we were planning on handling it to decrease any disruption it may cause. The student and I both agreed that to best educationally serve him and the other students, he would leave the classroom as needed (hopefully before he felt the onset occurring), no questions asked! Tests were given to him in private with some supervision. I provided him with notes as he often missed large portions of the class topics. He moved to the left side of the classroom where that side of the lights was turned off (many students joined him on that side as the lights apparently bothered many in the class). Again with his consent, it was suitable for not only the course—that is, developmental psychology, but also for the erudition of what I thought was a "best-teaching practice" for the soon-to-be teachers, we spent some time discussing several learning and neurological disorders— one of them was indeed ASD. The class became more understanding of the student's condition and how to accommodate not only this particular student, but other possible cases down their teaching roads. What was certainly disruptive to most, including myself, was mollified owing to communication and empathetic consideration by all parties.

Bernard A. Polnariev
LaGuardia Community College

What to Expect from Autism Spectrum Disorder/Asperger's Students:

- Mental health problems have some commonalities, but also have a degree of uniqueness to each individual. Be careful about applying broad strokes. Each student, regardless of whether they have ASD or not, needs individual attention and adaptation.
- Students with ASD may ask odd or repetitive questions that derail the lecture and distract the class. They do not do this to annoy. It is their natural way of communicating.

- They are often teased or laughed at by other students who pick on them or talk quietly behind their back.
- They may have poor hygiene or manners in class. This is related to their ability to empathize and connect to the feelings and perceptions of others (again, be careful not to generalize, other ASD students may take obsessive care of their hygiene).
- They may engage in odd dress or write on their clothes or arms. They may speak with strange inflections or use languages based on their reading or computer gaming.
- They may have odd interests (car motors, Victorian door hinges and vintage toys) that interfere with them connecting with their peers and engaging in more socially acceptable activities.
- They have difficulty reading social cues (standing to leave, subtle messages to stop talking, non-verbal signals). This becomes even more difficult when dealing with issues that are built upon subtle social cues such as flirting or social networking sites such as Facebook™.
- Their attempts to connect with peers will often seem flat or slightly off. Caring students help these types of students connect and overcome these "quirks." Students who are frustrated or stressed will often ignore or tease the student with ASD.

AUTISM SPECTRUM DISORDER/ASPERGER'S

What to Do

- When correcting behavior, provide caring, clear direction to students away from others who may overhear.
- Work with other students to decrease teasing and bullying behavior.
- Read and talk with those who understand ASD disorder and develop ways to improve your skills working with these students.
- Appreciate the strengths and uniqueness of each individual student.

What Not to Do

- Believe that students with Autism Spectrum Disorder shouldn't attend college to study and the best course of action is for them to stay home.
- Assume all students with ASD are the same and treat them equally.
- Yell or berate ASD students for their behavior and use embarrassment and sarcasm to correct them.
- Avoid confronting any behavior from an ASD student because they are protected by the Americans with Disabilities Act.

Frequently Asked Questions (FAQ) about Autism Spectrum Disorder/Asperger's

How should a professor address behavior that occurs in the classroom?

- Seek to minimize classroom disruptions by having a calm and consistent approach with all student behavior in the classroom.
- Avoid sarcasm or subtle social connections (for instance, pointing towards the door to ask a student to leave or asking "Are you sure you belong in this class?") These kinds of comments and approaches will not work well with students with ASD.
- Identify and address negative behavior or teasing that may be occurring early and consistently. Avoid the temptation to join in or allow it to continue through a lack of intervention. It may be helpful to talk to students alone or in a smaller group after class in a private setting.
- Build a positive classroom environment with open communication and a caring, supportive atmosphere in order to help students improve their attitude and interactions with ASD students.
- When working with ASD students, it is essential to offer clear messages to them. Try to avoid addressing multiple issues at one time.
- Your messages should be concise. They should be short and focused on the desirable action.
- Messages should be consistent over time. Messages that repeat the same information increase the likelihood that it will "sink in."
- Take the time to understand the world and interests of ASD students. This interest can build rapport and increase your success in working with them.

What are some ways to address teasing from other students? The best way to address teasing behavior is to directly talk with the students who are engaging in the behavior and explain to them why they need to stop. This is ideally done outside of the classroom setting without embarrassing the students in front of the class. Help them understand that their actions are having a negative impact on the target of their teasing and ask them if they understand why. A lecture to students to change their behavior is not as effective as a dialogue helping them understand why their behavior, perhaps unintentionally, is causing pain to another. Give them the opportunity to learn from their mistakes and behave differently in the future.

How do I know what is Autism Spectrum Disorder/Asperger's and what is just strange or odd behavior? It's hard. Actually, professional counselors and psychologists struggle with this distinction. As faculty, the *why* of a problem is less important than *what* you do to work with students. Much of the advice for working with an ASD student would work the same for those with personality disorders and social problems.

THOUGHT DISORDERS

Schizophrenia is one of the most upsetting and difficult mental health problems to address with a student. The media portrays those with schizophrenia as knife-wielding, crazy people looking to stab mothers walking their young children in baby carriages. Schizophrenics are seen as talking to themselves, responding to voices from another place, and present a danger to the community as a whole.

In reality, individuals with schizophrenia are very rare (less than 1% of the population) and are often so lost in their own internal logic and paranoia that they struggle to relate to those around them. They are often more scared of the world and overcome with worry that they will be hurt.

Students may be concerned and worried about the odd behavior they notice in other students who have schizophrenia and will need help to understand what the student is experiencing. They may worry about what the student may do and that they might act unpredictably or put others at risk.

Students with schizophrenia are in need of connection to mental health services such as therapy and psychiatry. This connection to services can help them monitor their illness and obtain medication to help with the symptoms they experience. Helping a schizophrenic student to access care for their disorder can be difficult.

Those with schizophrenia (which means "split mind") often have difficulty regulating their cognitions (thinking) and emotions. They may become upset by strange or unseen threats and need an instructor or other students to reassure them and to assist them when they are becoming overwhelmed. For schizophrenic students to be successful, it is essential they have a strong group of supports that have access to their treatment team in the case of difficulty. This often involves case managers and flexible communication among team members.

Faculty might also have to take on the role of educator and support for the student as they interact with other classmates. It may be that other students have not experienced an individual with schizophrenia before and are at a loss on how to communicate. Faculty can provide a much-needed buffer and assistance during crisis times when a schizophrenic student may struggle more with their communication, thoughts or emotions.

Individuals with schizophrenia may have difficulty in the classroom with dulled emotions or problems concentrating on the assignments and discussion at hand. They may wander off in their thinking or respond to odd or strange tangential issues. Students with schizophrenia who are following their medication regimen will be more likely to stay focused in class and will avoid drawing attention to themselves. Those students experiencing schizophrenic symptoms in the class-room will often derail the discussion and engage in off-topic lines of thought.

TROUBLE IN THE LECTURE HALL

Walking across campus at a major university, which includes not only undergraduates, but law students and medical students, can be an interesting and challenging experience. Teaching a course to law students entitled Law and Psychiatry is both fun and intellectually challenging; teaching a course to medical students can be priceless.

On my first day of class, unlike standing in front of rows of students seated the way we see the scene set in "The Paper Chase," walking into a medical school class puts me in a well, with students above me in rows, much like in "Grey's Anatomy" flashbacks. A different perspective, a different venue, a modified curriculum, but students in a professional school none the less. I could always tell the future litigators from the future researchers from the future mental health attorneys; now I had to tell the future surgeons from the future internists to the future psychiatrists . . . actually, not that difficult. I did though have to caution the students that this was a class on Legal Issues in Mental Health Law and not a psychiatric evaluation or consultation. Some days it was hard to tell the difference.

About three weeks into the semester, one of my students began to move from the front of the class to the rear, from sitting among her peers to sitting separate and apart from them. She participated less and less and became increasingly agitated during discussions about movie depictions of persons with serious mental illness, or examples of what patients present with in psychiatric emergency rooms or in-patient units. As my student's change in behavior escalated, so did my anxiety and concern about her. Her mid-term paper presented descriptions of people who were scary, out of control and ultimately violent toward themselves and others. My anxiety and concern became that much greater.

Treading lightly and using all of my knowledge, experience and years of expertise in mental health law and as a former hospital risk manager, I decided to ask my student to stay after class one day and just "chat." She seemed to be having a "good day" and was willing to do this. As we discussed my observations and concerns, she began to delve into a conversation that became increasingly disjointed. Her sentences went on and on, similar to a William Faulkner novel, with words flowing into words and no periods at the end of any sentences. The flavor of her conversations increasingly contained paranoid and delusional thoughts and her demeanor changed from sitting quietly in her seat, almost eerie in nature, to jumping up unexpectedly and going down and around rows of seats in the lecture hall. Finally, she stopped suddenly, looked around with a dazed expression and stood motionless in a corner of the room, not moving for minutes on end.

After calling the Dean's Office, campus Health Services and a psychiatrist friend who treats college and graduate students, we all concurred that 911 should be called and so they were. It was so sad to see my student placed on a stretcher and into an ambulance knowing they were on their way to a hospital and likely a psychiatric unit. But, it was also a positive feeling to know that my student would get the help she needed, hopefully insight into her condition, and take away from the experience the first-hand knowledge of being a psychiatric patient who could be evaluated and treated and live a productive life.

I heard several years later, while walking across campus, stopped by one of my former students, that the student from my Legal Issues in Mental Health Law was just starting her residency in Psychiatry.

Carolyn Reinach Wolf
Senior Partner
Abrams and Fensterman

Understand the disorder. Unlike some other mental health problems, schizophrenia is best understood as a biological/genetic problem that impacts the ability of an individual to accurately perceive reality. They may experience hallucinations (e.g., seeing or hearing things that aren't there), experience a worry or paranoia that others are out to harm them or exhibit a difficulty interacting with others.

Not going away. Schizophrenia is a life-long chronic illness that will not simply go away or be out-grown. Medication can help control some of the symptoms, but the medication can also have powerful side effects that make it difficult for the person with schizophrenia to stay consistent with their dosage. It is important for a student with schizophrenia to stay connected to their medical doctor and remain compliant with their medications. Some medications can be given by shot once a month and slowly lose their effectiveness over time. Faculty can help ensure the student seeks care when the medication begins to wear off.

Connections. An instructor can help a student with schizophrenia by encouraging them to form connections with those who can provide treatment such as psychologists, counselors and psychiatrists. Faculty can also provide assistance with communication between the student and their parents and peers when the student is having a difficult time. Faculty can also be helpful in monitoring a student with schizophrenia and making sure they seek help when they are having an increase in their symptoms.

Dangerous. Those with schizophrenia are more likely to be the victims of violent crime than they are to be involved in committing it. Despite the raving psychopaths featured in popular movies and TV shows, those with schizophrenia are often struggling more to keep themselves safe and mentally together. They rarely have the energy or stability needed to plot dangerous and violent attacks on others.

135

THOUGHT DISORDERS

What to Do

- Treat the student with kindness and caring. This is the best way to approach all students who are scared, worried or experiencing a perceived threat.
- Help the student form connections to their family, friends and treatment team (e.g., therapist, medical doctor, psychologist).
- Educate others about what they can do to help a schizophrenic student in a crisis.
- Pay attention to subtle signs and language that may indicate a student is off of their medication or struggling with voices, visions, delusions or hallucinations.

What Not to Do

- Find ways to argue that the student is too sick to be in the program and try to send them home.
- Ignore parents and family support that has likely been addressing this problem with their son or daughter for years.
- Treat the student as if he or she is broken and can't do things for him or herself.
- Embarrass or draw attention to the student in class. Tease the student for their odd behavior, speech and/or thoughts.

Frequently Asked Questions (FAQ) about Thought Disorders

Aren't they dangerous? No. People with mental illness are more likely to be hurt by others than they are to plan an attack or go on some kind of campus shooting spree. Media portrays those with schizophrenia as "crazy" and "dangerous" because their behavior is odd and difficult to understand. Through the confusion and difficulty, the public fills in the empty spaces with visions of crazed lunatics loading automatic rifles or running around like Norman Bates (the character in the movie *Psycho*) with a butcher knife. These are entirely unrealistic and do not accurately represent this disorder.

What are some ways to address teasing from other students? The best way to address teasing behavior is to directly talk with the students who are teasing the student with schizophrenia and ask them to stop. Oftentime, students engage in teasing behavior and don't realize the negative impact they are having on the other student. A caring confrontation with those who are teasing may help them to stop their behavior and perhaps even become an ally for the student.

QUESTIONS FOR FURTHER DISCUSSION

Here are some additional questions about mental health challenges in the classroom. These questions are useful for self-reflection or to assist in facilitating a group discussion during a faculty training or orientation session.

1. Discuss a time when you had to talk to a student with depression or suicidal thoughts in your classroom. What was the experience like? Did you refer the student to additional help? Why or why not? Given some hindsight, what would you do differently now?

2. What are some of the signs and symptoms of an eating disorder? We suggest caution in encouraging a student with an eating disorder to eat more healthily. Why is that? What have you found works when talking to a student with an eating disorder?

3. Talk about some challenges you have had working with mental health problems in the classroom. Some become frustrated that these difficulties keep instructors from teaching the content they need to complete in the course. What personal feelings get stirred up when you work with a student who has a mental illness?

Part III

Community Referral

Chapter 11

Communication

SHARE YOUR CONCERN, DON'T SILO INFORMATION

We are fans of those cop shows. You know the ones. Like *CSI*, *Law and Order*, *Castle*. If you watch these shows, you are familiar with the scene where our heroes are placed in a precarious position of chasing down a bad guy and end up having to make the decision to go into the dark and abandoned warehouse alone or wait and call for backup. You can imagine the obligatory scenes of a grizzled police chief shouting to where the heroes are standing by an ambulance, out of breath from their encounter with the bad guys. They are reprimanded for being a "wild card" and going in alone.

So, here's our message to you. Don't be a hero. Don't go it alone. Don't forget to call for backup and communicate with those who can help. When an instructor becomes concerned about a behavior, interaction or just has "that feeling" about a particular student—they should pass the information along immediately. A common mistake is waiting for things to get worse before reporting a behavior. Don't wait. Share the information. You can share it with the director of counseling, chief of police, your department head, the Dean of Students or your campus Behavioral Intervention Team (BIT).

This is a recent email from a faculty member about a concern they had in their classroom.

From: Professor
Subject: PSY 102: No Current Event Completed/Uploaded

Good morning!?? I just wanted to inform you that no current event paper was completed (uploaded to Blackboard on time) for PSY 102 and will result in a 0 for the assignment. Please let me know what happened to prevent you from completing this assignment. I do not want to see you fall behind in PSY 102.??
See you Monday.

Professor

From: Student
Subject: REPLY: PSY 102: No Current Event Completed/Uploaded

I've been meaning to get on here and contact you but I just haven't had a lot of free time. Last week I was diagnosed with breast cancer and was at the hospital all last weekend because I was far enough along that I had to actually have surgery. This past week with school starting, having a job, recovering from surgery, things have just been really crazy and hectic. I understand your policies and it was my responsibility to do the paper, but with everything going on and still being in a large amount of pain from everything I did the reading because I could see that on my phone but wasn't able to get back to a computer to do the paper. I assure you that I will be more on top of things now that things are starting to be less hectic and I'm getting back into my regular schedule. I really appreciate you contacting me and it was nice you took enough time out of the day to see what was going on.

Hope to hear back from you soon!

From: Professor
Subject: Reply: REPLY: PSY 102: No Current Event Completed/Uploaded

Thank you for the email. You have had quite a lot occur in your life in recent weeks. I understand that your goal is to continue with your classes this semester getting back to your normal schedule. With all that has occurred in your life, I encourage you to utilize the on campus Counseling Center to work through this stressful set of events. I am including their contact information below. I would be happy to make an appointment for you if you would like. Learning requires maximum cognitive focus and I know that stressful events tend to impede attentional focus. I want to see you as successful as possible in PSY 102, as well as your other courses. You might also want to consider focusing on work this semester while returning next semester or picking up some bi-term courses in order to give you ample time to adjust to your new situation. These suggestions are just that . . . suggestions. Please let me know what you decide. If you choose to continue with your classes this semester, I look forward to meeting you in class this afternoon.

Professor

We share this email with you for a few reasons. First, it highlights the importance of faculty sharing information with the campus BIT or counseling when they have a concern about a student. The information is then included in the student's counseling chart or BIT notes and the BIT or counseling center makes a decision to contact the student or wait and see how the situation develops. Second, the email displays the professor's willingness to engage the student and work flexibly with the situation. It demonstrates a proactive approach to managing students who are falling behind in assignments.

As you can see from this example, it is important to be proactive with students who begin to fall behind in your classes. It also serves as a further caution against making assumptions or putting students into a box when it comes to trying to understand why they aren't completing a paper or coming to class. While it may be that only 1 in 10 students have a horrific story like this one, these kinds of examples should be on our minds when responding to a student request. It's likely most students are simply poor planners, not studying or putting other activities ahead of their class assignments; however, this email serves as a reminder that some students are struggling with unimaginable stress that would qualify for a medical accommodation. Don't make the mistake of responding too quickly with harsh words.

ABSENT FROM CLASS

I had a student situation where a student had a severe psychotic break that turned into a high potential for suicide/homicide. While we were (luckily and barely) able to avoid the worst-case scenario (through a quick coordinated "hard" intervention), in the analysis of the incident after the fact, we found several faculty members—three in particular who stand out in my mind—who knew information and had failed to tell the BIT. There were staff and students who also failed to report, but the faculty members were interesting in their rationale. One told us that the student's increasing absence from class was "not [their] concern—[they] don't take roll. If students don't want to show up, they won't pass." Another wrote off the student's decreasing academic performance and engagement in class as "senioritis," a third decided the student's increasing propensity for lacking in self care (specifically bathing) was just "him being too lazy to bathe." (She actually sent him a "warning" email.) And I understand. Taken alone, these behaviors may seem relatively innocuous. But taken in the aggregate by the BIT (and with the other information subsequently uncovered), they would have painted a clear picture of a student deteriorating toward crisis.

W. Scott Lewis
Partner
National Center for Higher Education Risk Management

The publication *Inside Higher Education* (Grasgreen, 2012) suggests faculty are getting the message and sharing more with other departments on campus when they encounter medical emergencies, odd behavior, potential violence, threats and students of concern. Grasgreen talks with Victor W. Barr, director of counseling services at the University of Tennessee at Knoxville, about faculty communicating with the counseling center and BIT. She writes:

That's why Barr encourages faculty members to trust their gut, and not "discriminate" when it comes to making a call or referring a student. So when

143

an instructor notices a student is constantly missing class, or referencing suicide or homicide in essays, or has a sudden drop in grades, professors shouldn't overanalyze it—they can leave that to the counselors and BITs.

(p. 1)

Instructors should share information with other departments when it comes into their hands.

LAWS AND REGULATIONS: FERPA

A potential reason for faculty being hesitant to share information with other departments can be found in the federal regulations such as those found in the Family Education Rights and Privacy Act (FERPA) and, to a lesser extent, the Health Insurance Portability and Accountability Act (HIPAA), the Office for Civil Rights (OCR) Title IX.

Despite some potential misunderstandings of the law by faculty, FERPA does allow them to share information through a number of exemptions and policy clarifications. These include:

- *FERPA Emergency Exemption*: FERPA's health or safety emergency provision permits such disclosures, without the consent of the parent or eligible student, if necessary to protect the health or safety of the student or other individuals (U.S. Department of Education, 2012).

- *FERPA Dependency Exemption*: FERPA defines this as "a school may disclose information from an 'eligible student's' education records to the parents of the student, without the student's consent, if the student is a dependant for tax purposes. Neither the age of the student nor the parent's status as a custodial parent is relevant. If a student is claimed as a dependant by either parent for tax purposes, then either parent may have access under this provision" (U.S. Department of Education, 2012).

- *FERPA Personal Observations*: FERPA does not prohibit a school official from disclosing information about a student that is obtained through the school official's personal knowledge or observation and not from the student's education records. For example, if a teacher overhears a student making threatening remarks to other students, FERPA does not protect that information from disclosure (U.S. Department of Education, 2012).

  This is one of the most common examples of information shared from a professor to a campus BIT or department head. As such, it may be helpful to review an example. Imagine a student named Noelle, who is taking an introduction to public speaking class. She has talked with her professor at length about her dream of being a reporter and being on network television. During her first prepared speech, she makes several mistakes. The most notable is the repetition of the word "um" dozens of times. The professor stops her in mid-speech and tells her to stop using that word. She is flustered and upset, which leads to more uses of the word "um." The professor interrupts her again and tells her "I'll give you five more and then you are done." The professor then holds up his hand and raises a finger each time Noelle uses the "um" word. As she becomes more anxious, she uses the word more often. When the professor raises four fingers, indicating she only has one more chance, Noelle yells "You are such a god-damn prick! I should put a bullet in your head" and then runs out of the room, slamming the door hard behind her.

Leaving aside our obvious displeasure at this particular instructor's teaching method, steeped in embarrassment and shame, FERPA would allow for the professor to share the threat with counseling, the conduct office, the police, the BIT and Dean of Students under the personal observation exemption.

• *FERPA Legitimate Educational Interest*: FERPA defines this as the demonstrated need to know by those officials of an institution that act in the student's educational interest, including faculty, administrators, clerical and professional employees, and other persons who manage student record information (U.S. Department of Education, 2012). This may include a faculty member sharing with a student's advisor.

Imagine Aaron is a first-year student taking a 102 level introductory math course in preparation for his degree in computer science. Aaron becomes overwhelmed quickly with the work in the class and begins paying less and less attention to the lectures. Aaron starts talking and distracting other students in class, coming in late and eventually missing class altogether.

Aaron's professor would be able to share with his advisor and those staff members who are responsible for tracking first-year student retention risks under FERPA's legitimate educational interest policy. Aaron's advisor would benefit from knowing the problems he is encountering.

• *FERPA and Negligence*: Faculty should remember that FERPA is a law originally designed to protect information from being shared with individuals outside the institution, and allows for the institution to determine who has the "educational need to know" internally. And, by the very act of having the BIT (and/or TAT), the institution has made that determination. In essence, they have decided that the BIT not only has the need to know, but must know, as a matter of policy.

Failing to keep the BIT in the loop can actually have an unintended consequence—negligence. Imagine you know something about a student's condition or circumstance, but you decide that FERPA precludes you from telling them (or you just don't want to). Later, that student harms themself and/or someone else. In the inevitable lawsuit, it will (believe us) come to light what behaviors you had knowledge of, and you will be asked (perhaps in deposition) why you didn't tell the BIT. In this situation, the institution will not be able to defend your actions (or, more appropriately, inactions), as they created a BIT and reporting mechanism for all faculty and you failed to utilize it. In some instances, they will attempt to "sever" the institution from the lawsuit, leaving you alone to face the claim. This is not an enviable position to be in. While we hate to appeal to your sense of self-preservation as the primary reason to report what you know to the BIT—we clearly prefer the "it's the right thing to do" rationales—we also believe you need to know the potential outcomes that could be detrimental to you as well.

LAWS AND REGULATIONS: HIPAA

The Health Insurance Portability and Accountability Act of 1996 (HIPAA) (United States Department of Health and Human Services, 1996) is often quoted as another federal regulation that limits information among departments. HIPAA, however, only applies to medical and counseling treatment records in school settings where the health or counseling services bills a third party electronically for a student's care. This is a particularly rare occurrence on a college or university campus for counseling centers. While there may be some limitation with health or counseling staff sharing information back to a faculty member because of HIPAA, it is hard to imagine a scenario where HIPAA would have any application to a faculty member sharing information to a BIT or counseling center.

LAWS AND REGULATIONS: OFFICE OF CIVIL RIGHTS TITLE IX

The Office of Civil Rights (OCRs) Title IX protects individuals from exclusion or discrimination from any educational program or activity based on gender. Title IX would not limit a professor in reporting a concern to a counseling center or BIT. Title IX would actually encourage faculty to report behavior more often, rather than keep concerns related to harassment, discrimination or other threats.

LAWS AND REGULATIONS: OTHER CONCERNS

Another factor that affects an instructor's willingness to share information with the team is the lack of acknowledgment or perceived action on the part of the BIT, Student Conduct Office (SCO) or counseling center. Teams and counseling departments struggle with this communication back to the referring faculty member because there are some limitations within FERPA around what can be shared. Imagine a faculty member shares a concern with the team and there is little or no response. If the behavior continues in the classroom, many faculty will be reluctant to report the behavior again since there was little evidence of the BIT or counseling center addressing the behavior. It is more likely the professor will share with their colleagues, "don't bother calling them, they don't do anything." While the team or counseling center may be limited in what it shares back with the referral source, it would be wise to understand the potential impact of its silence following an initial report.

In most cases, a simple acknowledgment of the report and a notification the team is reviewing and investigating may be sufficient to honor FERPA's regulations as well as satisfying a staff or faculty member's desire to know that things are being addressed. At a minimum, the team should send an email back to the reporter (this can be automated with an electronic database). We suggest counseling centers, Student Conduct Offices, and BIT's use of the following (or a variation of):

Dear [reporter],

Thank you very much for submitting your report to our office. For more information about team members, protocols, and the rubric we use to evaluate behavior, please see our website at [www . . .]. Know that we are taking action and evaluating your report, and may be receiving other related reports. We may be reaching out to you, if appropriate, to assist the team or answer some questions about the report. Unfortunately, we are very limited as to what we can share about the reports we have received or any information we have gathered—please know that is not a reflection on you, but is the institution's procedure in conformity with federal law. Should you see any change in the student's behavior, either improvement or deterioration, please notify us as soon as possible by submitting another report or calling the chair at [PHONE]. Again, thank you for taking part in this very important caring and preventive process.

We would argue that BITs and SCOs (and Counseling Centers in certain situations), also owe faculty the "we are done for now" email. While they may not be able to share the details of the discussion or outcome (except for those provisions that affect the student's ability to return to or be a part of your class), it will at least serve to let faculty (and/or the reporter) know that the process has been followed. It may even ask them to keep an eye on the student and report any additional changes in behavior—positive or negative.

QUESTIONS FOR FURTHER DISCUSSION

Here are some additional questions about information sharing, FERPA and HIPAA. These questions are useful for self-reflection or to assist in facilitating a group discussion during a faculty training or orientation session.

1. We talk about the dangers of "siloed" information. Discuss a time that you have seen information siloed among departments. How was the situation resolved? What improvements would have helped to share the information?

2. FERPA regulations are often cited as a reason to not share information by faculty. FERPA allows information sharing for emergency exemptions as well as when a faculty member is sharing a personal observation. What is your understanding of FERPA? What potential misinformation have you heard about FERPA?

3. HIPAA limits information sharing through health services and "covered entities." Title IX requires faculty to share information if sexual harassment or assault is reported or observed. Discuss these two federal policies and how they apply at your institution.

Chapter 12

Know Your Resources

PEER SUPPORT

Remember Stephen's Kings masterpiece thriller *IT*? The story of *IT*, for those unfamiliar, is the story of a group of friends who take on a psychopathic, evil clown (are there any other kinds of clowns?). Without giving away the ending, their prospects for salvation fall on their ability to lean on each other to fight the ultimate evil.

While we sincerely hope the college or university experience is not as bad as being stalked by Pennywise the clown, the struggle itself certainly is more manageable with a group of friends to support those having a difficult time. We remember our own college struggles with grades and trying to find our place in the world. The one thing that we always could count on to help when we were feeling out of sorts was the friendships that surrounded us. Whether it was falling behind in classes, confusion about my major, a relationship that ended badly or the sheer panic about trying to figure out how to pass ancient Greek, friends provided a shelter against those many storms.

Friends, teammates and fraternity brothers serve as support networks. Faculty advisors can also be some of the most impactful people who helped guide us through a difficult experience by holding us accountable, but doing it in a very caring and compassionate manner. These advisors can still serve as mentors and role models to this day. In the best cases, we seek to pay forward these kindness experienced during our college years.

While it is not the role of an instructor or faculty member to play a sort of Tevye-like matchmaker for students to find their group of friends, faculty can be essential in offering advice and encouragement for students to connect with each other for support. These suggestions can be based on an instructor's own interests or involvements or can be related to positive social interactions an instructor had when they were in school. Perhaps a professor oversees the student newspaper, videography club or is involved in the international student association. It may be an instructor was once involved in a Greek system and could encourage students to pledge. Other instructors may have social connections with staff or faculty members who are involved in student organizations such as intermural sports, board games, role-play associations and movie or music clubs. Still others may have a shared experience with a student—being a veteran, an athlete, or maybe they come from their home state or country.

Schools often spend their student activity funds on speakers and performers that come to campus in order to educate or entertain. A professor could offer extra credit for students who attend an event and write a paper about it. An instructor could set up a meeting with an entertainer or educator to discuss the creative process before they give their performance or presentation. This kind of positive connection encouraging students to spend time together can be helpful in building positive social improvements in the classroom.

I'M RUBBER AND YOU'RE GLUE

Roy sits alone in the corner. I watch him as I stand in front of the classroom and I know that college has been a difficult transition for him. He's an older student, in his mid twenties and struggles to connect with the younger students around him. I watch him in his bubble of quiet, looking around and then looking down at the chapter we are reviewing for the upcoming test. He tries to look busy and may fool some of the other students. He doesn't fool me, though. I've seen his eyes tear up when some of the other students have teased him. They call him "the old man" and snicker when he asks questions.

It's time for the class to be dismissed and I tell them as much. I ask Roy to hang around after for a minute or two and he happily agrees. He's one of those students in class who is first to have his hand up, which contributes to the other students pushing him to the outside of their discussions before class. The class empties out. Roy and I are alone.

Me: "Roy, let me ask you something. I've been very impressed with your knowledge in class. You seem to keep up well with the readings and have aced the past two tests."

Roy: "I like your class, that's for sure. I'm hoping to do something in psychology when I graduate. All of this is really interesting to me."

Me: "That's great to hear, Roy. I'm really glad about that. One thing that I notice—and perhaps it's because I studied psychology so long—and maybe I'm reading into this, but I wonder how are you doing outside of the class?"

Roy: "I'm doing well in my other classes, if that's what you mean . . ."

Me: "I'm glad for that, and not surprised at all. But I was thinking more about getting along with other students, enjoying the college life. How's that kind of stuff going, if I can ask without being too pushy?"

Roy: "Well, that isn't really too important to me. I'm really here to get the grades I need and move on to graduate school."

Me: "That's kind of what I thought. I don't want to tell you what to do, but I wonder if you would heed some advice from an older guy like me."

Roy: "Of course. I respect your opinion."

Me: "I know you're older than most of the other students in my class. I also know that it might not be easy for you connect with them. Perhaps you don't have much in common."

Roy: "That's true. I'm just not into the party scene here. I've already done that and I'm back at school to get the grades this time. I know they think I'm old. I know they think I'm some kind of nerd. But I'm going to be right in the end. They'll see when I graduate with a 3.8."

Me: "Well, your academic goals are important and seem to be going well. I know for me, one of the positive memories I have from college isn't just the classes, but it was getting to meet some cool people, hang out in the halls, Denny's at 2 a.m. . . . you know, that kind of stuff."

Roy: "Well, I live off campus so I don't see too many students outside of class."

Me: "What kind of stuff do you like to do when you aren't in class, Roy?"

Roy: "Well, I'm a fan of video games. I just got the new Borderlands 2. It's pretty sweet."

Me: "Nice. Did you know we have a club on campus just for gamers?"

Roy: "No, I didn't know that."

Me: "Might be cool to try out. Just give it some thought. They have a webpage about meetings on the main campus website."

Roy: "I'll check it out."

Me: "Excellent. I think you might like it. And it will give you some other people to talk to instead of just claptrap, minion."

Roy: "Claptrap? Minion? Hey—that's from the game!"

Me: "Hey—this old guy can still play some video games, you know."

Roy: "Right . . . well, see you next week."

Me: "Sounds good, Roy."

Brian Van Brunt
Director of Counseling and Testing
Western Kentucky University

DOUBLE DOWN

I notice in my 500 level class—a class designed for fifth year seniors or first year master's level students—that two of the students are designated as "U2" meaning they are in their second year of college. After the first day of class, I ask them both— Cris and Erin—to come down so I can talk to them for a moment. I learn they are friends and decided to take this class together; they are both 4.0 students, they are both pre-law, and Erin is pretty highly strung (she shares this).

Lewis: "You know that this class is designed for 5th year seniors or 1st year master's level students. Most of these students have taken Jurisprudence, Constitutional Law, and other classes that would establish a base level of knowledge."

Cris: "Yes sir." *[Erin nods yes.]*

Lewis: I certainly do not doubt your intellectual ability, and [smiling] certainly not your gumption, but I wanted to be sure you understood the nature of the class.

Erin: "I'm not sure I understand, there are no prerequisites listed."

Lewis: "That is true—they are not required, but most of these students have taken those classes—they have been here for four years. And, since, as you heard, the class grade is one final all essay exam and one research paper—I am concerned that the other students are starting from a knowledge base that is deeper than yours, and since I don't grade on a curve . . ." *[I notice Erin tightening up.]*

Erin: "So what do you mean?"

Lewis: "What I am saying is that, while I am sure your work has the potential to be excellent, there is not a 'points for effort' in here, and, as you are both great students with GPAs that are certainly better than mine was in college, I wouldn't want you to take a class that might negatively impact that for the wrong reasons. That being said, I don't want you to think that you can't pass this class—for all I know, you both may do exceptionally well."

Cris: "Thanks for being straight with us; do you mind if I think about it and get back to you next class?"

Lewis: "Absolutely not."

Cris: "Can I email you about it too?"

Lewis: "Of course, I know the add/drop clock is ticking."

Erin [tensing up]: "Well I don't need to wait, I can't have my GPA ruined. But I'm screwed. My schedule is set and I am really limited on what I can take with my work schedule."

Lewis: "Erin, I get your situation. Let me propose this: take a look at the course schedule and let me know if there is a class that might work instead of this one."

Erin: "There was one other, but it was full."

Lewis: "Okay, let's see who teaches it and maybe we can reach out to them together to get you in."

Erin: "You would do that for me?"

Lewis: "Not for you, but with you. How about you, Cris? I am willing to work with you if you need me."

Cris: "No, I just want to think about it."

Lewis: "Okay, great."

I think of this story as an example of a "prevented" BIT situation. Had Erin stayed in the class, she might have gotten more and more upset if she hadn't done well and deteriorated. (She didn't. She ended up dropping this class and another, so she could shift her schedule around and take my 300 level "controversies" class and add a different elective at this time slot. She got an A. Fortuitous, I know. She also ended up never taking the class. She switched her major to Social Work, and is now teaching. To give you closure: Cris stayed in the class. She sent me an email asking for "other books she should read that would help her catch up to the others in the class." I sent her a bibliography, and she read them. All of them. And she got an A. Her work as a sophomore—like her maturity level as you can ascertain from the conversation—was well beyond her years. There are not a lot of Cris's in the world, I know. That's probably one of the reasons why she ended up at an Ivy League law school and is back in her home state practicing. Why do I know so much about these two? This established a mentoring connection that continued throughout their college years and beyond (an unintended benefit.)

W. Scott Lewis
Partner
National Center for Higher Education Risk Management

PARENTAL INVOLVEMENT

We've all heard the stories.

"Listen. You need to call my son on his cell phone if he doesn't show up for your 8am class. He does this all the time, staying up too late and then not getting to class. If you just call him I know he will get to class. Can I give you his number? Hello? Hello?"

"I need you to give my son the final exam before finals week next Tuesday. We have planned our family vacation to Cabo for finals week and I have already bought the ticket. I'd really appreciate your help."

"The admissions counselor said professors were willing to help Jennie succeed at college. She always had an Individualized Education Plan (IEP) in high school so her teachers knew about her learning style preferences. I was told that each professor was willing to work with my Jennie to succeed. If you aren't going to work with her, I'm going to have to call the president of the school and share my concerns with him."

There are times when parents live up to their reputation as "helicopter parents." They can be over-involved. They can be frustrating, rude and can't seem to let their child go. They can be pushy, demanding and annoying.

Yet, we suggest this is not the majority of parents. Most parents care about their son or daughter and merely want them to be successful—just like you do. They become overwhelmed by fear that they aren't doing enough—just like you can. They are concerned about their child—just like you are. It wasn't so long ago when faculty and staff at colleges complained that parents were not involved enough—now they are.

Parents receive a mixed message from most colleges and universities. It goes something like this. "Let your child go and grow. Don't over-parent or hover. Let them have their own college experience." These messages are then augmented with "This is your child. You need to be involved in the solution to this problem. They haven't been going to class. They had a suicide attempt. They have had three alcohol violations. You have to take them home now." Parents can easily get confused on how involved they should be.

We believe these messages cause some degree of fear and neurosis for parents about how they should be involved in helping their child be successful. Should they call and check in? Would this be seen as over-involved? They worry their son isn't going to class. Is it OK to call a professor to check on that? They were told that FERPA prevented instructors from talking to them. But then they were just told that FERPA doesn't apply when a student is declared on their parents' taxes.

This is all set against the backdrop of high school. Parents are expected to be on the booster club and Parent/Teacher Association (PTA). Parents are supposed to assist with an Individualized Education Plan (IEP), make sure their student is working on their homework and getting enough sleep. As educators, we know that this is supposed to change when a student goes to college. That message doesn't sink in immediately for parents. It's unrealistic to think decades of care and concern are going to magically change during the 45-minute orientation program entitled "Letting Go." The reality is the transition happens slowly over four years.

Parents and students are in a transition phase when the student goes away to college. The student is reaching for independence and learning new and amazing concepts. They are just as likely, however, to be bringing their laundry home and still seeing their pediatrician because "they really like Dr. Mike," reminiscent of the Ross Geller character from the TV show *Friends*, still seeing his pediatrician at 30.

The professor should help educate parents as well as the students. We aren't arguing that you sit parents in your classroom and explain to them the details of find the area under a curve or elaborate on Degas' painting method. Instead, we are arguing for some developmental education for parents about their new role in being an advocate for their son or daughter while at college.

You can reinforce the message they (should have) heard in orientation:

"You've done the hard work so far of raising your son. What I'd like to ask now is that you allow them the space and distance to be able to stand independently. Give him some room to struggle and maybe even fail. It is through this struggle that he will develop the inner strength to succeed. Remember, a bad grade is not the end of the world—it is a learning experience."

You can and should see whether your college has an orientation for students and parents. You should attend it; see what message parents and students are getting. You will likely find it enlightening. Then you can ask the parent/guardian whether they attended it, so you know where their knowledge base is. We have both had the advantage of being a part of orientations, often presenting to students and parents.

It's important for faculty to make the referral to the right person rather than try to handle the problem by themselves. An example would be:

"I understand your daughter has had individual support in high school for her learning difficulties. At college, we don't have IEPs. Instead we have an office for students with disabilities (ADA) where she can apply for accommodations in the classroom. I apologize that the admissions counselor gave you the impression that each professor will change the rules of their classroom to accommodate each student's learning style. While I try to teach to a variety of learning styles, I realize there may be some other needs your daughter has. Can I put you in touch with the ADA office?"

Good professors involve parents, but always at an appropriate and minimal level—remember, you have support from Student Affairs (who often chair the BIT)—use them. They set limits on communication and encourage student responsibility, but they do this with grace, mercy and understanding for the difficult and confusing developmental process both parents and the student are going through. Good professors don't make megalomaniacal statements such as "I don't talk to parents—FERPA won't let me talk to you," or "this is college, not middle school, let your student grow up." It *is* okay, however, to let them know that their son/daughter has access to all the grades, assignments and syllabus, as well as all the support resources of the institution.

These kinds of statements do more to stroke the professor's ego and avoid the difficult work of helping a student and parent work together toward the student's success. The statements are often centered in a desire for the instructor to work less and punch out at the end of the day—or at least they sound that way to the parent.

MOM AND POP

When I was asked to share all the grades with a mom (this has happened more than once), I let her know that I post all the grades on the campus' online system. She said, "I know, but my son won't let me see them." At this point, I am at a crossroads. In one instance, Mom added, "And I am paying for all of this anyway, so I have a right to know." I reminded her that the same password that lets her pay for meals, housing, and to add "bucks" for books, etc. is the one that lets her see the grades. We had a chuckle when I asked her if she understood "leverage." She didn't know the access points were the same.

In another instance, I told Dad that I post all the grades on the campus' online system and asked why his daughter wouldn't let him see the postings. He told me that she says that she's an adult and is paying for this herself with loans and a job, and he has no right to "monitor her." (Note: technically, under FERPA, she may very well be correct.) He added, "she tells me she is doing well, but I don't trust her to tell me the truth— I know you will." Now Dad has put me in a precarious position. There is a parent–child gap that is not unusual, but not one I should be serving as the counselor for. In this case, I told him that, given his concerns, he should talk to her, and that he may have to just trust her, but that I cannot serve as the go-between and release information. I told him that I hand back all assignments, some on paper, some via email, and, since she says she is doing fine, he could ask to see her work to perhaps offer (appropriate) help. I could tell this frustrated him, but he understood. I ended our call by telling him that he was not alone, and that he could commiserate with other parents (our campus had a parents' Facebook group), and maybe talk to a counselor in his area for strategies.

W. Scott Lewis
Partner
National Center for Higher Education Risk Management

IMPORTANCE OF REFERRAL

A week and a half ago (March 10, 2012), the day after the school shooting near Cleveland, a student stood in the doorway of my Bronx college classroom. He was eating half a bagel with cream cheese. It was a month into the semester, 45 minutes into the class period. I didn't remember ever having seen him before.

He had been staring into my room, watching us through the small rectangular window next to the heavy metal door. He seemed to be looking for something. I motioned to him. He opened the door and said he wanted to talk to me.

156

I was tight on time, trying to finish discussing a chapter before giving a test the next time the class met, so I refused. But before I could tell him to email me or wait to talk after class, he said, in front of all the students, "Something big is going to go down at the test." Then he disappeared.

(Ravenelle, 2012)

Ravenelle's account in the New York Times shares a powerful vignette about referrals. Should a professor refer an incident like this? What kind of information should be shared? Who is the information shared with on campus?

This account ends with the professor sharing information with his supervisor and campus safety and there turns out to be no event that occurs on exam day. The author writes:

The levels of trust and openness that are necessary for teaching are diminished every time someone opens fire in a classroom. Idle comments become vaguely menacing threats. Classrooms are no longer just about learning but also about observing—watching to see who seems upset, uninvolved, angry.

By all accounts, it's a sad commentary on the current state of the classroom, albeit an accurate one. Instructors are increasingly asked to share information with various departments concerning potentially at-risk students. This creates a few challenges. First, instructors have to be able to identify at-risk behaviors and sort them out from run-of-the-mill college student behaviors. What is obsession and what is passionate interest? What is passion and what is aggression? What is critical thought and critique and what is pushy and rude behavior? Most professors don't have the luxury of also being a counselor or psychologist, a conduct officer or a cop.

One overarching suggestion for all referrals is the importance of including contact information for various departments on your syllabus. A sample paragraph from Western Kentucky University reads:

Students are encouraged to seek support at the various campus services located around campus. Counseling services is open Monday through Friday from 8–4:30 and the best way to make appointments is to call 270-745-3159. You can learn more about counseling services on their website at www.wku.edu/heretohelp. In the event you require academic support or ADA accommodations (www.wku.edu/eoo/ada/uas.php) please contact campus tutoring services located at Downing University Center (DUC) (www.wku.edu/tlc). Asking for help is never easy, but at WKU it's important to realize that many staff are here to help you be successful in your academic career. Make sure to use these services.

This process helps students self-refer to services before they dig themselves so far into an academic hole they can no longer see their way out of it. Assuming students will depend on you to refer them for assist and/or out of concern for their behavior, it begs the question: Who gets referred?

We suggest adding a section to your syllabus with contact information (websites and phone numbers) for all support services—Academic Support, Counseling (on campus and community agencies, e.g., suicide hotlines, rape hotlines, shelters, etc.), Disability Support Services, Student Conduct, Title IX officer, Financial Aid, etc. I think of this section as the "car owners manual" part of my syllabus. It lets them know that the institution is here to help, and that you are a referral agent.

WALK A MILE IN MY SHOES

To assist a diverse, nontraditional student population enrolled in developmental courses within an open access public community college setting, we developed the "Fresh Start Initiative." The purpose of this one-hour orientation workshop (before the official college's New Student Orientation) is to provide students in two- or three-week immersion courses with information regarding the resources, attitudes and beliefs necessary to be successful in college. Consequently, one key issue that we address is "mindfulness"—the concept of being present in the moment, and especially *during class.*

The approach we have taken to introduce this issue is the following: we ask students:

> If you came to see us [counselor/advisor/faculty member] in our office for help, how would you feel if we checked our email or surfed the web or were speaking on the phone about what movie we watched the other night while you were trying to speak to us?

We then ask students "would you feel respected and listened to and would you want to come back to see us for help again?" Invariably, the students say no, they wouldn't have felt respected nor would come to see us again. We then shift the perspective by asking students "how do you think a professor feels when you are sitting in their class, paying attention to your phone/iPad/etc.?" Invariably, students nod in recognition. We then spend a few minutes explaining "the culture of Higher Education expects mature, professional behavior just as a boss would expect on the job." We then further explain that if they have "concerns or problems that make it difficult to focus and/or pay attention then they should come to the counseling center for assistance." It has been our experience that students get the point more effectively when we ask them to "walk a mile in the professor's shoes" and reflect on "how they would like to be treated when seeking help from someone at the college."

Mitchell A. Levy
Bernard A. Polnariev
LaGuardia Community College

REFERRAL: COUNSELING

Counseling services are varied at different colleges and universities. Some are non-existent; some are no more than academic and career support centers that also can address some minor mental health wellness issues such as stress, time management or organization skills. Other centers provide top-notch psychological testing, assessment groups and individual treatment, as well as facilitate in-patient admissions for suicidal students. Some schools have nothing. Some out-source counseling to an Employee Assistance Program (EAP) or Campus Assistance Program (CAP).

Issues referred to counseling run the full gamut: from anxiety disorders to depression to drug abuse to schizophrenia to academic stress to trauma; if it happens in the "real world," it happens on campus. A quality director of counseling should be glad when calls come from professors who share concerning emails, upsetting classroom behaviors or simple requests for consultation or a presentation in the classroom. Poor directors see these phone calls as frustrating annoyances; taking them away from their important work. Referrals work better when you have a receptive director of counseling.

One approach is to invite counseling staff into your classroom to give a lecture or presentation about their services or a topic related to a particular content area. This is easier if you are an instructor who teaches introduction to psychology, communication or a general education class. It is more difficult to think of a content area for those in science or math. However, most counseling staff are comfortable talking about stress and how to juggle academic priorities.

REFERRAL: CONDUCT

An instructor rarely refers students to the Student Conduct Office (SCO). Some schools choose to handle academic dishonesty such as cheating or plagiarism through the Code of Student Conduct. These reports are sent to the conduct officer, a meeting is scheduled and sanctions are given or a formal hearing is scheduled. Alternatively, some colleges and universities choose to handle academic integrity issues through an academic process internal to the department.

Most schools encourage faculty to handle minor classroom disruptions such as technology misuse, cross-talk and minor rude behavior directly with the student. If the behavior continues after appropriate management techniques have been attempted or it increases in severity, a referral should be made to the SCO for review. Immediate referrals (phone and online incident reports) are expected to the SCO and/or the campus conduct or the police if a student is threatening, violent or aggressive in a classroom setting. Campus conduct referrals may also happen quickly for racism, harassment or excessively odd or strange behavior that disrupts the academic environment.

Examples of Counseling Referrals

Counseling referral	What not to do	What to do
Student expresses suicidal thoughts after class to a professor. "I not sure I'm feeling very well lately. I think I may do something soon. Either way, I won't have my paper that is due next week."	Professor responds, "College requires hard work. If you are so depressed you can't complete the assignments or come to class, then maybe you aren't ready to be in school."	Instructor responds, "I'm worried about you. Maybe that's just me being maternal/paternal, but I worry about students in my class who say they aren't sure they are going to be here. Does that mean something more serious? Are you thinking about suicide?"
A student becomes irrational and frequently upset and angry with other students in class who bring up legitimate counterpoints to his arguments.	Professor shares, "Listen, college requires you to behave a certain way. The way you are behaving in class isn't it. If I was you, I'd change or you aren't going to make it at college."	Instructor meets with student alone and shares, "It seems like you are having a hard time hearing other students' perspectives on these topics. Does that happen in other areas of your life as well? Is it something you ever would consider talking to someone about? Did you know we have staff and counselors who work with students on these issues? But you still need to follow the class rules regarding open debate and be respectful."
A student becomes anxious and tearful at the prospect of giving an oral presentation in class.	The instructor says, "Everyone gets anxious before giving a speech. Just practice and you will be fine."	The instructor offers a referral to the counseling center and suggests talking to them about ways to reduce anxiety and potentially a medication to help calm them before presentations.

Examples of Counseling Referrals (*continued*)

Counseling referral	What not to do	What to do
A student talks constantly in class, is extremely distractible and can't focus on the lecture.	The instructor embarrasses the student and calls him "Antsy George" in front of all the other students.	The instructor has a private conversation with the student and suggests a counseling assessment or testing with ADA to see if there is a more serious attention problem the student is struggling with in college. Also, a referral to the Disability Support Services may be in order, either by referring the student or sending them a note to see whether they know the student.
A student smells of alcohol during class, makes poor eye contact and falls asleep in the back row.	The professor corners the student after class as other students are still around. He says, "It seems like you are an alcoholic and I think you would benefit from going to Alcoholics Anonymous (AA) before you destroy your life."	The professor meets alone with the student and shares, "It seems to me that you have been drinking before class. I may be wrong here, but maybe talking to someone in counseling could help. Either way, you need to be awake and focused in my class."

REFERRAL: AMERICANS WITH DISABILITIES ACT

Students often struggle with academics in the classroom because of a disability. These disabilities are protected under the Americans with Disabilities Act (ADA) and students can obtain an outline for reasonable accommodations through their campus Disability Support Services Office (DSSO)—a centralized office charged with responsibility for determining appropriate accommodations for students who have registered and qualified for those accommodations (NOTE: it is NOT the purview of the professor to determine what accommodations are appropriate—doing so may put the professor and the institution at risk of violating the ADA or other discrimination laws). These accommodations may include note-takers, extended test time, a change in seating location or access to specialized textbooks.

While it is a student's responsibility to obtain these accommodations through the DSSO, many students don't understand how to go about obtaining an assessment or setting up a meeting with the ADA office (despite the information sent to them and given during orientation, this may shock you—they don't always read everything we give them to read). Students may also be concerned about being stigmatized as a "student with a disability" and therefore have a desire to be successful in their coursework on their own. This may be a noble gesture on their part; however, as the class becomes more difficult and the work more challenging, students may find themselves quickly treading water far from shore. A caring professor can share their point of view on accommodations (and should in their syllabus) early in the semester and even invite the ADA coordinator to spend 15 minutes of class time explaining their services to the students.

KUNG FU PANDA

I'll share a story from my own life in terms of accommodations. I've done very well in my own academics, writing and scholarship. Much of this has come easy to me and is simply the product of determination and hard work. One thing that didn't come easy to me was learning forms (or katas) in Kung Fu.

I began Kung Fu training about three years ago and enjoy the intricate movements, graceful imitations of animal's movements and the swinging about of large, dangerous and pointy weapons. The idea of weapons pulls me in closely and I was able to learn the spear, broadsword, straight sword and kwan do (a big long stick with a curved sharp blade on the end). The learning, however, did not come easy to me.

I often found myself lost in class, which was a new experience for me. Our sifu (teacher) would carefully demonstrate several moves in the form, showing us where to place our feet, how to hold our hands, which direction to point the weapon and how you transition into the next step. The movements were quick and then follow with repetition and practice. The problem occurred when I fell behind or became stuck on one aspect of the form. I became confused and lost. Uncertain whether I was supposed to spin the weapon around my back while taking a step, or complete the spin and then take a step. I became disoriented about where I should place my foot as my arm moved forward into a strike.

This was hard for me partially because learning, and to a similar degree—teaching, came easily to me in the past. Feeling lost and out of step is a strange and awkward feeling that quickly had me thinking, "I should just drop out" and "this is too hard, I'm never going to learn it." For me, it wasn't a matter of working hard. It was a matter of getting home and just not knowing what to practice. When I was in class I tried to keep up, but I would fall behind. When I was at home, I could start some small part of the form, but then became confused and didn't have a way to get back on track.

The stroke of brilliance came when I asked the instructor if I could tape him demonstrating the form at the end of class. This helped me watch him when I was at home and then practice the movements until I got them right. It ended up helping me in class keep up with the other students. It helped me so much, I moved to the front of the class, ahead of other students in the form. This was an exhilarating change from always being last.

Quality accommodations for students are like video recording in my Kung Fu class. It allowed me to be able to process the information in a different way and then be more successful in mastering the lesson. It helped me by matching my particular learning style with a more effective teaching style. It didn't let me work less or enable me to slack off. It helped me work smarter and more effectively master the material.

Luckily, I knew to ask for the help and possessed the age and wisdom to appear like an idiot in order to learn something that was important to me. I can understand, however, why students who struggle in the classroom are reluctant to ask for help. It's hard to overcome that stigma of not being able to keep up with everyone else or feeling as if you are asking for something special in an entitled way. It's important for college professors to understand the complicated and often embarrassing process of asking for an accommodation.

Brian Van Brunt
Director of Counseling and Testing
Western Kentucky University

LEGAL EAGLE

After undergraduate and graduate school, I felt sure that law school—while difficult— would be manageable. But right away I struggled with focusing on each subject for a long period of time (for those of you who don't know, there is a tremendous amount of reading during the first year of law school). Luckily, as a former instructor and student affairs professional, I knew to reach out to counseling services. I was medication averse, and, like many students, didn't want to get accommodations if I didn't "need" them. The counselor gave me some "life skills" to utilize to overcome what turned out to be a disability, and encouraged me to register with the DSSO. (In retrospect, I should have, but didn't. I know, I know . . ."practice what you preach" and "physician heal thyself."). The life skills helped tremendously (and still do), and I finished law school. The point here is that even a person who knows what services to use and how to use them can be reluctant—imagine how daunting for someone who does not know how to navigate the waters (or, in the cases of some students, are too proud to, for cultural or other reasons—we see this in some veterans, "I handled two tours at a Forward Operating Post on a hill in Afghanistan, I can handle college").

W. Scott Lewis
Partner
National Center for Higher Education Risk Management

REFERRAL: CAMPUS BIT

Referring students to the campus BIT depends on the policy and procedures, rules and regulations your particular campus has set up in terms of reporting expectations. The rule of thumb for faculty about reporting behavior to the campus BIT goes something like this: "Do it."

Most campuses want information shared with their BIT and see a well functioning BIT as one that analyzes and triages potential reports into low, moderate and high levels of concern. The BIT (and/or in some cases, Threat Assessment) then takes the information and sorts through it to develop some kind of action plan. There are times when this action plan results in the team taking no direct action with the student but taking a "wait and see" stance. Other times, a team may seek to gather more information from available resources such as other professors, an advisor, admissions officer, residence life, campus safety or the counseling office.

Some suggest having faculty be more restrictive in terms of what they report. While sharing an incident where a student text messaged in class is probably a solid example of over-reporting, it becomes quickly evident that most other disruptive and disrespectful behavior may contain some of the early signs or indications of a potentially more serious behavior problem. This isn't always the case. Students can often be eccentric, frustrating, annoying or difficult and present no need to be involved with a campus BIT action plan. However, it is our opinion that the campus BIT is in the best position to sort through this data from professors and then make a decision about next steps based on their process.

So, when at a loss about what kind of behavior you should report to the BIT, in the end it comes down to just this: "Do it." A more detailed discussion of faculty working with a campus BIT is included in the following chapter.

REFERRAL: TITLE IX

The same type of reporting exists under Title IX. When a faculty member learns of any gender-based discrimination (which would include sexual assault, harassment, bullying, relationship/domestic violence, etc.)—even if the incident is dated—they should notify the Title IX coordinator. The good news for faculty is this: telling your SCO and/or BIT will likely get the information to the Title IX Coordinator. Some campuses have provided faculty a brochure to give to students who may be the victim of discrimination—check with your Title IX Coordinator (you have to have one by law) for more information. But, like BIT the rule of thumb here is, "when in doubt, report."

CLOSING THE CIRCLE

All this has happened before. All this will happen again
—Battlestar Galactica (BSG)

Many of the problems we encounter in higher education are circular in nature. Those who work in higher education appreciate the unique nature of the "college student stories"; though we also know many of these stories remain the same. Students push against authority. They test limits. They behave in immature ways. Some are isolated and angry at the world. Some are bullied. Some are teased. Others are clearly not ready yet to get the most out of their college experience.

Think of every referral you make to counseling, conduct, the ADA office, the campus BIT as a start of a circle. Think of the initial referral as an arc drawn on a piece of paper. The other half of that arc is making sure the referral "sticks" and the outcome is satisfactory to you as the referral source. Think of closing the circle.

At the heart of this, we are talking about an exercise in personal responsibility paired with a little healthy paranoia. Don't assume that the problem has been dealt with because you haven't seen the student for a while. Attend to the silences, and to never letting a student "fall through the cracks." To assume that a student is doing better because no one has heard from him in a while is a fatal flaw in follow-up. Instructors need to be thoughtful and concerned with student behavior in the classroom and are on the front lines when it comes to violence prevention in higher education. While reporting concerning behavior in their classroom is a first step, following up on the reports to ensure that some kind of action or next step has been taken and/or sending a report on how the student is doing (better, worse, the same) to the BIT helps to ensure the closing of the circle to prevent any students from falling through those cracks. Don't be surprised if the BIT checks with you to see how the student is doing—there may be no "new" issue, it is just a follow-up.

So say we all.

QUESTIONS FOR FURTHER DISCUSSION

Here are some additional questions about connecting to students, parental involvement and referring students to additional support. These questions are useful for self-reflection or to assist in facilitating a group discussion during a faculty training or orientation session.

1. Discuss a time that you went above and beyond to connect with a student. What drove you to that action? What was the outcome?

2. We suggest the importance of including parents as part of the discussion when working with disruptive or dangerous students. What are your thoughts on involving parents? What are the positive aspects of including parents? What are some drawbacks?

3. The chapter reviews the importance of referrals to counseling and ADA. Discuss what kind of behaviors you have referred students to campus services for in the past. Talk about the importance of "closing the loop" when it comes to referral to ensure the referral is successful.

Chapter 13

Behavioral Intervention Teams (BIT)

HOW TO USE YOUR BEHAVIORAL INTERVENTION TEAM (BIT)

Faculty need to report concerning behaviors to the group on their campus charged with gathering this information, analyzing it and developing a plan to work with the student to mitigate the risk. These teams have been called Threat Assessment Teams (TATs), Risk Assessment Teams (RATs), Behavioral Intervention Teams (BITs) and a whole host of names specific to the institutions managing them (campus partners, networks, student at risk committee to name a few). Sometimes, campuses have many of these teams—there may be a BIT and a TAT. For the purposes of this book, we will refer to these teams as BITs.

So what is the mission of a team? Deisinger et al. (2008) suggest the following for a mission statement for a TAT: "Identify a student, faculty member, or staff member who has engaged in threatening behaviors or done something that raised serious concern about their well-being, stability, or potential for violence or suicide" (p. 47).

The mission of a BIT is broader, and will encourage reporting of behaviors that may not rise to the level of "threat" or "risk" such as minor classroom disruptions, excessive absences, etc. This is why we encourage reporting of the behaviors we are discussing—even the minor ones that are managed—to the BIT or to a member of the BIT. BIT and TAT membership may have overlap, and generally speaking, reporting or documenting incidents with the Chief Student Conduct Officer will likely get the information to the BIT.

BITs most commonly meet weekly and are made up of various departments on campus. The Campus Safety and Security Project (2009) reports the most frequent members on a team include academic affairs, campus safety, counseling, campus police, health services and human resources. Eells and Rockland-Miller (2011) suggest teams include counseling, student conduct, campus safety, health services, residential life and academic affairs. The *Book on BIT* (Sokolow et al.,

2011) and *Ending Campus Violence: New Approaches to Prevention* (Van Brunt, 2012) recommend student conduct, counseling services/mental health professional, and security/law enforcement at a minimum.

In 2012, the National Behavioral Intervention Team Association (NaBITA) released the first large-scale survey on how college and university BITs operate (Van Brunt, Sokolow, Lewis & Schuster, 2012). Study highlights include: 92% of schools have student of concern teams. Teams are typically run by the Dean of students, Vice President of Student Affairs (VPSA) or student conduct officer. Most teams meet weekly to discuss cases. These cases are made up of about 70% psychologically natured problems.

A central purpose of a BIT is to improve communication between the various departments on campus to better identify and mitigate risk when it is reported. Meloy et al. (2011) define the danger of individual departments doing their best without working together:

> There is always the risk of a "silo effect"—different domains of behavior are never linked together or synthesized to develop a comprehensive picture of the subject of concern, conduct further investigation, identify other warning behaviors, and actively risk-manage the case.
>
> (p. 19)

Randazzo and Plummer (2009) write:

> one of the biggest pitfalls to avoid was to the usual tendency of higher education institutions to operate in information "silos," with different departments and offices taking steps on their own to handle situations without knowing the bigger picture or factoring in steps that other departments may be taking. One of the most important roles that Virginia Tech envisioned for its threat assessment team was to facilitate information sharing across departments and offices and to break down some of those silos.
>
> (p. 56)

Faculty is crucial in helping with this process. By reporting information to a centralized group, schools have a better opportunity to get out in front of potential issues and crises and ensure students have access to the care they need to ensure their safety and (potentially) the safety of the campus community. It is, however, understandable that faculty may struggle with the reporting of student behavior to a centralized team. They may fear an overreaction by the team or being seen as "ratting out" a particular student to the campus administration and authorities. They may generally be against the concept of any group that may resemble some kind of Orwellian, *1984* reporting structure that monitors student behavior. They may worry that this trend in reporting may impact students' creativity and rights to individual expression.

However, we will fail in our efforts to help students reach the assistance they need and that is appropriate to their situation, as well as to prevent campus violence, without enlisting the support of the faculty who are in a unique position to observe student behavior and report it to the BIT. The U.S. Secret Service (Vossekuil et al., 2000) found in 81% of their cases (*n*=37) at least one person knew the shooter was thinking about or planning the incident, and in 59% of the cases, more than one person knew about the planning. In 93% of the cases, "the attackers engaged in some pre-offense 'disturbing' behavior that created concern in those around him" (Meloy et al., 2011, p. 7). It is imperative that a team seeks referrals from the entire campus community and encourages reporting of concerning behaviors—including even those minor behaviors that move away from the student's aforementioned baseline.

Faculty has a key role in sharing their concerns. Kanan (2010) writes, "The need to break the code of silence that surrounds potentially dangerous behavior must be reinforced with students: telling keeps people safe" (p. 24). BITs are most effective when faculty know when and how to report their concerns and are encouraged to share information. This is similar to the current Transit Authority campaign in New York City, "See something, say something," that encourages information sharing from the community to those in a position to process and analyze the intelligence and address the potential threat.

DADDY'S LITTLE GIRL

I took over as Beth's faculty advisor during her sophomore year of college when she decided that her major would be English. Two years later, now entering her senior year, I'd already received several phone calls from faculty colleagues about Beth. During her junior year her classroom behavior resulted in two Behavioral Intervention Team (BIT) referrals. The BIT reviewed two resident life reports where Beth displayed aggressive posturing, was loud and verbally threatening to others. She was also under the influence of alcohol. In both cases the BIT determined staff from residence life would talk to her, document the conversation and place a "verbal warning" in her housing file. Three nights after she received her second verbal warning, Beth was found wandering drunk on campus. Her erratic behavior caught the attention of campus public safety. Officers approached her and Beth was sent to the hospital for alcohol overdose and a mental health evaluation. Beth returned to campus from the hospital the next day. As her advisor this meant I knew more about Beth then most students I advise.

In my classroom late in the spring semester, it became clear that Beth's behavior was changing. An assignment required students to write about their earliest childhood memory of reading and how they felt about reading as a child. Beth received a C for that paper; the paper submitted lacked insight, did not meet the assignment parameters and was simply not well written. Beth showed up late to the next class, sat at the edge of her front row seat and stared at me "aggressively." It is hard to explain, but she sat with an angry expression, crossed arms with her legs stretched out in front of her. When she did speak, it was in clipped and abbreviated sentences. Beth sat in the front row and "stared me down" from that point forward. Occasionally Beth would mutter derogatory comments under her breath, and shared these opinions in whispered tones with other students. Other members of my department faculty reported similar aggressive behaviors in conjunction with a sudden drop in academic performance.

One of her suite mates, who was also my advisee, reported more aggressive behaviors including sudden anger outbursts, periods of time spent without speaking, staring with an aggressive posture, leaving notes in the kitchen and on doors that threatened "retaliation" if things were not done to Beth's specifications. After encouraging that student to report the behavior, I decided it was time to talk more directly with Beth.

I contacted the counseling services office and talked through my concerns. The decision was made for me to meet with Beth with one other department faculty member present. I set a specific time, made sure the door was kept open and discussed the meeting with my department chair. When I was finally able to meet with Beth she walked into the office looking fragile and tired. Without preamble Beth talked about the loss of her mother four years previously, how close she is to her father, how he just announced that he is getting remarried to a woman Beth barely knows. Beth shared episodes including excessive spending, drug and alcohol abuse, high-risk sex with male and female partners, stealing, property damage and pathological lying. Somehow throughout these crises, Beth maintained good grades. She willingly admitted that it was her academic success that kept her in therapy, on her medication and focused. Now that her academics were becoming more difficult she was having trouble finding balance.

Upon hearing her history and current mental well-being, I determined that a referral to counseling services was critical. Documentation of the meeting needed to be submitted to the BIT, department chair and the counseling service. At times the conversation was difficult but we agreed that specific behaviors would stop immediately; glowering at professors, sitting aggressively, whispering in class and making inappropriate hostile comments during class discussion had to stop. In terms of her academic work, we set up a meeting with the academic support services with an agreement that we would meet once a week until mid term. The other faculty member present had worked with Beth in numerous courses and was able to reassure Beth of her great potential as a student. At first Beth was uninterested in the discussion and asked if she was failing or being asked to leave college. I reassured her that her behavior was a concern but she had an opportunity to avoid further repercussions. We continued to follow up for the remainder of the Fall semester.

M. J. Raleigh, Ph.D.
Director of Counseling
University of North Carolina Pembroke

QUESTIONS FOR FURTHER DISCUSSION

Here are some additional questions reporting information to the campus BIT. These questions are useful for self-reflection or to assist in facilitating a group discussion during a faculty training or orientation session.

1. Does your campus have a student of concern team or a BIT? Do you know how to make a referral to the team? What obstacles are in the way of making a referral to the team?

2. Discuss some reasons why you might be hesitant to share information with the campus BIT. A central concern for many is the need of the individual student balanced against the needs of the greater community. Is this an issue for you as well? Why or why not?

3. What are the merits of having a BIT on campus that also reviews faculty and staff behavior (not only students). What are some of the obstacles to having a BIT review staff and faculty behavior?

Chapter 14

From the Student Conduct Office*

"I'VE GOT THIS STUDENT . . ."

Every faculty member has stories of individual student successes as well as stories about students that fell through the cracks, harmed themselves or others, or left school due to unmanageable personal crises. Each year I meet new faculty who are excited to learn that there are student affairs practitioners who can help guide them through student behavioral issues. I also meet faculty who have been teaching for a long time and who, as they learn about the student conduct process, the campus BIT, and suggestions for talking with students, say "Wow—I wish I had known about this before!"

Some faculty and staff see student conduct or the Dean of Students' Office as a dumping ground for all things behavioral. Others try to avoid dealing with student behaviors by ignoring them and hoping the problems will go away or by forcing students out of class. In response, I try to remind my campus colleagues about what it means to be educators. Just as we want students to graduate who can conduct research and write quality documents and solve complex equations, we also want graduates who can respect boundaries, communicate effectively in group settings and effectively navigate dialogues when they disagree with authority. We have a unique opportunity and responsibility to influence students and help them learn how to recover from mistakes. With the generation of Millennial students—many of whom have grown up with a great deal of privilege and entitlement—we also have a duty to teach them how to fail. As Dr. Jean Twenge describes in *Generation Me: Why Today's Young Americans are More Confident, Assertive, Entitled—and More Miserable than ever Before*, "It's often difficult for young people to make the transition from the more certain world of college to the working world—or even graduate school—where 'doing your best' isn't always enough, and choices aren't always clear" (2006, p. 119).

"I'VE GOT THIS STUDENT . . . WHO CREEPS ME OUT"

There is a mantra I strive to pass on to faculty—*students have a right to be odd*. I have received phone calls about everything from students who look at a faculty member oddly, to students who wear furry tails (yes, actual tails. This is not a tuxedo reference), to students who talk to themselves during class breaks or pass gas in class. Certainly any behavior can become disruptive in a classroom if it affects the teaching/learning process and is not addressed adequately, but faculty also need to recognize that all kinds of students (with all sorts of habits, identities and experiences) come to college. Each campus should have some sort of guidance about when to refer to the campus conduct process, when a Dean or chair might have a conversation with a student, and when to refer to the campus behavioral intervention team. For those faculty concerned about student privacy—FERPA allows for sharing within the institution when there is a "legitimate educational interest" in the information. Certainly, any consultation with the campus conduct office or BIT that is designed to promote individual student success or improve the classroom learning environment falls into this category.

I've noticed that faculty (especially at elite institutions) are often less tolerant of "odd" behaviors, unless the student is studying in their academic department, or is an advisee, or has received a scholarship. This makes sense—often those students that we consider odd are the students that we know the least. It is more difficult for an adjunct faculty member teaching a blended course to understand their students than it is for a faculty member who sees a student majoring in her academic discipline who also attends departmental events. On the other hand, when it comes to reporting or addressing behaviors in the classroom, community college faculty seem more likely to tolerate those behaviors that literally drive them crazy or cause them stress than their counterparts at four-year institutions. I speculate that this is due mainly to the nature of open-enrollment institutions, as well as specifically a lack of training, resources, and well-developed procedures. In the absence of such things, faculty can still take basic steps to maintain control of their classrooms. Even the simple act of learning and using a student's name not only makes students want to succeed more in the class, it also reminds students that they are noticed as individuals and are accountable for their individual behaviors. This can lead to the student being more likely to trust and open up to the faculty member, sharing insights and providing information about baseline behaviors.

"I'VE GOT THIS STUDENT . . . WHO MAKES ME SCARED TO WALK ALONE TO MY CAR"

Some faculty members—especially new or tenure track—are afraid of revealing or even acknowledging that they are not classroom management experts. They may believe that having to refer a case to student conduct shows weakness on their part. While I don't intend to speak for conduct officers or behavioral intervention team members everywhere, it is hard for me to imagine any such professional who wouldn't welcome a phone call to consult about a student issue that causes fear or stress for a faculty member. Two things you should *never* hear from the student behavior experts on your campus:

> "No—please—DON'T tell me something concerning about a student."
>
> —Your campus BIT or threat assessment team

> "What!? You want to talk to me about ways to help students behave and respect the policies!? Why would I do that? I'd rather students get in trouble first so I have to do paperwork and they have to meet with me!"
>
> —Your campus student conduct officer

Some common behaviors that create fear for many faculty members include challenging a faculty member's authority repeatedly in front of the class, not taking a hint when the faculty member changes the subject or asks that all questions be held until the end of class, and making statements such as, "I'm not paying tuition for you to preach your political views to me" and "If I get one more D, I'm going to have to take things up a notch." These behaviors may seem even more concerning when exhibited by those from whom we least expect them—the polished student, the usually shy female, the older male returning to school after decades of working.

In cases such as this, I often work with faculty to *plan for both extremes*. In 99.9% of cases, the student will change his/her behavior once confronted, or the situation will get resolved through usual means (conversations, classroom management techniques, a behavioral intervention investigation, etc.). However, I still want faculty to plan for the 1%, 100% of the time—to prepare for the worst while they expect the best outcomes. In the above examples, the faculty member and I would discuss the situation to come up with a plan for a conversation that includes how and when to confront the student in a way that feels the safest and minimizes risk of escalation. It may involve having a colleague or a campus public safety/law enforcement officer present or meeting in a public location. We will also explore ways the conversation can start to go badly, so that the faculty member can recognize that and alter the situation (often by leaving the room or calling campus police). No matter what the outcome, the faculty member feels better prepared about the interaction with the student after making plans for many possible outcomes.

"I'VE GOT THIS STUDENT . . . WHO MAKES ME DREAD COMING TO CLASS"

If a student is causing you to dislike coming to class because you don't want to deal with him/her, you should listen to this feeling. This is a call to action coming straight from your gut. Confrontation and holding each other accountable is not a normal part of most of our lives, but *people rise to the level of your expectations*. I often tell people that my role on campus is like being a judge on the latest trendy reality TV show—the bottom line is about giving people feedback about their behavior. This isn't rocket science to me or most conduct officers or hall directors. We spend countless hours talking to students to help them understand how others might view or experience their actions, the standards for behavior on campus, and the consequences if they don't follow the campus rules. However, for the faculty member whose area of expertise might actually be rocket science, such a conversation with a student might feel like being asked to speak in a foreign language. This is where the collaboration with student affairs colleagues can prove to be invaluable. We don't want to come into your classroom if you don't want us there—we want to give you the tools to repair it yourself.

The other important thing to learn here is this: no matter how inappropriate you think a behavior is or even if you think that you have mentioned general guidelines to the class as a whole, students may not know that their behavior doesn't meet your expectations unless you tell them. With an increasing number of students with varying levels of cognitive functioning or ability, entitled or privileged upbringings, or different cultural backgrounds, the things that you might think are basic components of respect still need to be articulated to students. One often unexpected challenge in an open-enrollment campus setting occurs when middle-aged White males exhibit disrespect toward the class and challenge the authority of a younger female instructor. You never know your students' life journeys, and you can't presume they will read your mind when it comes to what you expect in the classroom compared to what your colleague teaching down the hall expects. Whether it is not answering phones in class, not interrupting, taking breaks only when scheduled, not wearing tails in the classroom, or any other number of behaviors that can distract from a quality learning environment, students need to be told what you expect. Providing clear guidance also gives relief to many students, who may wonder everything from "When will we take breaks so I can use the bathroom?" to "Do I ask questions during class, or wait until the end?" to "Do I have to raise my hand or can I just speak up?" Once even the most basic expectations have been communicated, it is much easier to hold students accountable when they test your boundaries—which they will.

"I'VE GOT THIS STUDENT . . . WHO KEEPS ME AWAKE AT NIGHT"

This might be the one thing that most concerns faculty and staff at college campuses today. Whether it be a student who sends an email saying she can't come to class anymore because her husband is abusing her and she can't take it anymore, the student who drew a picture of a handgun in art class and seems hostile toward students in class with different viewpoints, or the student who has a sudden change in appearance and academic performance and submits irrational writing assignments—each of these situations can cause even the most senior faculty to lose sleep. In each of these situations, a faculty member has an opportunity to not only learn more about the student's struggle, but also to influence and intervene. These cases are prime examples of situations to refer or report to the campus BIT. In each of these, the BIT will likely do further investigation and assessment to determine a level of risk. Then an appropriate intervention will be determined, and the BIT may solicit your assistance in talking with the student or managing the situation.

The power of a conversation is one of the most underestimated assets we have in better understanding, supporting and assisting students with concerns. There are some simple questions that a faculty member can ask, such as "Is there someone on [or off] campus that you trust and can talk to?" or "Is there anything you need help with?" Faculty *cannot* be afraid to engage students in conversations about their struggles and their lives outside of the classroom. We see students (and non-students) engage in violence due to struggles both on and off campus. Students do not experience life in silos, and we cannot serve them as educators if we deny this reality of the student experience. Talk to your students. If you don't know the answers, let them know you will check and get back to them with more information. This often goes against the grain of training within academia, where you are expected to be the "expert," but the reality is that in order to be an academic expert in a specific discipline, you most likely don't have the time, energy or training to be able to fully resolve all of your students' problems. Students don't expect you to be perfect; however, ignoring them when their behavior warrants intervention, is a perfect mistake.

"I'VE GOT THIS STUDENT . . . WHO STILL WON'T BEHAVE EVEN AFTER I CONFRONTED HIM"

In cases where you have already talked with the student about specific behaviors, followed up about the conversation and your expectations via email, and provided forms of support that you and the student agreed upon, a student may still be disruptive. Whether the student chooses his behavior (such as continuing to kick another student's desk just to be spiteful) or you aren't sure whether the student can help his behavior or not (such as a student who challenges you by raising his voice or interrupting when he thinks others are wrong), it may be time to refer the case to student conduct for disruption, failure to comply or another such violation. It is crucial that you read your campus conduct code so that you know the kinds of behaviors that constitute disruption on your campus. While a student has a right to be odd, they don't have the right to disrupt the educational mission of the campus. This statement is framed for the individual, because the conduct process is about individual students recognizing *the impact, not just the intent* of their actions.

One of the most common questions I get from faculty is "At what point can I kick a student out of my class?" Instructors should be aware that once a student is admitted to the college or university, they have certain procedural protections provided through the campus code of conduct and other such documents. However, a student doesn't have a right to infringe on the learning environment of others. When that starts to happen, the faculty member has an obligation to address the behaviors. My hope is that you can take proactive steps to avoid getting to that point. Many campuses allow for interim action, depending on the nature and the seriousness of the incident, while an issue is being resolved. Talk to your departmental colleagues as well as your campus conduct office to learn what the practices are at your institution, what types of behaviors warrant such action and who is authorized to issue it.

As the spectrum of possible student behaviors is so varied, there is no perfect chart of who to call, when and how. While today's examples include students wearing tails and students texting in class, tomorrow's forms of disruption or concern may vary. However, there are some basic guidelines I can offer:

- If it keeps you awake at night, creates significant or repeated disruption for you or other students, or causes fear—don't ignore it. Respond. This includes things such as: sexual harassment, vague or direct threats, or significant and measurable disruption.
- Consider whether you want to be the last or only person with the information. Determine when to inform your department chair, dean, student conduct office, Dean of Students, and/or campus BIT. Sharing information does not necessarily result in a formal action, but might help to inform the

177

campus' understanding of a student. No one person or office experiences all aspects of a student's behavior, so your information may help to complete the last piece of a puzzle.

- A "response" can vary from a conversation about campus resources to an email clarifying your expectations to walking a student over to the campus health center or calling the police/public safety.
- Learn how to describe and document *behaviors* and their impacts. You don't want your students to feel "SOLD out" so don't use stereotypes, opinions, labels, or diagnoses.
- Behavioral intervention teams are designed to help a student *before* they get in trouble. Student conduct processes are typically used *after* disruption has already occurred.
- When in doubt, call. You have allies in your educational mission. Student affairs practitioners bring a series of skills that support and complement the academic engagement that you provide in the classroom. Use their expertise with students to help you continue to excel as an expert in your classroom.

While I would like to presume it is already understood, I recognize the importance of practicing what I preach by clearly articulating my expectations. *When it comes to addressing or managing student behaviors, the worst thing you can do is nothing.* Just like you wouldn't give a student a passing grade who didn't deserve it for his/her academic work, don't pass on an opportunity to address a student's behaviors—whether they are disruptive, concerning or threatening. You have failed your student if you let an opportunity to teach pass you by.

QUESTIONS FOR FURTHER DISCUSSION

Here are some additional questions based on Laura Bennett's thoughts in this chapter. These questions are useful for self-reflection or to assist in facilitating a group discussion during a faculty training or orientation session.

1. Laura Bennett discusses odd and weird behavior from students. Discuss some strange student behavior you have encountered. What factors helped you distinguish the "merely strange" from the "potentially dangerous?"

2. Have you ever experienced a wakeful night or panic about a student who scared you to the point that you were worried for their safety? Discuss the situation. Would Laura's advice in this chapter be helpful? Why or why not?

3. Where does your college or university fall on the faculty question "At what point can I kick a student out of my class?" How supportive is your school in backing up faculty decisions? What are some of the classroom disruptions or dangerous behaviors that have caused you to want to remove a student from the classroom?

ACKNOWLEDGMENT

* Our thanks to Laura Bennett, Student Conduct Officer at Harper Community College, who contributed this chapter to address what kind of behaviors faculty should be reporting and the importance of this collaborative work.

Part IV

Final Thoughts

Chapter 15

The Most Essential Things

TEN CORE CONCEPTS

There are some people who start reading at the end of the book. Perhaps it's one of those habits picked up writing theses and dissertations or having to read through piles of journal articles on a monthly basis. So, if you are one of those people—this chapter is for you; those who read from back to front looking for a concise summary of all we have discussed so far in this text.

This chapter pulls together some key ideas, theory and the technical, practical aspects of classroom management. We'll do our best to lay this all out in ten clear, straightforward sections. Work on these ten areas and you will be more effective in handling both disruptive and dangerous classroom scenarios that you come across. If you share any single chapter of this book with other faculty—this is the one to share.

1. CONFIDENCE

We know it's a bit unfair to start with confidence as a concept since this is one of the few concepts we discuss that can only be achieved through experience, trial and error and time. The reason we start here is because nothing is more effective than a professor, instructor, educator or teacher who possesses a sense of confidence and has the ability to follow through with their students with poise and equanimity.

Confidence starts with a strong knowledge of the content material being taught in the classroom. Have you ever had a new lecture topic assigned out of the blue or had to make up a presentation without enough time to prepare? If so, you know well how hard it can be to feel confident in front of an audience when you haven't obtained a mastery of the lecture material you are covering. This is why it can be difficult for new professors and instructors to excel at classroom management while trying to also deliver the course material in the most effective way.

Imagine you are driving in an unfamiliar city. You have a general understanding of where you are going, but lack the on-the-ground familiarity to remember landmarks, look at your map and retain more than one or two segments of the trip. GPS gives you some more specific directions and you have some basic idea of where you are ultimately headed, but these things are a far cry from being comfortable with navigating.

In this kind of situation, trying to also appreciate the landscape of the city or the diversity of the people are far from your mind. Finding the next stop sign or the turn sign that indicates where to get back onto the highway takes up all of your attention and focus.

It can be the same for a new professor in the classroom or an instructor teaching new material for the first time. The more they are focused on the content, the less they are focused on the management of the overall classroom. More seasoned professors learn to do this over time. The same way more seasoned drivers and travelers can better appreciate the journey once they know where all the turns and landmarks are. An instructor who is more confident with the classroom material will be in a better position to manage disruptive and dangerous behavior.

Another very important aspect of a successful professor lies in their ability to keep the class engaged and interested in the course content. It's not enough to read from the textbook or recite PowerPoint slides to your students. Instructors who receive positive classroom evaluations are often the ones who keep their students interested in the material and the learning process. These instructors often have fewer classroom disruptions or distractions to face from students as they are primarily focused on learning the material in front of them.

It brings up the image of that old Billy Joel song, *The Entertainer*. Simply put, professors who "entertain" their students while teaching the materials are more effective, receive higher marks on course evaluations and, in our subjective experience, tend to be more satisfied with their role as a teacher and in their interactions with their students when compared to those who police their classrooms with an iron fist and see the education process as a "dumping" of knowledge from the top of the hierarchy to those receptacles below.

Perhaps we've picked one of the most polarizing words here to drive this point home. Let's leave the term entertainer and instead define this as those instructors who offer some degree of charisma, sparkle or excitement for their topic. They make even the seemingly mundane interesting. Imagine the dreaded Statistics 303 course. It's overwhelming until the professor takes each concept and applies it to sports, election predictions, cards, and even our grades and birthdays. These are the kinds of classes you never miss. It's these teachers who encounter fewer management problems with their students. When an instructor knows the material well and shares the material in an innovative and resourceful manner, they tend to run into fewer problems with disruptive and dangerous behavior in the classroom (there is also less likelihood of academic integrity issues).

184

We're not suggesting that professors should just be entertaining, you know, like a clown juggling balls in order for students to behave well. We're not suggesting that instructors who fail to entertain students are then responsible for creating the idle hands that then end up engaging in disruptive or dangerous behavior. Students are in school for the privilege to learn and bring with that undertaking a responsibility to behave properly in the classroom.

We are suggesting educators who know their classroom material well and share it with their students in a creative and interesting manner often spend less time dealing with classroom disruptions since many of the students are focused on the content of the class. Also, knowing your students can reduce the likelihood of these issues as well. There can be times, certainly, where a particularly innovative debate may backfire and create an argument between students. But most of the time, inventive and energetic delivery of course content leads to the development of a more positive learning community.

LAND OF OOO

A colleague of mine approached me with some concern over her poor course evaluations. She had been professor for several years and was very smart and knowledgeable in her field. As we talked, it turned out the problem was related to her delivery of the material. Students complained about lengthy reading assignments, her efforts to review the same material in PowerPoint slides and the overall "dryness" of her lectures.

I shared with her that some of my higher evaluations came from attending to some of the more unseen phenomena that I encountered in the classroom. My students were less frustrated because I always let them go five minutes early instead of holding them five minutes late; trying to teach some essential concept at the end of the class. My students laughed and enjoyed my attempts to explain who Oscar and Felix were in the TV show *The Odd Couple* and my inclusion of *Adventure Time* (a popular cartoon for college students that takes place in the Land of Ooo) references in my slides.

I told her that I saw my role not just to deliver the material, but also to do it in a way that increased the likelihood that they would remember the concepts I was trying to share. The inclusion of YouTube™ clips in my lectures and spending some time at the start of class talking to my students about how their weekend was helped build a connection between us and develop a more positive learning community. My students still learned the essential concepts and did well on the standardized departmental learning goals; I think the difference was they weren't always aware that they were learning because they were lost in enjoying the concept.

I struggle to this day with the inherent dichotomy between professor and entertainer. Trying to find a place somewhere between Jon Houseman from the *Paperchase* and Mr. Schoop from *Summer School*. In my experience teaching over the years, I find myself continually returning to a kind of Mary Poppins approach; trying to educate while keeping track of how my audience, my customers, my students are engaged in the material. I stop myself if I become aware that the majority of the class has "tuned out" or if I am racing to finish a content chapter near the end of the class so I can check it off my list. I try my best to be genuine and present during my teaching and remind myself how I retained information better in classes where I had professors who were similarly engaging, creative and confident, and excited about the material they were sharing.

Brian Van Brunt
Director of Counseling and Testing
Western Kentucky University

2. HUMILITY

This is a hard one to write about. We'll say that up front. It will be hard to hear us, who you likely don't know, basically tell you not to be an arrogant jerk in the classroom. But we're going to take a shot at it because it is really important. Some professors have a blind spot here and we're willing to bet no one in their department is going to bring it up (like bad breath and body odor). People don't like conflict; and what's more, giving advice to someone who isn't interested in the advice is kind of wasted time. But we are going to take a shot at it because it is really, really important.

Let's take Bob. He's been teaching forever. He still has notes for his lectures on that blue mimeograph machine paper somewhere in his office. He measures how long he has been teaching a particular class in decades, not years. He's set in his ways, unwilling to change how he teaches. He has poor evaluations that he doesn't read because he has tenure and nothing to learn from those bright-eyed students sitting in front of his class. His lecture and exam methods are esoteric at best and are seen as trials to be bested rather than opportunities to demonstrate knowledge mastery.

Bob ignores students' questions he finds too simplistic or idiotic to answer. He is sarcastic and treats most students with an air of disdain. He offers few comments on his exams and simply writes a single letter grade on the top. A student confronts him during class about his grade on one of his exams.

Student: "What is this supposed to mean?"
Bob: "It's the letter D. Fourth letter of the alphabet."
Student (frustrated): "I mean, why did I get a D on the paper? I worked a really long time on that."
Bob (thoughtful): "Tell you what. Go outside and dig a hole. Then fill it up. Dig it again. Fill it in again. In the end, you haven't really accomplished anything. Same thing with your paper. Time and effort don't seem to be a factor in moving ahead in terms of a final product."

Some students laugh uncomfortably at this. One says, "Oh snap."

Student (angry now): "You are a real son of a bitch, you know?"
Bob (suddenly cold and angry): "Get out of my classroom you ill-mannered, arrogant whelp. I will not abide you talking to me that way."
Student (standing): "How about you make me?"

Other students shuffle uncomfortably.

Being an educator carries with it an element of responsibility and respect for the learning process. Insulting students, not communicating around grades and generally taking a holier-than-thou, arrogant stance is not only "karmicly" a horrible way to exist in the world; it also increases the risk of violence in the classroom. In the scenario, the student could attack Bob. Another student could try to defend Bob by tackling the first student. Disrespect has no place in the classroom; whether it be from student to professor or professor "Bob" to the student, and, as Bob learned: the way you treat students is the way they will treat you. Be professional, and they will treat you like a professional.

Sadly, there are some who teach with Bob's approach. The likelihood of them coming in contact with an inflexible, angry student is really just a matter of time. In this case, the faculty community may have some responsibility to "police its own" by having some conversations with the Bobs out there who are waiting on retirement, rude and insulting to each new class of students and unwilling to learn anything new. The unwillingness to learn goes against the core of what it means to work at an institute of higher education.

Let's take one more example.

Dennis teaches accounting and is best described as a "stickler for the rules." His syllabus is ten pages long and contains page after page of class policies, expectations and requirements for the course. Dennis is introverted and very rigid in his teaching style. He references the syllabus when any student tries to ask for assistance. Dennis feels these students can go to academic affairs for tutoring help, counseling for mental health support or the DSSO for a disability accommodation. Everything is neat and in its own place. Some students like Dennis and find his clear rules and procedures comforting and predictable. Other students find him infuriating, unreasonable and inflexible.

A student confronts Dennis after class about missing four classes. Dennis takes out the syllabus (he always has a copy near him) and begins:

Dennis: "It says very clearly here that you have three absences. You can miss three classes for any reason including: sickness, personal days, and emergency or other unforeseen circumstances. You have missed four classes. That means you have failed the course."
Student: "You don't understand, my mother was sick and I . . ."

Dennis: "That is why you are given a number of absences. You have used more than you are allowed. I can't make any exceptions. The policy is very clearly stated here in the syllabus. Every student had a copy at the start of . . ."

Student (growing panicked and angry): "You aren't listening to me! My mother is sick and I didn't have a choice!"

Dennis: "I'm sorry. You've missed four classes. You can talk to someone at our counseling center if you need assistance with what is going on with your mother."

Student (fists clenched): "You are like some kind of freaking robot! Are you kidding me! My mom has fucking cancer!"

Dennis: "I'm sorry about that and you are welcome to talk to someone in counseling. You missed four classes. There isn't anything I can do."

The lesson here, of course, is you can be right as an instructor and also be courting disruption or violence. In Chapter 4 we discuss the importance of understanding how a discussion can transform into an emergency. Dennis misses some clear signs of escalation in his student's behavior while holding firm to a set of rules and procedures. We advise taking a step back to consider having this discussion at another time. We also would caution a professor like Dennis, who might be tempted to see his syllabus as the end of any further discussions, to be more open to a dialogue with his students. Dennis would be smart to suggest some kind of appeal process with an impartial third party such as a department head or hearing board to deflect some of the student's anger. He might even suggest an accommodation review with the ADA office depending on the severity of his mother's medical condition. A forward thinking professor may even piece together that this might not be the only class the student has missed and a referral to the campus BIT or Dean's office might be helpful to connect the student with support services.

3. TIMING

Like a good stand-up comedian, "timing is everything." This also applies to classroom management. Choosing the right time to handle a disruptive student can make all the difference in how they hear and, hopefully, internalize the message. If the instructor's goal is to set a limit for a disruptive behavior and move on with no regard to whether or not the message was received or internalized, then timing doesn't matter much. The professor can just say what they choose and move on with the lecture. It's our hope and suggestion that the instructor should be more aware of how the message is received.

Students who are upset don't respond well to strict, inflexible limit setting. They respond better to a subtle, clear message about their behavior and a request to discuss it later in a more private setting. The public nature of the classroom creates a theatre for the student to perform. This is not the ideal environment to sustain an argument with a student in the middle of class. As we learned in Chapter 4, the techniques of motivational interviewing can help a faculty member roll with a student's resistance and avoid argumentation with them in the classroom setting.

Timing is important when we feel a pressure to address an issue immediately rather than developing a more thoughtful and measured approach. Beginning an intervention with a student when our buttons are pushed, when we are seeing red or experiencing rising heart rate and blood pressure is a bad idea. Like a parent doling out punishment on the fly, this *Judge Dredd* approach to classroom management is another example of a trap instructors can fall into. While we don't want to ignore disruptive or dangerous behavior as it occurs, we should avoid saying to ourselves, "Well, now that they've stopped my lecture there is no time like the present to have this argument and finally correct this bad behavior." This pressure to address the problem in the moment becomes even more intense when the disruption has gone unaddressed for several class periods with the hope that the student will spontaneously take responsibility for their actions and get themself in check.

To be clear, we are not advocating for professors to disregard disruptive or potentially dangerous behavior in the classroom because the student isn't ready or willing to hear our corrective action. We are arguing against a lengthy, public classroom discussion that only has the potential to make matters worse with an upset, defensive and irrational student. Remember, your syllabus did not have as the topic for the day's lecture, "Dole out a lesson in civility to the student who annoys me." Stick to what you set for the day—or at least get back to it quickly. In a YouTube™ video, we can watch a student in Milwaukee arguing back and forth with a well-meaning professor about a grade on her paper. This public argument ends with the student escalating and the police being called, who then proceed to tackle the student in the classroom (Esser, 2010). The lesson here is to address the professor's focus on defending her grading policy and arguing with the student rather than a primary focus on redirecting the conversation to another time and place.

For those who struggle to pull out of the moment when confronting a student and avoiding a further argument, it can be helpful to ask yourself "Is what I'm about to say going to achieve my goal of focusing back on the lecture?" If not, we would suggest saving the further elaboration with the student during a private meeting after class or during office hours when you have a higher chance of success of having a conversation where the student gains a better understanding of your perspective on the matter.

Perhaps some sample phrases such as these can be helpful in redirecting students to continue the conversation at a different time.

189

"I want to talk to you more about this after class or at the next free time we both have available."

"What you have to say is important and I want to make sure I understand it. Right now, I feel distracted and focused on getting through my lecture. I would rather talk later when I can give you my full attention in a private setting."

"I can see that you are upset and I'm starting to feel a little upset as well. Let's hold onto this until after class when we can both talk about your concern."

[Calmly] "While I can understand you are frustrated with [Insert situation here], we need to focus on the topic for today. I am happy to talk with you after class or during office hours, but for now we are going to go on. If you continue to disrupt class today, however, you will have to step out for the remainder of today." [Then go on with the lecture.]

4. GRACE AND MERCY

And suddenly the chapter takes a turn and begins to sound more like a good old-fashioned revival with concepts such as grace and mercy from the Lord! Rest assured, you haven't lost your place or found a new yourself reading in a new book. While there are certainly religious connotations to the concepts of grace and mercy, we believe there are some very real practical applications of these concepts when it comes to teaching students in higher education and managing disruptive and dangerous behavior.

We should not enable disrespectful student behavior and hand them the keys to the school. We should not lower standards and give in to their demands when we are faced with a student who falls short in terms of living up to the expectations in the classroom. There *is* a need for faculty to engage students with caring and respect—especially if the student is not displaying these qualities themselves. The heart of institutes of higher education is the education—teaching the course content, and the equally important qualities of respect, caring, empathetic listening and the truth of the old golden rule: "Treat others how you wish to be treated."

Our admonition to those working with disruptive, frustrating or annoying students is to understand the strength and power inherent in the demonstration of grace and mercy when encountering those who try our patience, and to behave in a way that demands a caring, developmentally appropriate corrective action. Addressing rude, entitled and frustrating student behavior is one way to prevent this behavior from festering and escalating into violent or dangerous behavior.

Perhaps there is also an argument here for treating students fairly. By this we mean following that golden rule and treating them how you would like to be treated in a similar situation. The issue is not one of giving them what they deserve, but instead offering them an opportunity to climb their way back out of the hole they have dug themselves into. Perhaps recalling times in our own scholarship and schooling where professors shared some of this grace and mercy with us.

Imagine a graduate student comes to you after class, distraught about her grade on a quiz. She explained she was having some serious health issues, but didn't want to withdraw from the class. You encouraged her to talk to the Dean of Students Office to see if there was any assistance they could offer since the condition was medical. She said she would, but even if she took an abbreviated load, she wanted to stay in your class—hence her panic over her quiz grade. She asked whether there was any way we could meet during your office hours to go over the concepts and whether you would mind if she emailed you when she felt she was struggling. You agreed to both, and went one step further. You connected her with an older student who had done exceptionally well in your class to see whether her peer could help her with the concepts. They met, it helped, and her work improved. Her email questions waned as she improved. A cynical professor might think, "Look out, she will take up all of your time." As it turned out, she picked up the material and helped others who were struggling. She, in essence, became an advocate, and her talking about your compassion to others served to a) keep other students engaged, b) reduce the likelihood of any disruptions, and c) keep her in school and motivated.

GRACE

I was about two-thirds into my doctoral program at the University of Sarasota in Florida. This was a blended program that required students to complete half of the coursework through online classes and the other half of the program required the students to travel to Florida to complete the courses in a traditional classroom.

I signed up for the psychology course in the classroom entitled "Treatment Planning and Clinical Diagnosis." I began the class and purchased the text several months before I traveled down to Florida for the classroom portion. I completed all the reading assignments and several essays and reflective assignments. I went down to Florida, unpacked in my hotel, had a nice dinner and then drove myself to the campus the next day to meet my friends and begin the week of learning.

As it turned out, I had signed up for a master's level course instead of the doctoral course entitled "Clinical Treatment Planning and Diagnosis." I realized my horrible mistake about ten minutes into the class and approached the professor to try to drop this class (which I didn't need) and sign up quickly for another class offered in Florida that I needed for my doctoral degree. The professor excused me from his class and I rushed over to the registrar to see what could be done.

It turned out there is another course entitled "Advanced Individual Treatment" I needed for my degree and the registrar handed me a slip to sign up for the new class. All I needed to do was get the professor teaching the course to sign it. In other words, have the professor who I had not met, and having not purchased the textbook, done any of the pre-class assignments and to whose first class I am now showing up 40 minutes late, give me permission to come in late. No problem, right?

As it turned out, it wasn't a problem. I waited until the first break and approached the professor. I explained my stupidity of signing up for the master's course instead of the doctoral course in treatment planning, my need to take this class in order to stay on track for my degree and the cost I had already put into coming down to Florida in terms of my airfare, vacation time away from work and time away from my wife and two children. He profoundly said, "Sure. We can work it out."

I found the textbook that night at a local bookstore and did quick outline reading of the material. I caught up on some of the pre-class assignments and each day of the week-long class allowed me to move closer and closer to catching up with the rest of the students. I ended up making an A in the class and I will never forget the professor who allowed me to be added to his class.

You see, I did something wrong. I failed to sign up for the right class and deserved to be sent home to sign up again for the correct class. I was not entitled to any special accommodation for my situation. But this one professor chose to show me some grace and mercy in this situation. To this day, I don't believe he understands what a profound impact that decision had on my life when I teach, present and write about education. I encourage you to offer some grace and mercy to your students as well.

Brian Van Brunt
Director of Counseling and Testing
Western Kentucky University

5. AWARENESS

Remember the term from your research class that involved exploring the "plausible rival hypothesis?" No? Let us remind you. It's the idea of seeing what else could be going on in your experiments that could be causing the effect. Instructors should adopt this same approach to being aware, alert and watchful with their classes. They should look for disruptive and potentially dangerous behavior and be curious about the potential motivation and factors that are contributing to making the situation worse. For example:

- Why is a student always getting into arguments? What might you be able to do to get ahead of this problem? Maybe if you talk to them after class about their perspective. Then again, maybe they just come from a family that argues a lot and that is normal for them. Even though you may have never argued in your family. This might just be a matter of perspective.

- You wonder whether the student is having some kind of emotional problem. They seem really sad and withdrawn from the rest of the class. You go to check in on them and see whether you can't refer them to counseling services. You think you should be careful, though, maybe they are just being quiet.
- The student gets teased frequently in your class and seems lost with much of the material you are covering. You wonder whether there is some kind of learning problem here that is preventing them from understanding what is going on. Then again, they might just not be putting the effort into studying when they aren't in class. Either way, you are going to talk to them after class and see whether you can't offer some help.

We aren't arguing for professors to be detectives or social workers here, but instead, they should have some interest and awareness of their classroom before things take a turn for the worse. This is at the heart of prevention: getting ahead of the problem rather than focusing solely on intervention and management. Be aware of what kind of behaviors and motivations for these behaviors are occurring in your classroom and look for ways to get ahead of potential problems and disruptions. In all of the above situations, a note to the BIT is a good idea.

There are few classroom management problems that occur suddenly and without warning signs. Like a flint striking steel throwing sparks onto kindling to start a campfire, the precursors for most disruptive behavior give off their own sparks before catching fire. Professors who are the most successful at preventing violence in their classrooms are aware of their students, assess problems before they happen and intervene early before a look or mumbled comment escalates to a disruptive behavior or dangerous action.

SMALL CLUES

Craig was a student in my Pre-Law University 101 class. He started off the class trying to be funny (sometimes successfully), and relentlessly flirting with the girl next to him. He was clearly smart enough to manage the academic work, and he knew it. Leading up to midterms, I had noticed that he was answering fewer questions and was less engaged in class. (Before, he was quick to raise his hand and try to be both right and amusing). Then he asked if he could move seats. (I use a "get comfortable and that's your seat for the semester" seating chart—it helps me learn their names and reduces the likelihood of disruptions. And cheating.) I didn't ask why, as class was starting, I just let him move to an empty seat. I followed up with an email, just asking how he was doing. He told me he was fine, but I wasn't buying it. I gave his name to the BIT, and they followed up through his resident director. She learned that his girlfriend (the girl in class) had "been caught" by him cheating on him, and she (the girl) was posting personal things on Facebook about him. Tack onto this his parents had just let him know they were splitting, he had failed a test in another class he thought he was acing, and he was clearly in a bad place. I could have written this off as him having a bad day, and done nothing. Instead, I ended up being the conduit for the BIT to reach out to him.

W. Scott Lewis
Partner
National Center for Higher Education Risk Management

6. ACTIVE LISTENING

Listening is one of the most effective ways of de-escalating a disruptive or dangerous student. The simple act of not talking encourages a student to share what they are upset about helps reduce the student's desire to raise their voice, yell or become more frustrated with the situation happening around them. People yell when they are not feeling heard or understood. When an instructor takes the time to listen to a student who is upset, it conveys the message they are paying attention and reduces the student's urge to escalate their behavior in order to be heard.

Admittedly, it does require a bit of patience to listen to someone whose viewpoint is so far off from your own. Students try to make a case for a classroom exception (extra credit or turning in a paper late) or explain away a behavior (cross-talk or misuse of technology). It's normal for an instructor to want to shut the conversation down quickly with a "well, that's not the way it is." While this kind of statement is an accurate representation of the situation at hand (and no amount of arguing on the student's part will change the professor's mind), we need to allow the student to feel understood so they aren't tempted to "raise their voice" through more disruptive or dangerous actions.

Another aspect of handling a disruptive student is having the discussion apart from an audience. This audience tends to "add fuel to the fire" and ends up escalating the student behaving in a disruptive or dangerous manner. If you have ever watched the TV show *COPS*, you are familiar with the first step when the police show up to a domestic violence scene. One officer directs the guy in a ripped white t-shirt over to sit on the curb to tell his side of the story. The other officer talks with the wife at the kitchen table to listen to her version of the story. Like fire and gasoline, as soon as they get back together the couple is back at each other's throats.

The classroom audience follows this example. A professor is always in a better position to have a conversation alone with a student in order to give them the space and attention they need in order to feel heard. The exception here is when the student is threatening or unsafe for the instructor to be around in a closed, private area. This requires the professor to always be concerned first with their personal safety when handling a disruptive or dangerous student. (For those of you who started the book at the end, there is a whole section on "Staying Centered" in Chapter 3; for those who didn't, you may want to re-read it. Please know that it is the short version of a workshop we teach.)

ATLANTA INTERNATIONAL AIRPORT

I travel as part of my consulting practice and this is how I found myself in the Atlanta airport on a Tuesday afternoon. I waited in line to use one of those airlines check-in kiosks that let you type in your confirmation number and then you get a copy of your ticket. I waited and watched a 65-year-old gentleman struggle with the machine. From where I stood, it looked as if he was typing in his number over and over again and the machine was not accepting his code. The line was rather long and an airline representative came over to help the traveler figure out what wasn't working with the machine. The exchange went like this:

Airline representative: "Sir, I'd be happy to help you. What seems to be the problem?"

Older man: "I keep entering my number and this damn thing isn't working. It won't let me enter the entire code." He shows her a printout of his ticket order.

Airline representative: "Allow me." She reaches for the printout.

Older man: "I've entered it already five times and each time it stops and won't let me enter any more numbers. I don't know why you have all these computers around if they aren't . . ."

Airline representative: "Sir, I'd be happy to . . ."

Older man: ". . . working. I mean, I pay all of this money and in my day there was a thing called customer service."

Airline representative: "If you would just give me the printout you have . . ."

Older man: "You aren't listening to me! I already typed that in."

Airline representative: Looks around frustrated at the back-up in the line. "Sir, if you just let me see your paper there, I can fix the problem."

Older man [now disgruntled]: "I don't know what you are going to do differently. I followed what it said to do." He holds the paper out.

Airline representative: Takes the paper from his hand. "Here, you just have to enter the confirmation number, not the ticket number." She types quickly and then his ticket comes out of the bottom of the machine.

Older man [grumbling]: "I don't see why this all has to be so complicated."

While the representative meant well, she tried to solve his problem before listening to his frustration. People who are upset about something want other people to understand why they are upset. Sure, they want a resolution to their problem, but they also want to be understood and cared about. Instructors would have an easier time working with disruptive students if they first listen to the problem and allow them the chance to explain their frustration. They should seek to do this in private, as long as it can be accomplished safely, and should use open-ended questions to help the student explain why they are upset. These questions could include: "Tell me more about why you are upset?", "What have you tried so far to solve the problem?" and "What would you like me to do in order to help you?"

Brian Van Brunt
Director of Counseling and Testing
Western Kentucky University

7. CLARIFY

Setting clear expectations in your syllabus and during your first class meeting can go a long way to head off disruptive behavior in the classroom. Each professor has their own personal feelings about what kind of classroom behavior they would like to see. Some become very upset at the idea of a student texting in class. Others find a baseball cap or hat worn in class to be disrespectful. Some want students to raise their hands in class before talking. Others encourage students to jump into conversations without raising their hand and being recognized.

There is nothing wrong with any of these preferences. However, good instructors realize students often experience some different messages from faculty in terms of what behavior is acceptable in the classroom. Professors who explain their personal expectations around classroom behavior and civility set the stage for students to have a clear understanding of how they should behave in their class.

- What are your rules on attendance and punctuality?
- What about academic integrity issues?
- Do you allow food in your classroom?
- How do you handle frequent bathroom visits or any getting up?
- Do you encourage students to interrupt the lecture with questions or do you prefer them to wait until the end of class?
- How are students recognized? Do they "have the floor" or are you in control?
- Does gum chewing set your teeth on edge?
- Is a quick glance at a cell phone permitted or seen as a sign of disrespect?
- Are cell phones allowed at all?

Whatever your expectations for behavior in the classroom, clearly outline them during one or more of the first class sessions to remove any doubt about how you expect students to behave in your classroom. In fact, start off a new course with a discussion during one or more of the first class sessions (some faculty like to wait until add/drop passes) to build a successful, positive learning community. Know that simply putting it in your syllabus and hoping they will read and understand it may be a recipe for disaster.

Some examples of these questions could include:

- Why did you decide to take this class?
- What made you interested in the course material?
- Is this a class for your major and future career or an elective you have to take?
- What are some things you expect to take away from this class?
- At the end of the semester, what standard would you use to measure whether this class was a good one?
- What are some of the things past instructors have done (no names, please) that have detracted from your learning?
- How do you learn best? What is your preferred learning style?

TAKING PERFECTION OFF THE TABLE

While I have faced various classroom management challenges during my 11 years of teaching, I do think I have fewer "wild stories" to share than most. That likely stems from many factors that have nothing to do with me, but I do highly value an open, low-stress classroom. We have serious work to do in class, but I believe people find great freedom to think and ask questions in relaxed, open environments.

Every course I teach is based on a critical thinking model that my institution has adopted (see the Foundation for Critical Thinking at *www.criticalthinking.org*. While a "critical thinking model" might sound highly structured and rigid, I have found that it serves to act more as a key that unlocks doors for college students. This model moves students from focusing on and worrying about "knowing the right answers" toward "asking better questions." This model defines critical thinking as "thinking about how one thinks with the goal of improving the thinking process." Further, it contends that questions are the hallmark of critical thinking. For most, this is quite freeing and even calming because it takes perfection off the table. Education becomes more about seeing the questioning and critical thinking processes happening in all of their classes and in their various disciplines.

Many of my students talk about their educational experience before college mainly as test-performance driven. For a great number of them, school truly was about getting as many right answers as possible. They even had pep rallies for big standardized test days in high school. So much is at stake for these schools in the way of prestige and funding. And much of that process focuses on learning the correct answers to questions. Most students also describe this type of testing in negative terms.

The nature of the Net and our unprecedented access to information makes finding answers to questions relatively easy. The work of thinking comes in the questioning of those answers including but not limited to their accuracy, quality, depth, or usefulness. Almost daily, I tell my students that the quality of their questions matters more than the "rightness" of their answers. In fact, some of the items on their in-class quizzes are questions that ask them to identify major questions addressed in the reading or I might ask them to write some questions that push the discussion further. To be sure, I ask them to define and illustrate important concepts found in readings, but I also ask them to write questions about the implications of the issue at hand or about the evidence included in an argument.

Most students find this both intellectually stimulating and empowering. There is no perfect question, but practicing the questioning process makes them "players" in the class and not just passive receivers of information or "performers" of tests. It makes class a time to refine thinking rather than only receive information. Questioning also fosters creativity by encouraging students to create something rather than simply memorize or master content. This is in no way to denigrate learning content (also part of critical thinking!), but rather to take what is learned and ask deeper, more meaningful questions about the issue at hand.

The questioning process never ends and therefore can never be perfected. Given this reality, many students find the freedom to ponder, create and think in new and exciting ways. And, hopefully, they begin to shift their view of the classroom from a place where they passively receive information toward seeing the classroom as a place to produce ideas through the thinking and questioning process. Thinking is a creative act, and by valuing questions, encountering any sort of content presents an opportunity to create.

Cort Basham
First Year Program/General Education Professor
Western Kentucky University

The following is a sample paragraph used in a sociology of deviance class. This class discussed difficult and often controversial material and the professor wanted to ensure that students understood his expectations around civil discourse.

You have signed up for a course in the sociology of deviance. This course contains some graphic visual material, questionable language and often will offend or challenge your comfort zone or worldview. Given the nature of the course, it's likely we will have some impassioned debates and discussions. I would ask that during these times we focus on the issues at hand, be respectful to one another and avoid any personal attacks, raised voices or talking while someone else is making a point or expressing their opinion. The point of this class is to be challenged and learn new ways to see the world from a different perspective. The best way to accomplish this is through listening and respectful dialogue with others who see things differently.

In a heavy discussion class such as Controversies in Law and Politics class, the professor may spend a fair amount of time on the aspects of principled and respectful debate, since the class is heavy on discussion. In a class that is more lecture based, the professor would spend more time on the "regular" rules. In all cases, it is useful to remind students they have paid for the opportunity to be in this class, but they should not mistake that as this being "their classroom." This is more likely to be accepted by students in a humorous way, but also in a way that ensures they get the message.

8. KNOW THYSELF

This popular Greek proverb was inscribed on the Temple of Apollo at Delphi. While some see it as an admonition against boastful behavior exceeding what you have accomplished, it applies here for educators to understand how past experiences have effects on their current expectations in their classrooms.

We all are the product of our experiences in the world. Faculty are not exempt from this. Instructors should develop an understanding about their expectations, biases and past experiences. Here are some questions we encourage faculty to explore as they think about their approach to teaching and classroom management.

- What are your biases when it comes to expectations for students' behavior in your classroom?
- Think about your own college and graduate school experience. Who were some of your favorite professors? What qualities did they possess? What aspects of their approach to teaching and classroom management have you adopted?
- Who were some of your least favorite instructors? What qualities did they possess? What aspects of their approach to teaching and classroom management have you avoided in your own experience?
- How was discipline and authority handled in your early childhood experiences in your family? In what ways do these early messages inform your current expectations for your students' behavior in your classroom?

- What are your feelings about the incoming class of first-year students at your institution? How do these feelings influence your teaching or classroom management style?
- What are the most difficult students for you to work with in the classroom? What kinds of behaviors push your buttons?
- What attitudes about classroom management come from your institution and departmental colleagues? How do these shape your approach to teaching and classroom management?
- What students do you feel more connected to in your classroom? How do you treat them differently than the students you do not enjoy as much?

Tired? Good, that's a lot of self-reflection right there. The point of the exercise is to help faculty explore what kind of factors influence how they handle classroom disruption. Our past experiences can influence our current practice for the good or bad, depending on what kind of messages we received and how we internalized these messages.

I'M GETTING THE ARTICHOKE DIP!

Each semester, I offer students in my classes from the previous semester a chance to sit down with me—usually at a local restaurant, appetizers are my treat. In that session they know grades are in, evaluations are done, and there is nothing at stake. I call it the "debrief" and ask them to give an honest assessment of what they learned, the course itself, the text, my teaching style, etc. I know, you are thinking that only the ones who loved it will show up. Not true. I get a pretty good attendance (might be the food), and they are remarkably candid. It does not turn into a "bitch session" either—they don't let it. I talk to them about how I developed the material and remind them about the learning outcomes for the course and then I let them know that I use some of what they say to continue to improve my style and material. I also find it helps me learn a lot about my "market."

W. Scott Lewis
Partner
National Center for Higher Education Risk Management

9. CONSULT

The basic premise of all education centers on the idea that we are always acquiring knowledge and learning new ways to approach the world we live in. Consider looking to other professionals and colleagues to see how they approach similar situations you may encounter in the classroom. This is essential for new professors to learn how to approach classroom management, as they have no past teaching experience to draw upon.

This can also be helpful for experienced instructors who have not seen a particular behavior in their classroom before. This could be working with a student who has a developmental delay or handling an emotionally fragile student who struggles with anxiety or depression. It is unrealistic to expect educators to have full knowledge related to their field of content and also have some mastery of the wide collection of behavioral problems they may encounter in the classroom.

It is also helpful to call or email your counseling center director or student conduct officer for advice on how to handle disruptive classroom behavior that may overlap in their fields of expertise. Asking for advice or consulting with a fellow faculty or staff member should be seen as a positive action, not a sign of weakness.

10. EXERT CONTROL

In some extreme cases, a disruptive student resists any attempt at a professor's redirection or attempts to shift or end the argument. Like an individual who "trolls" and "flames" others on the Internet with inflammatory comments, the student looks for a public reaction and attention and will not be dissuaded or talked out of their prize. In these rare instances, the professor is left with only one real alternative: Dismiss the class.

Dismissing the class is not an easy proposition for many instructors. They have carefully planned and timed lectures that are tied to exams and the syllabus. Instructors are concerned over the prospect of allowing one student to force the rest of the class to miss a lecture. The class may meet infrequently and a single missed class equates to a loss of over 10% of the class content. But nothing you were going to talk about that day was worth relinquishing your control of the classroom—and that, in essence, is what you may be doing.

Continuing a class when a student is focused on disrupting is a dangerous proposition. A better approach is to cancel the class and report the concerning behavior and student to the department head, SCO *and* campus BIT. This report should be in the form of an email or online incident report *and* a phone call to the SCO. At the very least, the student is likely in violation of the student code of conduct in respect to following through with a faculty or staff member's request for compliance to no longer be disruptive. If the student is allowed to return to class—and it is standard operating procedure on almost every campus that they will not be allowed to until they have met with the SCO—clear expectations are then set on the behavior with consequences for future non-compliance. If the student attempts to return the next session, and you have not heard from the SCO, the conversation should go something like this (see Hold the Line).

HOLD THE LINE

You are waiting by the door, as you have not heard from the Student Conduct Officer (or you heard from them that the student has ignored their requests—and likely your email follow-up) and you want to catch the student before they get in.

You [seeing them in the hall, you approach]: "Mike, good to see you, I need to talk to you over here *[off to the side or, in some cases, down front—try to avoid an audience as best you can]* before class starts."

Mike: "Yeah, what's up?"

You: "As you know from my email, I had to refer the incident from last class to the Conduct Office, and they have been trying to get a hold of you."

Mike: "Yeah, I know, we keep missing each other—between my work and other classes, I haven't been able to get with them."

You: "Well that presents me with a problem."

Mike: "What's that?"

You: "Well Mike, I can't let you into class today without their permission." *[Note: See how this makes you the "good cop"?]*

Mike: "What do you mean you can't let me in?"

You: "Well, the rules are pretty clear. Since the disruption from last class caused me to cancel class, it would be against the rules for me to let you in until they give me clearance. I hate to be rigid, but I don't want to get both of us in trouble."

Mike: "So what am I supposed to do? I mean you can't really stop me from going in."

You: "That's true; I won't even begin to try. But if you do go in, I will have to call security or law enforcement to remove you—and that will be more disruptive, and likely get you in trouble. It may be embarrassing for you as well."

Mike: "You don't HAVE to call them. I will try to call the SCO tomorrow."

You: "Actually, I do have to. I don't want to, but I have to follow the rules or else I will get in trouble." *[Note: more you as good cop/messenger.]*

Mike [irritated]: "Well, what am I supposed to do about the work I miss? We have a quiz today!"

You [staying calm]: "I know, and I get your frustration. That's why I think you should probably call them now or go over to the SCO right now and address this. If there is work we need to make up and/or you need to get the notes, I will try to help you with it as much as I can, but you need to take care of this as soon as possible so you don't miss any more classes."

Mike [not pleased, but walking away]: "Fine, I will head over there now."

You take out your cell and call the SCO and let them know he is on his way. This is critical, as they may know more about him and his outbursts (or this may be an anomaly; either way, give them a heads up).

W. Scott Lewis
Partner
National Center for Higher Education Risk Management

There are a dozen variations on this, but the end result is the same. You are the messenger of what will/must happen, not the cause.

*

We will close with this. Hopefully, this book has provided you with information you may have already known, but shown in a different light. We also hope it gave you new insight and tools to use. The work we do educating students is critical to the future. It can feel like missionary work at times, and we appreciate your dedication and expertise! And believe us, the students do too—they just don't always show it. We spend a good amount of time traveling the country giving in-person workshops on this subject, and get questions and role-plays that accentuate this material. If there is ever anything we can do for you, please don't hesitate to reach out to us!

References

Albrecht, S. (2010). Threat assessment teams: Workplace and school violence prevention. *FBI Law Enforcement Bulletin*, *21*, 15–21.

Alvarez, S. & Schneider, J. (2008). One college campus's need for a safe zone: A case study. *Journal of Gender Studies*, *17*(1), 71–74.

Ancis, J. R., Sedlacek, W. E., & Mohr, J. J. (2000). Student perceptions of campus cultural climate by race. *Journal of Counseling and Development*, *78*, 180–185.

ASIS International and the Society for Human Resource Management (2011). Workplace violence prevention and intervention: American National Standard. Retrieved from *www.asisonline.org/guidelines/published.htm*.

Associated Press (2010, February 13). Shooter kills 3 faculty at Alabama university. *Toronto Star* (Canada).

Association of Threat Assessment Professionals (ATAP) (2006). Risk Assessment Guideline Elements for Violence (RAGE-V): Considerations for assessing the risk of future violent behavior. ATAP.

Ben-Ari, A. (1998). An experimental attitude change: Social work students and homosexuality. *Journal of Homosexuality*, *36*, 59–71.

Blankstein, A. & Faturech, R. (2009, October 14). UCLA student is charged with attempted murder in attack. *Los Angeles Times*.

Bonner F., Marbley, A., & Hamilton, M. (2011). *Diverse millennial students in college: Implications for faculty and student affairs*. Sterling, VA: Stylus Publishing.

Boyes, R. (2007, November 9). YouTube killer shocks a grieving nation into breaking the silence. *The Times* (UK).

Boysen, G. (2012). Teacher and student perceptions of microaggressions in college classrooms. *Journal of College Teaching*, *60*, 122–129.

Burd, S. (1996). Murder of 3 professors at a thesis defense causes a stunned campus to ask, why? *Chronicle of Higher Education*, *43*(2), A14.

Byrnes, J. (2002). *Before conflict: Preventing aggressive behavior*. Lanham, MD: Scarecrow Education.

Campus Safety and Security Project (2009). Results of the CSSP. Retrieved from www.nacubo.org/Documents/Initiatives/CSSPSurveyResults.pdf.

CBS News (2012). Colo. massacre prosecutors: James Holmes threatened professor before shooting. Retrieved on November 23, 2012 from www.cbsnews.com/8301–201_162–57522294/colo-massacre-prosecutors-james-holmes-threatened-professor-before-shooting/.

Chao, R. & Good, G. (2004). Nontraditional students' perspectives on college education: A qualitative study. *Journal of College Counseling*, 7, 5–12.

Choe, J. Y., Teplin, L. A., & Abram, K. M. (2008). Perpetration of violence, violent victimization, and severe mental illness: Balancing public health concerns. *Psychiatric Services*, 59(2), 153–164.

Chonody, J., Rutledge, S., & Siebert, D. (2009). College student's attitudes toward gays and lesbians. *Journal of Social Work Education*, 45(3), 499–512.

Coomes, M. & DeBard, R. (2004). *Serving the millennial generation: New directions for student services*. San Francisco, CA: Jossey-Bass.

Daulerio, A. (2010). NYU business school professor has mastered the art of email flaming. Retrieved on November 14, 2012 from http://deadspin.com/5477230/nyu-business-school-professor-has-mastered-the-art-of-email-flaming.

Deisinger, G., Randazzo, M., O'Neill, D., & Savage, J. (2008). The handbook of campus threat assessment and management teams. Stoneham, MA: Applied Risk Management, LLC.

Dill, P. & Henley, T. (1998). Stressor of college: A comparison of traditional and nontraditional. *Journal of Psychology*, 132, 25–32.

Dobuzinskis, A. (2011, January 15). California student arrest may have averted disaster. Reuters.

Doughty, D. (2010, May 4). UVa lacrosse teams rocked by student death, arrest. *The Roanoke Times*.

Drysdale, D., Modzeleski, W., & Simons, A. (2010). Campus attacks: Targeted violence affecting institutions of higher education. United States Secret Service, United States Department of Education and Federal Bureau of Investigation.

Dunkle, J. H., Silverstein, Z. B., & Warner, S. L. (2008). Managing violent and other troubling students: The role of threat assessment teams on campus. *Journal of College and University Law*, 34(3), 585–636.

Eells, G. & Rockland-Miller, H. (2011). Assessing and responding to disturbed and disturbing students: Understanding the role of administrative teams in institutions of higher education. *Journal of College Student Psychotherapy*, 25(1), 8–23.

Elam, C., Stratton, T., & Gibson, D. (2007). Welcoming a new generation to college: The millennial students. *Journal of College Admissions*, 195, 20–25.

Ellis, A. (2001). *Overcoming destructive beliefs, feelings, and behaviors*. New York, NY: Prometheus Books.

Esser, T. (2010). UWM student arrested in class. Retrieved on November 2010 from *www.examiner.com/article/uwm-student-arrested-class*.

Gearon, C. (2008). Back to school days for adults. *US News and World Report, 144*(10), 46–48.

Glasser, W. (1999). *Choice theory: A new psychology of personal freedom.* New York, NY: Harper Perennial.

Gossett, B., Cuyjet, M., & Cockriel, I. (1998). African Americans' perception of marginality in the campus culture. *College Student Journal, 32,* 22–32.

Grasgreen, A. (2012). No longer afraid to consult. Retrieved from www.inside highered.com/news/2012/04/16/counselor-faculty-consultations-rise-virginia-tech#.T5AoQ0lpyAM.email.

Greenhaus, J. & Beutell, N. (1985). Sources of conflict between work and family roles. *Academy of Management Review, 10,* 76–88.

Grossman, D. & Siddle, B. (2000). Psychological effects of combat. In L. Curtis & J. Turpin (Eds.), *Encyclopedia of violence, peace and conflict.* New York, NY: Academic Press.

Haiken, M. (2013). Suicide rate among vets and active duty military jumps— now 22 a day. Retrieved from www.forbes.com/sites/melaniehaiken/2013/02/05/22-the-number-of-veterans-who-now-commit-suicide-every-day/.

Hart, A. (1995). *Adrenaline and stress, the exciting new breakthrough that helps you overcome stress damage.* Nashville, TN: Thomas Nelson Publishers.

Harvard Medical School (2003). *Understanding depression.* Boston, MA: Harvard Health Publications.

Harvard Mental Health Letter (2011). *Mental Illness and Violence, 27*(7), 1–3.

Heggins W. & Jackson J. (2003). Understanding the collegiate experience for Asian international students at a Midwestern research university. *College Student Journal,* 237, 379–391.

Hooper, J. (2002). Killer's secret behind revenge attack. *The Guardian,* UK.

Howard, P. (1999). *The owner's manual for the brain: Everyday applications from mind-brain research* (2nd ed.). Austin, TX: Bard Press.

Huffington Post (2012). Jonatha Carr, Florida Atlantic University student, has violent outburst in class discussing evolution (Video). Retrieved on November 14, 2012 from www.huffingtonpost.com/2012/03/21/jonatha-carr-fau-student-class_n_1369739.html.

Hyun, J., Quinn, B., Madon, T., & Lustig, S. (2007). Mental health need, awareness, and use of counseling services among international graduate students. *Journal of American College Health, 56*(2), 109–118.

Kanan, L. (2010). When students make threats. National Association of Secondary School Principals, *NASSP Bulletin,* 24–29.

Keith, P. (2007). Barriers and nontraditional students' use of academic and social services. *Journal of College Student Development, 41*(4), 1123–1127.

King Greenwood, J. (2009, August 7). Sodini called mom just before killings. *Pittsburgh Tribune Review*, PA.

Kohler-Giancola, J., Grawitch, M., & Borchert, D. (2009). Dealing with the stress of college: A model for adult students. *Adult Education Quarterly*, *59*(3), 246–263.

Langman, P. (2008). The search for the truth at Columbine. Retrieved from www.schoolshooters.info, pp. 1–15.

Laur, D. (2002). The anatomy of fear and how it relates to survival skills training, integrated street combatives. Retrieved from www.lwcbooks.com/articles/anatomy.html.

Luck, L., Jackson, D., & Usher, K. (2007). STAMP. Components of observable behaviour that indicate potential for patient violence in emergency departments. *Journal of Advanced Nursing*, *59*(1), 11–19.

Martine, E. (2009). Jason Michael Hamilton's rifle jammed after 2 shots in Northern Virginia College shooting, say cops. CBS/Associated Press.

Meloy, J. (2000). *Violence risk and threat assessment: A practical guide for mental health and criminal justice professionals*. San Diego, CA: Specialized Training Services.

Meloy, J. R. (2006). The empirical basis and forensic application of affective and predatory violence. *Australian and New Zealand Journal of Psychiatry*, *40*, 539–547.

Meloy, J. R. & O'Toole, M. E. (2011). The concept of leakage in threat assessment. *Behavioral Sciences & the Law*, *29*(3), 513–527. DOI: 10.1002/bsl.986.

Meloy, J., Hoffmann, J., Guldimann, A., & James, D. (2011). The role of warning behaviors in threat assessment: An exploration and suggested typology. *Behavioral Sciences and the Law*, *30*(3), 256–279.

Miller, W. & Rollnick, S. (2002). *Motivational interviewing: Preparing people for change* (2nd ed.). New York, NY: The Guilford Press.

O'Brien, K. (2010). The empathy deficit. Retrieved on January 26, 2013 from www.boston.com/bostonglobe/ideas/articles/2010/10/17/the_empathy_deficit/.

O'Neill, D., Fox, J., Depue, R., & Englander, E. (2008). Campus violence prevention and response: Best practices for Massachusetts higher education. *Applied Risk Management*, LLC.

O'Toole, M. E. (2002). The school shooter: A threat assessment perspective. Federal Bureau of Investigation.

O'Toole, M. E. & Bowman, A. (2011). *Dangerous instincts: How gut feelings betray*. New York, NY: Hudson Street Press.

Payne, D. (2006, September 22). Gunman kills one, injures 19, in shooting spree on Canadian campus. *Chronicle of Higher Education*, *53*(5), A44.

Poyrazli, S. & Lopez, M. (2007). An exploratory study of perceived discrimination and homesickness: A comparison of international students and American students. *Journal of Psychology*, *14*(3), 263–280.

Price, C. (2009). Why don't my students think I'm groovy? *The Teaching Professor*, *23*(1), 7.

Prochaska, J., Norcross, J., & DiClemente, C. (1994). *Changing for good*. New York, NY: Harper Collins.

Rai, G. (2002). Meeting the educational needs of international students. *Journal of International Social Work*, *45*, 21–33.

Randazzo, M. & Plummer, E. (2009). Implementing behavioral threat assessment on campus: A Virginia Tech demonstration project. Printed by Virginia Polytechnic Institute and State University, Blacksburg, VA.

Ravenelle, A. (2012). Each teacher wonders, is this the one? Retrieved from www.nytimes.com/2012/03/10/opinion/teachers-need-trust-and-security.html?_r=1&ref=opinion.

Rothstein, W. & Rajapaksa, S. (2004). Health beliefs of college students born in the United States, China, and India. *Journal of American College Health*, *51*, 189–194.

Ruderman, W. (2007, October 27). Teen's plan for a massacre. *Philadelphia Daily News* (PA).

Sokolow, B., Lewis, S., Manzo, L., Schuster, S., Byrnes, J., & Van Brunt, B. (2011). *Book on BIT*. A publication of the National Behavioral Intervention Team Association (NaBITA).

Strauss, W. & Howe, N. (2007). *Millennials go to college: Strategies for a new generation on campus* (2nd ed.). Great Falls, VA: Lifecourse Associates.

Sue, D. (2010). *Microaggressions in everyday life: Race, gender, and sexual orientation*. Hoboken, NJ: John Wiley & Sons.

Sue, D., Capodilupo, C., Torino, G., Bucceri, J., Holder, A., Nadal, K., & Esquilin, M. (2007a). Racial microaggressions in everyday life: Implications for clinical practice. *American Psychologist*, *62*, 271–286.

Sue, D., Bucceri, J., Kin, A., Nadal, K., & Torino, G. (2007b). Racial microaggressions and the Asian-American experience. *Cultural Diversity and Ethnic Minority Psychology*, *13*, 72–81.

Sue, D., Lin, A., Torino, G., Capodilupo, C., & Rivera, D. (2009). Racial microaggressions and difficult dialogs on race in the classroom. *Cultural Diversity and Ethnic Minority Psychology*, *15*, 183–190.

Tseng, W. & Newton, F. (2002). International students' strategies for well-being. *College Student Journal*, *36*, 591–597.

Turner, J. & Gelles, M. (2003). Threat assessment: A risk management approach. New York, NY: Routledge.

Twenge, J. (2006). *Generation me: Why today's young Americans are more confident, assertive, entitled—and more miserable than ever before*. New York, NY: Free Press, A division of Simon & Schuster.

United States Department of Education. (2012). Family Educational Rights and Privacy Act (FERPA). Retrieved on November 19, 2012 from www2.ed.gov/policy/gen/guid/fpco/ferpa/index.html.

United States Department of Health and Human Services. (1996). The Health Insurance Portability and Accountability Act of 1996 (HIPAA). Retrieved on November 19, 2012 from www.hhs.gov/ocr/privacy/index.html.

United States Postal Service (2007). Threat assessment team guide. Retrieved from www.nalc.org/depart/cau/pdf/manuals/Pub%20108%20(2007-Mar).pdf.

Van Brunt, B. (2012). *Ending campus violence: New approaches to prevention*. New York, NY: Routledge.

Van Brunt, B., Sokolow, B., Lewis, W., & Schuster, S. (2012). NaBITA Team Survey. Retrieved from www.nabita.org.

Van Brunt, B., Woodley, E., Gunn, J., Raleigh, MJ, Reinach Wolf, C., & Sokolow, B. (2012). *Case management in higher education*. Publication of the National Behavioral Intervention Team Association (NaBITA) and the American College Counseling Association (ACCA).

Vann, D. (2008). Portrait of the school shooter as a young man. *Esquire*, *150*(2), 114.

Virginia Tech Review Panel (2007). *Mass shootings at Virginia Tech: Report of the review panel presented to Governor Kaine, Commonwealth of Virginia*.

Von Drehle, D., Altman, A., Steinmetz, K., Brock-Abraham, C., Calabresi, M., Gray, S., & Thompson, M. (2011). 1 madman and a gun. *Time*, *177*(3), 26–31.

Vossekuil, B., Fein, R., Reddy, M., Borum, R., & Modzeleski (2002). The final report and findings of the safe school initiative: Implications for the prevention of school attacks in the United States. Retrieved from www.secretservice.gov/ntac/ssi_final_report.pdf.

Vossekuil, B., Reddy, M., Fein, R., Borum, R., & Modzeleski, M. (2000). *USSS safe school initiative: An interim report on the prevention of targeted violence in schools*. Washington, DC: US Secret Service, National Threat Assessment Center.

Wallis, D. (2012). Coming home from war to hit the books. *New York Times*.

Whitlock, C. (2008, September 24). Gunman kills 10 students at school in Finland. *Washington Post*.

Wilson, R. (2000). The murder of a professor. *Chronicle of Higher Education*, *47*(3), A14.

Woodford, M., Howell, M., Silverschanz, P., & Yu, L. (2012). "That's so gay!": Examining the covariates of hearing this expression among gay, lesbian and bisexual college students. *Journal of College Health*, *60*(6), 429–434.

Index

Page references to Tables are in *italics*.

210

211